Praise for M

"More than any other musician I've [...] 1
Cohen maybe), Bob Wiseman has [...] to put
together two ideas so different and so seemingly unrelated, they hardly
belong in the same brain, let alone the same sentence. And that, I've
since discovered, is what great music is all about."

— BRUCE HEADLAM, CO-HOST OF BROKEN RECORD

"Wiseman's *Music Lessons* belongs beside Sei Shōnagon's *Pillow Book*,
John Cage's 'one-minute stories' and Eduardo Galeano's collections of
stories. Equal parts wisdom and whimsy, these are 'lessons' for musicians,
parents, artists and anyone who wants to learn better to pay attention."

— CHRIS CAVANAGH, STORYTELLER,
THE CATALYST CENTRE POPULAR EDUCATION CO-OP

"Reading *Music Lessons* is like listening to the finest of mix-tapes,
curated by that disarmingly philosophical friend who knows way
more about music than you do. A must-read for musicians, students
of music, parents of students of music and anyone who's ever thought
an MRI machine sounds like industrial ambient rock."

— CAROLYN TAYLOR OF BARONESS VON SKETCH

"o my, this is fucking genius!!! making me smile like a 2 month old
baby farting!!! real fucking cool style of writing. i'm sold on being
amazed by page 2!" — RAMI JAFFEE OF FOO FIGHTERS

"You can say what you like about Bob Wiseman, but I would like to
see you try and make it stick." — PETER PAUL VAN CAMP, POET

"Inspired by the mysterious and the ordinary, Wiseman offers insight-
ful observations about the musician's life. Whether he is passionately
listening to music, to his daughter's questions, to struggling students,
or to industry professionals, Wiseman delivers the playful musings of
a skillful story teller." — LEANNA MCLENNAN, WRITER AND EDUCATOR

"Like most of Bob Wiseman's artistic endeavours, his book *Music Lessons* flows effortlessly, teeming with all the honesty, insight, curiosity, humour, integrity, originality, quirkiness, and mischievousness you've come to expect from this amazing, singular voice."

— GREG RICHLING, MUSIC PRODUCER,
FORMERLY OF THE WALLFLOWERS

"Now that these entries have been published, I have no more use for FB." — STEVE JORDAN, FOUNDER, POLARIS MUSIC PRIZE

"*Music Lessons* has taught me to never underestimate the keyboard virtuosity of its author, whether it be via a piano tsunami, or a typed tirade well-tempered by poetry and wit." — JOHN OSWALD, COMPOSER

"Bob embodies the Toronto I lived in for ten years. Self deprecating, artistically puritanical, and totally comfortable wearing overalls at the bank." — GRAHAM WAGNER, WRITER FOR *THE OFFICE* AND *PORTLANDIA*

"Each little bonsai-essay, exchange, or pedestrian encounter (the sweet lemon-drop, the subtle caramel, or the tart Swedish Fish) makes you glad Mr. Wiseman took the trouble to write these memorable, provocative, and deeply intelligent/inquisitive/poetic/philosophical improvisations."

— DAVID GAINES, WRITER/ACTOR/TEACHER

"Wiseman's bite-size anecdotes, koans, allegories and highly stylish fragments, torn either from his memoirs or the pages of user manuals for unknown appliances, are super-smart, hilarious, highly addictive and persistent in their insistence on lingering in the reader's mind long after first encounter! Bravo, Bob!" — GUY MADDIN, FILMMAKER

music
lessons

music
lessons

bob
wiseman

Published by ECW Press
665 Gerrard Street East
Toronto, Ontario, Canada M4M 1Y2
416-694-3348 / info@ecwpress.com

Cover design: David A. Gee
Cover image: Bob Wiseman

LIBRARY AND ARCHIVES CANADA CATALOGUING IN PUBLICATION

Title: Music lessons / Bob Wiseman

Names: Wiseman, Bob, author.

Identifiers: Canadiana (print) 20190229608
Canadiana (ebook) 20200181947

ISBN 978-1-77041-512-6 (paperback)
ISBN 978-1-77305-495-7 (PDF)
ISBN 978-1-77305-494-0 (ePUB)

Subjects: LCSH: Music—Philosophy and aesthetics. | LCSH: Wiseman, Bob. | LCSH: Musicians—Canada—Biography.

Classification: LCC ML3800 W814 2020 | DDC 780.1—dc23

The publication of *Music Lessons* has been generously supported by the Canada Council for the Arts which last year invested $153 million to bring the arts to Canadians throughout the country and is funded in part by the Government of Canada. *Nous remercions le Conseil des arts du Canada de son soutien. L'an dernier, le Conseil a investi 153 millions de dollars pour mettre de l'art dans la vie des Canadiennes et des Canadiens de tout le pays. Ce livre est financé en partie par le gouvernement du Canada.* We acknowledge the support of the Ontario Arts Council (OAC), an agency of the Government of Ontario, which last year funded 1,737 individual artists and 1,095 organizations in 223 communities across Ontario for a total of $52.1 million. We also acknowledge the contribution of the Government of Ontario through the Ontario Book Publishing Tax Credit, and through Ontario Creates for the marketing of this book.

PRINTED AND BOUND IN CANADA

PRINTING: FRIESENS 5 4 3 2

For my background singers
Magali and Esmé

One day a man took his son aside and said to him:
"Children talk to god — the awakened, to life."
He seemed to reconsider what he'd just said, then added:
"It's not so much that they talk to life as it is that they listen to <u>life</u> talk —
with no comment of their own."

really

Little girl asked if I could show her Mary Had a Little Lamb.

No problem.

Really?

Really, select a note any note.

She pressed F. We started ma/ry/had (F, D#, C#), she worked it a few times.

She said I like to make things up.

That's a sign of a composer. Let's make something up.

Really?

Really.

We played a little improvisation then she changed her mind, returned to Mary Had a Little Lamb. Kept attacking the notes vertically with her fingers and wrist in the same line like a knife stabbing. Asked her to try balancing a miniature plate on her hand which made her hands horizontal with the keys more pianistic but this was also a little exhausting. Took a break and made small talk, she has a lot to say. Wishes she could speak French but her school won't allow it until she's in grade six. She said her parents both speak other languages and when she was younger in daycare she could count to 30 in Chinese.

Could I hear you count in Chinese?

I don't remember anymore. You know what else? My parents were going to take me to China one time but they changed their mind at the airport so we didn't go.

Really?

Really.

Did you know the black keys on the piano are a scale that is used in a lot of Chinese music?

Really?

Really. Let's make something up on the black keys, play anything just black keys and I'll back you up.

Really?

Really.

Proceeded to make something slow, melodic and pentatonic. Her mother noticed from the kitchen and walked into the room listening and beaming that her daughter was doing this.

I said to the mother I heard you guys almost went to China. She looked at her daughter and then me.

We've never been to China. I don't know why she invents things like that.

Should I or shouldn't I tell her? Kid's a composer, just practising making it up.

nanton, alberta

Sitting in a coffee shop with many seniors in Nanton, AB, one afternoon while touring that area and a Chris Isaak song came over the little restaurant speakers. The clientele started to argue about which Blue Rodeo song this is. At a certain point I couldn't take it any longer and piped in that it wasn't Blue Rodeo, it was Chris Isaak. One guy with anchor tattoos and Popeye forearms looks me in the eye expressionlessly and tells me it's definitely Blue Rodeo. Imagine the ace I held up my sleeve which if I tried to use would only confirm to him and his pals that I am a delusional fool, cruisin' for a bruisin'.

the day

Yesterday I ate celery eggplant curry. I recommend. I listened to a homeless old guy on a bench tell me about seven morning workers he suspected of being up to no good and repaired a broken piano bench leg. I made a smoothie using the $1 bag of strawberries I froze, spotty bananas, mint, peaches, maple syrup & vanilla extract and stood in line at Home Depot to get a refund on my bill statement and wished the in-store music, Two of Us by the Beatles, was replaced with Revolution #9. Would anyone notice, so busy tapping their sandals, balancing fidget spinners, waiting for their turn to complain to someone who is only a cog in a wheel waiting for shift change. It was revealed when I opened my daughter's bag from summer camp that she ate everything from her lunch. I'm winning. Noticed being in the present and the long gaps between next time's noticing. Exported poppier music for gangster doc which the director was curious about after our last meeting. Does what works for me work for him — can't tell. Just get to him fast so he has time to consider. I chaperoned the girl on training wheels, stopping only to squeeze a cedar's leaves then smell our hands. Didn't drink the grey water from the Tranzac but finished the vegetable stock into the new hummus. Best hummus ever. Will have to check schedule when the call comes in from Hummus Monthly wanting to do a cover story. Music lesson on Skype with woman in Kelowna who uses Mister when she talks to me. I like her song about inequality, don't have the heart to tell her it's a hit.

b part

Piano student: how do you make a B part?
Me: you just do something else but vary it from the A part.
Piano student: how do you do that?
Me: like this (makes something up).
Piano student: how did you do that?
Me: I thought about the A part and did something different that didn't sound like A but was in the same key.
Piano student: can you show me that?
Me: sure, but you can do it yourself too. do anything.
Piano student: no way.
Me: yes you can.
Piano student: no way.
Me: yes way.
Piano student: but you already know how.
Me: you just did it.
Piano student: what?
Me: saying "no way" was your A part then saying "but you already know how" was your B. they were in the same conversation and you varied it.
Piano student: you're fucking with me.
Me: you just made a bridge (sings "you're fucking with me").
Piano student: no way.
Me: back to A.
Piano student: can you just show me that B part?

Me: can I put this on Facebook?
Piano student: no, don't do that.
Me: why not?
Piano student: because I'll look stupid.
Me: I won't say your name.
Piano student: that's our outro.

g

There was a Toronto pianist who hated G# so much that she decided to never play it ever again. This made it awkward for other musicians to play with her, it even cost her some jobs. Someone at Musicworks wrote an article about her peculiarity and a few months later it must have been noticed by the President of America because he started mentioning her in speeches and calling her music the best music ever written in the world — superior and strong — he favoured white keys. Next she was offered a job in Washington making interstitial sequences for Presidential speeches. She was also offered a sports car, her own recording studio and a hassle-free P2 visa. She liked the new life.

Then one day while waiting at a railway crossing idling her purple AMG C-Class Cabriolet she noticed the hum of railway cars and it reminded her of a pattern she used to play in F. This led to thinking about the fingering that never felt right in G#. And then she imagined an alternative way to whiz thru G# — eureka. As soon as she got home she tested the daydream and it worked. Now she could skate around G# as easily as F or D or A. This changed everything and she returned to playing in all keys. Meanwhile people had started publishing articles about the 11-tone octave concept. Music clubs had started programming festivals without G# and in certain circles one ran the risk of great embarrassment to admit they still listened to anything in G#. When people heard about her new perspective they called her a sellout. The president was also displeased and fired her and told *Fox and Friends*, "I always had a bad feeling about her." They launched an audit resulting in financial penalties and forfeiture of the car and rescinded her visa.

She moved back to her parents' house in North York and wrote a memoir, *Thoughts on Accidental Accidentals*. In it she explained that following her instincts was all she was doing and the strangeness of finding so much judgment about her process which was only about being true to her music instincts. Later, CBC asked her to audition to be a Q host and the Polaris prize asked her to be a judge. Netflix approached her to turn each chapter into a 13-part miniseries. She wondered why people equated notoriety with musicality?

star wars

Student: I'm going to see Star Wars tomorrow, episode six, *Return of the Jedi*, I haven't seen this one but I know everything about Star Wars.

Teacher: You know Akira Kurosawa?

Student: What is that?

Teacher: That is the guy whose film Star Wars is based on.

Student: Star Wars isn't based on another film.

Teacher: Yes it is, it's called *The Hidden Fortress*. It was made in the 1950s, black and white.

Student: I think you mean the lightsaber fights because those are based on something from Japan.

Teacher: Yes, like that movie.

Student: I don't think you're right.

Teacher: Google.

Student: I've been watching it since I was eight, I think I would know.

Teacher: What do you think of the music in Star Wars, like when they are in a bar and there is a band playing?

Student: I think it is realistic.

Teacher: Based on what?

Student: Based on what music in the future would sound like.

Teacher: But we've never been to the future.

Student: Yes I know, but I still think that is what it would sound like.

Teacher: What else do you know about the future?

Student: That we all die.

Teacher: Now we agree on something.

Student: What is that?

Teacher: We all die.

Student: Right, but first I'll make a band and we'll tour the world and I'll make a lot of money and buy a house and help my parents.

Teacher: That shouldn't be a problem.

Student: I've been working on this dream a long time.

Teacher: Good luck.

Student: Don't need it.

Teacher: Why is that?

Student: I don't believe in luck.

Teacher: What do you believe in?

Student: My dreams — I believe in those.

Teacher: And if they don't work out?

Student: Maybe I'll be a teacher like you.

miles davis

The idea that so-and-so is the son or daughter of someone famous doesn't mean they have any of that talent, it just means their earlobes might look the same. People get behind that line of thought in politics all the time, like birth is a permission slip. Miles Davis picked Chick Corea, Keith Jarrett, John Coltrane, Tony Williams and Bill Evans as side players because of their talent, not their connections.

the job market

the film I am scoring came about because an editor at the company worked with me two years earlier and recommended me when they wondered who to call.

the film before that came about because I scored the director's previous film and that one came about because five years earlier his girlfriend wanted me to score a film she wrote.

the film before that came about because I started talking to an old acquaintance at a wedding and he told me about a film he had been working on and I said I score films.

the film before that came about because the director's son and my daughter were at the same preschool and we would talk about what we were doing.

the film before that was written by a woman who's a friend of mine and she told the director they were using me.

the film before that was for a couple comedy guys who moved to new york and didn't yet know any new york composers.

the film before that came about because the director started making a documentary about me and then he had other films to finish so hired me.

the film before that came about because the producer thought I could act the part of a musician in one scene.

the film before that came about because I knew the director years earlier and then read about her making this movie she was making and wrote her.

the film before that came about because they needed someone for free.

the film before that came about because the person who lives upstairs knew I did this sort of thing.

deciphering

Once heard someone not from North America remarking about popular music all sounding the same. I can appreciate that. At music school they spoke about the differences between Indian ragas and I couldn't follow what they meant. Now as I walk into busy Future Bakery, barely hear three notes of a song over the Saturday night crowd, instantly tell it is Stevie Wonder's harmonica and a second later I realize it is Boogie On Reggae Woman even though most other musical elements are obliterated by the people eating, drinking and flirting. Never ceases to amaze me how few combinations there are of three or four notes and yet many of us recognize distinctions instantly.

making life

Good improvisers get to experience making life. If audiences get it, they do too.

slo mo

My daughter scooters to the bus stop after asking, "Can I scooter to the bus?" I remind myself any second she will start telling me the way things are instead of asking permission. There was a character in a Richard Brautigan book who used to count everything because it was boring and when he was bored it felt like things happened more slowly. He concluded he would live longer if in a sustained state of boredom. I try to watch her scoot in slow motion. There are things I pull off on the piano, probably won't be able to do in older age, assuming I live to have an older age. I try to savour them as they are happening, watch it in slow motion for my imaginary self-of-the-future, in case right now he is wishing he could go back in time.

teleportation

Sometimes I can get my left hand to solo and my right hand to accompany. It wouldn't be accurate to say it's just a reversal of the usual relationship. When it's really happening it's like Star Trek, I'm experiencing teleportation.

best concert, james tenney

Interesting to hear more land acknowledgements this year. Opening remarks at public events stimulate thought even though some people read it without much life in their voice. Guess you can't force people to wake up but you can supply information, not be silent, let them do with it what they will.

When I was young, studying with Casey Sokol, if he recommended something I wouldn't forget. Once, he came to class stoked about a concert the night before, music by James Tenney. "I love the way that guy hears music," said Casey. Note to self — James Tenney.

I only got around to exploring him this year when the Music Gallery presented a retrospective of his work. It was my fave concert with one caveat, they removed Ain't I a Woman (based on Sojourner Truth's 1851 speech). I looked it up and read Tenney's notes from 1992, "Black women have always been doubly disenfranchised in our society, and Sojourner Truth (1797–1883) was one of the earliest and most eloquent voices speaking out against both racist and sexist forms of oppression. The composition is based on string instruments imitating the human voice, specifically her speech . . . In this piece I have tried to simulate certain acoustical properties of the words in Sojourner Truth's speech, as read and recorded for me by Michele George. . . . The fundamental (or first harmonic partial) of the voiced sounds is taken by the first cello, while the first formant region in the spectrum is represented by the violas, and the second and third formants by the celesta and violins, respectively. . . . These various acoustic components of the speech sounds are introduced gradually — incrementally — in an effort to facilitate both an 'analytical' and 'synthetic' hearing of the material — and perhaps a more profound meditation on the social implications of the text."

I get a little thrilled when musicians travel down political roads, because most hide under rocks and I believe art can effect change so I was excited. "A more profound meditation on the social implications of the text." Incredible, adventurous, unusual, revolutionary music. Just what the Music Gallery is about . . . right?

I think the public explanation was that they removed it because there was concern about stories of Black people being told by White people who have not had to struggle with some issues like accessibility, racism, etc. But isn't that partly why he wrote the piece? Why then didn't they remove his anti-war piece Viet Flakes despite the fact that he wasn't Vietnamese or a soldier? They didn't remove the anti-nuclear piece Pika-Don despite the fact that he wasn't identified with the people from whose accounts he quoted. He wasn't a scientist, priest, general or a Japanese woman or a Japanese child or someone who actually experienced a nuclear bomb.

Nope, he was just a guy who wanted people to think about real shit.

The evening started with a land acknowledgement that makes people consider colonial history, consider the bigger picture re: what happened and where we are. Didn't understand then why not apply same sensitivity before performing Tenney's piece if understanding the background was the point.

I do love the Music Gallery and I think the people currently at the helm have been making it compelling which is awesome but something about deleting a piece from a retrospective didn't sit right. Left thinking about Kurt Vonnegut and his story about the future where smart people wear earpieces and loud sounds go off every 20 seconds to interrupt their line of thought and make the world a more level playing field intellectually.

memories of being destroyed on first listen

You Know My Name (Look up the Number)/Beatles
Let X = X/Laurie Anderson
The Revolution Will Not Be Televised/Gil Scott-Heron
Fuck and Run/Liz Phair
Old Grey House/Kyp Harness
Sweet and Dandy/Toots and the Maytals
Life Is Unbelievable/John Southworth
Non-Alignment Pact/Pere Ubu
Watermelon Man/Herbie Hancock
Hungarian Rhapsody #6/Franz Liszt
New York New York/Nina Hagen
Teentown/Jaco Pastorius
The Windup/Keith Jarrett
All I Want/Joni Mitchell
I Zimbra/Talking Heads
Subterranean Homesick Blues/Bob Dylan
You Beat Me to the Punch/Mary Wells
All Day Sucker/Stevie Wonder
Who Killed Phillip?/Kathleen Yearwood
Walk on the Wild Side/Lou Reed

attitude problem

Want to trade cds?

No, it's okay.

What do you mean?

I heard you play earlier, not my thing.

That's so mean.

Isn't it mean to say yes I'll take your cd when not interested?

You should see a shrink.

Because I'm not into your music and admitted it?

One should always find something positive to say about the art of someone else.

Have you never heard something you didn't enjoy? Did you lie to their face and tell them it was great?

I would try to say something constructive. Not everybody has the courage to take the stage. Maybe I would say something about the fact that they took the stage.

You're the one who should see a shrink.

Because I don't want to hurt people's feelings?

Because you lie to yourself.

I didn't really want your cd anyway.

Great.

Great what?

Great you are being honest.

You have an attitude problem.

Why?

Because people need encouragement.

If people need encouragement, why are you discouraging me from being me?

You did it again. You have an attitude problem.

You just want to be flattered.

I want to help people achieve their potential.

Very sensitive of you.

Are you making fun?

No, just realizing you want to help people and the truth is you have some great songs, I bet you could change the world.

That's my plan.

Keep on doing it, man. You have something special. It isn't easy to take the stage like that.

I know. That's what my publicist says too.

I bet they offer you a reduced rate because they really love your stuff.

How did you know?

Lucky guess.

unconscious

Kid: Why is it when I try to play something that is tough, after a long time practising over and over, I can do it?

Teacher: I don't know, but true it works like that.

Kid: It's like it goes from my conscious mind to my unconscious mind.

Teacher: Like learning language.

Kid: Why isn't it quicker?

Teacher: Some say it is muscle memory, like the muscles are learning and then remember at a different speed than the speed of your mind.

Kid: Muscles don't have speed.

Teacher: Why not? . . . snails, hummingbirds, trees, flies all have different tempos, why not people?

Little kid: You lost me . . . but I'll consider that over and over and then maybe it might make sense.

Teacher: I see what you did there.

Kid: Thanks.

pitch

Teacher: You're out of tune with the keyboard, could you check your tuning?

Student: Why don't you ask her?

Teacher: Her keyboard has preset pitch already established.

Student: You could go to the portamento settings.

Teacher: That doesn't alter the fact that the keyboard is already at A440 and your strings are not.

Student: But I like it this way.

Teacher: But this is a school, not exactly conducive for working in a group to have someone sharp or flat.
Student: So what.
Teacher: If it was a philosophy class I would consider your point, maybe.
Student: I'm into micro-tonality.
Teacher: I'm into not being out of tune, at least not here.
Student: Have you ever heard King Crimson?
Teacher: Have you ever heard Mood Jga Jga?
Student: Have you ever heard Henry Cowell?
Teacher: Have you ever heard Anhai?
Student: Have you ever heard Eugene Chadbourne?
Teacher: I toured with Eugene Chadbourne.
Student: You win.
Teacher: Then you'll tune.
Student: Okay.
Teacher: Why are you so difficult?
Student: I was born this way.

now you take my cd, please

Student: here's my cd.
Instructor: thanks but maybe you should give it to someone else.
Student: won't you take it?
Instructor: you can leave it but no guarantee. why don't you ask (suggests another teacher) instead I bet they would love it.
Student: but i want you to hear it.
Instructor: to be honest most things I hear I can't stand.
Student: then why do you teach?
Instructor: hearing too many cds and not liking so many doesn't mean I don't like teaching.
Student: do you like Drake?
Instructor: Drake who?
Student: are you serious?
Instructor: maybe you shouldn't give me your cd.
Student: what kind of music do you like?

Instructor: if it blows me away I like it.

Student: melody or lyric?

Instructor: either or other things . . . authenticity gets me.

Student: you don't think Drake is original?

Instructor: maybe he is. I don't know. my opinion doesn't matter.

Student: why not?

Instructor: it's subjective. I never liked Elton John but someone out there probably played Crocodile Rock for the first dance at their wedding. but between you and me he's only about as good as Drake.

Student: you're evil.

Instructor: evil's my middle name.

Student: (hands him cd) I'd really feel honoured if you listened to this.

Instructor: no no no don't say that.

Student: why not?

Instructor: chasing outside acknowledgement is not going to help you.

Student: but you've won awards, I see them on your wall.

Instructor: well if someone gives you an award sure you can use it to help continue playing the game but "beware of outside acknowledgement" means not being submissive to people judging. don't waste time with that. focus on your work instead of imaginary opinions of imaginary people. you know any people on panels who vote on awards?

Student: no.

Instructor: you might be surprised, some of them know less about what they're judging than the people who actually make it.

Student: thanks for the advice I never asked for.

Instructor: and if you don't mind my saying so make sure you avoid the opposite.

Student: avoid not winning awards.

Instructor: avoid feeling humiliated by a bad review about you or your work. don't be fooled into getting down about that. it doesn't mean anything and neither does getting an award that says you're the best-dressed violinist in the month of June. these things are a game.

Student: so how do you make music and not care what people think?

Instructor: it's a secret.

Student: yeah so . . .

Instructor: first you make music, second you don't care what people think about it, third you make more music again. keep that quiet okay?

one less bridge

Got a call from a music magazine some years ago asking me to review a product — a Leslie amplifier simulator.

They didn't pay musicians for these requests. They subscribe to a line of thought that people who add to a corporation's profit by providing creative content should feel good getting free publicity. The fact that the owner gets free publicity plus earns revenue from selling that creative content isn't part of their explanation for why contributors should be satisfied only with publicity.

I had plans for promoting my record production work so I asked him how about I run a classified ad for some weeks in exchange for my review? He said they don't usually do that. I said okay see you later. He called back and said they would make an exception. I checked out the Leslie simulator. I didn't like it. I wrote a review about how inadequate it was.

You would think I stabbed someone from behind if you heard his voice after he read my review.

"Don't you understand the inventor of this pedal is an advertiser?" he said as though I was hard of hearing.
"Didn't you want me to write a review of my experience?"
"Yes I did but wasn't there anything positive?"
"If you think something sounding like a chorus pedal is a Leslie, then that's positive I guess. But if someone hoped it would sound like a Leslie, then I have to say it doesn't."
"Well we can't use this," he said as though I should feel bad about this situation. I didn't.

rate on

Student: Why the low mark?

Teacher: It didn't rhyme.

Student: She's my only mom, known her all my life, we were young and had to run, known her all my life.

Teacher: What's your point?

Student: It rhymes.

Teacher: In which universe?

Student: (sings) Mom (pause) ron.

Teacher: You're using the word "run" as in jogging, moving through space fast. Ron isn't run. You don't ron from something, you run from something. You had to run you didn't have to ron.

Student: That's how I speak.

Teacher: You really say ron instead of run?

Student: (nods head)

Teacher: Hmmm, even if that's really how you talk, "mom" and "ron" are not truly a rhyme. You understand? For our purposes let's achieve simple, clear, unchallengeable rhymes before we push the envelope, okay?

Student: Okay, I'll make it . . . more clear.

Teacher: Exactly, thanks.

Student: Rate on.

Teacher: Seriously?

Student: What's your problem?

the agent business

Ten years ago after playing the Ironwood Stage in Calgary, the owner, Patrick, was hard to contain after the show. He liked it a lot and didn't understand why I didn't have an agent. (I booked it myself, usually did.) He thought I should have more corporate representation, like the other acts he usually received. Appreciating his enthusiasm I thanked him but explained that most of the usual agents don't like me, or don't like my work, or they don't like me personally.

He said no no no you have to meet Fred at the Agency, he's different. Next day Patrick wrote an introductory email for Fred and me and Fred responded inviting me to contact him. I followed up with a phone call.

Hi Fred, Bob Wiseman here.

Hey Bobby how are you? Love your stuff!

Thanks.

Bobby I got to tell you we're pretty full up right now, it's a tough time.

No sweat, I was just honouring the introduction Patrick made.

Look Bobby, let me know next time you come to town, I want to see your show.

Toronto?

Yes.

I live in Toronto. I'll be playing the Tranzac Wednesday.

Shit Wednesday I have racquetball but any other Wednesday Bobby I'd really like to know.

How about the 27th?

Shit that's POP Montreal.

Okay.

I gotta go Bobby but do keep in touch man, for real okay? And please please please let Patrick know we spoke.

I will.

I called Patrick, tried to not act I-told-you-so but he changed the subject — you gotta talk to Shelly at Paquin Entertainment. She's so great and she's really different than the others yada yada. Within the hour he made another email introduction. I wondered if his confidence stemmed from his relationships, like if these agents encourage club owners like him, who are pivotal, to believe they have sincere friendships and that their opinions are taken very seriously by the agents or if that was just an act, something they high-five each other for back in the office after the client hangs up. My guess was the latter; so far I didn't think I was wrong. A couple days later I was talking with Shelly.

Hi Bobby, sorry for the delay it's a zoo around here. I am very familiar with your work, so what are you doing these days?

Just the usual, making records, touring.

Nice real nice. So what can I do for you?

I don't know, I was following up to your response email after Patrick from the Ironwood wrote to suggest you work with me?

Oh yeah, right. Thanks yes okay. So who do you work with now?

Just myself.

Right okay yes well I would love to help where I can. Unluckily though I am just too busy to take on any more artists. I would not be able to spend enough time on the project to do it proper justice. I mean it's really really *really* hard you know what I mean?

I know.

Why don't you send me your work?

I thought based on the exchange with Patrick you might want to work with me but actually I'm okay, I'm good. I don't have the things in place that probably are preferable for you like an ordinary manager or an ordinary record company.

You have no label support?

No, I don't.

Oh.

Okay, well, I'll get going.

Okay sure, thanks a lot for calling Bobby and please let Patrick know we spoke. Okey dokey?

Okey dokey.

I called Patrick back and told him what happened, now it was almost a week after the show that excited him. I expected him to give up by now but he did it again. He said Bob Wilson at Live Tour Artists, you have to speak with him. He's different. (How many people can be different?) Okay, sure, I said. Once again he wrote an introductory email but then my phone rang.

Hi is Bob there?

Hi, I'm Bob.

Hi, I'm Bob Wilson, I got your number from Patrick at the Ironwood, I remember you from years ago. You want to meet for a drink and discuss what you're doing now?

Sure, when's a good time for you?

Tonight?

See you tonight.

And he was great and we did a bunch of work over the next three years and he got me paid much higher than I do by myself and then my daughter was born and I rearranged my life to be a stay-at-home person. She just turned five, I might be due to try again now.

reincarnation

More than one friend believes in reincarnation and one in particular is absolutely convinced — anyone who plays very well means they had previous lives playing. What can you say to someone who thinks like that except fart and walk away . . . but I liked him too much, so I tried to be straight up.

"Anyone can play good."

"No, not true."

"You think I play the way I do because of past lives?"

"I know it."

"How do you know it?"

"I just do, Bob, it's obvious."

"But I know I can show anyone how to do whatever I know how to do."

"And do they?"

"If they do the work."

"And do they?"

"Not usually but they don't usually do the work. It doesn't mean that doing the work doesn't get them to where I'm pointing."

"You did all this in another lifetime, maybe more."

"Can you prove it?"

"Proof is what you do. Ordinary people can't do that."

And so it went, over years like ping-pong.

He died since then. He once told me he hoped he comes back as a cat. That makes sense. A cat would be very experienced in being stubborn.

little big

Little person starts to cry, confronted with my impatience. Impossible for her to understand that the dance class starts at a certain time. She can't tell time and she loves the dance class. Was ready to go moments ago but then the dust. Busy now exploring pieces of dust. What is my problem, these are amazing pieces of dust. She was even trying to collect them on tape and make me a gift. Ungrateful grown-up. Can't say anything to reassure her, now wailing at higher decibels. It is me that has to change, not her.

The first time I recorded Mary Margaret O'Hara I hit record, she sang, I liked some parts but not every part, she came into the control room and I explained my opinions about what was good and what wasn't, then I played it back to prove my point but had an unexpected surprise, heard more in playback than I recalled during recording. Felt awkward but stuck to my initial feedback, after all I'm in charge and I'm going to prove how smart I am. Mary Margaret isn't someone I ever saw be frustrated or angry. She went back genially to the microphone and we repeated the experience. The fact is after each playback, what I felt so certain about kept proving incorrect. Decided to shut up and collect her improvisations and study the recording over time. Make decisions later. Stop disrupting her instincts since they're more complex than my immediate process; it was me that needed to change.

umwelt

My evil plan is working. Returning to school, finishing my master's, nose to the grindstone, show up, do the work, *poof*, first semester done. No degree, just a bunch of Junos, which as it turns out are pretty good when placed over bass strings if you play prepared piano. Seems like nobody notices I am an imposter. Certain people understand life can be war and we can be spies. When the class looked at Umwelt, it wasn't a new concept as much as it was a new word for an old idea. My younger self couldn't handle material I didn't agree with. Fast forward decades, it is a cinch. Now so familiar with situations or ideas that I don't agree with — if my inner voice wasn't silenced, then who cares about different opinions? My father returned to school in middle age. I'm where he was 30 years ago. It's like having a new connection with him, like time travel. As far as spies go, he deserved his own shoe-phone. Naturally, I'm studying music, though not in the music department.

did you get the joke?

Little person is into knock-knock jokes. As far as she understands, the point of the jokes is just to have a last line which could be anything. For instance, knock knock, who's there, dog, dog who? dog and popcorn ha ha ha ha ha ha ha ha ha ha and it is really hilarious every time. Way funnier than the joke of being an opening act.

We want you to open for (insert famous person). Sure, how much does it pay? Sorry, it doesn't pay. But your tickets are $25 and this place holds 200 people. Yeah, but our expenses are crazy, so you want to do it or what? I'll throw in a couple drink tickets (and dinner at half-price).

Guy in coffee shop tells me the code to their wifi is 11111111. I said one sec, I'll write it down. He says don't worry, it's on all the tables. People who don't get the joke, that's life.

stanley cowell

A group of jazz musicians from Philadelphia and New York came through Winnipeg in the mid-70s. They gave workshops before giving a big concert. I signed up for the piano session. It was with one of the first musical monsters I ever met, Stanley Cowell. He spoke to us (seven young pianists) about what was happening on the piano in New York. Watching him play it was apparent this situation was over-kill, like hiring Evel Knievel to discuss how to balance on a tricycle. He didn't make us feel awkward, he was a gentleman, he said where I come from people are trying to have an independent left hand. I got that message and even though it was a long time ago, that idea remains never too far from my piano mind.

90

Sometimes, on the road, when she was telling the same story for the 90th time to whatever audience was in front of her, this one artist used to also think, this situation has nothing to do with why I started writing music in the first place.

loop pedal

In the movies, the person sentenced to death is never offered a last piece of music. In real life, it is worse. They can never stop hearing the same song between their ears right up until the fat lady sings.

on hold

I got her off script for just one moment. Can you please not play the horrible music while I'm on hold? She laughed and said no music? Yes, I'm a musician. She laughed again, no problem, I hate it too.
No doubt as surveillance cameras, wherever she is stationed, caught the unsanctioned response, she probably got fired.

mensch award

When I lived in the country it took 90 minutes to get there from Toronto. A zillion people told me they would like to see it. Jumped on that curiosity and invited them over right then, right now. Then they would say they had "no time" but maybe later. All but one time, that is.
Gord: Hi, I wasn't sure if I would get you or an answering machine. Heard you moved outside the city.
Bob: Yeah, it's 45 minutes past Hamilton.
Gord: What is it exactly that you bought?
Bob: It's an old blacksmith shop.
Gord: So you're making horseshoes?
Bob: Not exactly (both chuckle). I have a studio set-up, you want to come over? I could put you to work engineering.
Gord: Like right now?
Bob: Sure.
The Juno committee never acknowledged Gord Downie's technique

for pressing record and play, on a Tascam MSR-16. But he should have been nominated for Best Impromptu and the 1995 Mensch Prize.

who else would it be?

I played a piano song at the Tranzac open stage. People applauded. Asked did I play too much (because usually people do two songs but I might have played too long) — a woman at the bar said do eight more. The host told me it would be fine to do one more. I started one more but heard someone loudly talking, as though the music was in the way of their conversation. An annoying stumbling block for improvising. I looked up, it was the woman who said do eight more.

ginkgo

I never saw ginkgo trees growing up, nor heard of them. Didn't notice until 15 years ago around High Park when Daeren pointed them, out extolling their medicinal virtues. Love the look of the crazy ginkgo leaf, like nothing nowhere. Someone told me they are prehistoric, I don't know what that means but I added it to the list of reasons to be in awe. Rarely saw big ones until last week at Queen's Park and same day in front of Hart House (east side). Like a skyscraper. What a pattern and what a leaf. If I write a song about this tree, most probably Ringo, Bingo, Lingo and Carmaig's son will find their way into my rhyme scheme.

kombucha — steve gadd

Made kombucha about eight times, only one batch so far exploded, I would like a badge. Never obtained the top badge in swimming, the bronze medallion, but did get my red seniors. At the seniors' residence in the north end with my dad we visit his old uncle Isaac, and he sneaks in a flask of whiskey and a sandwich from Oscar's to share with his uncle. I liked the skinny, concave, toothless 94-year-old guy. Even though I was four, didn't mind him kissing me and the gleeful sounds he made as secret nourishments were revealed. Sneaking is an art form. The better musicians are good sneaks, the lesser ones heavy-handed. The great drummers sneak in all sorts of things that I don't see coming. Gleeful all around. Shaking hands with Steve Gadd in 1991, unexpected and ridiculous but there he was, small and thin saying hello. I felt like Mike Myers in *Wayne's World* when he meets Alice Cooper, on his knees muttering "I'm not worthy."

secret

There was a student from a small town who said all the people they ever wished they could see live would never come there because it was too tiny but now that they moved to the big city, everyone they ever wanted to see comes through each year. Who have you seen, I asked? No one, he replied, if I go to the actual concert it will depress me. But I thought that was your wish? I'd rather keep it to a dream, if I do it for real it will only remind me where I'm not. Is that your secret? He smirked, You realize you are asking me a question whose answer destroys itself? Waitasec, I think I got this relationship backwards.

is but a joke

Got to the class a little early and found one of the guys practising Make You Feel My Love, he's maybe 22 years old. Don't know any of these people well but my sense of this particular guy was that he would have thought Adele wrote the Dylan song.
"Do you know who wrote that song?" I asked, eager to surprise him.
"Bob Dylan," he answered.
"That's right," I said, disappointed at not getting to prove my cred as the teacher. "Do you know much of Bob Dylan's music?"
"I know he's written lots he doesn't get any credit for, it's a real shame."
"You think so? Like what?"
"All Along the Watchtower," he replied.

tiff

At a TIFF premiere, Q&A with director, and I got the last question. I asked what his process was like with the composer.

He answered the composer was a big shot who he didn't anticipate being able to work with but surprisingly the composer approached him. They tried some cues blah blah blah basically he said it was fantastic to watch the composer develop the score. No fights. No dilemmas. Didn't have anything to say that was critical.

Then everyone claps, says goodnight. As I made my way out, taking the long way, I noticed by the elevators the director was still talking to fans and so I approached and reminded him I was the last question and had one more question — was it really so easy for them to work together? He said no it wasn't, but I'm not going to say that out loud in a Q&A.

What's the point of the Q&A? It doesn't mean you have to insult someone if you had disagreements, it's just a way for us to gain insight. So this was the insight, that he's chicken.

bad song

Many students had similar questions in the songwriting course when assigned the following problem: write a bad song.
"What's that?"
"You tell me."
"Is it supposed to be out of tune?"
"Sure, that would be bad."
"Is it bad rhythmically?"
"Sure. That could be bad."
"But for who?"
"You mean for who is it bad?"
"Yes."
"That's it, isn't it?"
"We can do, like, anything?"
"Make it bad, don't let me hear anything good."
"Why are we doing this?"
"Because I'm in charge."

"But what's the point of writing a bad song?"

"How could we be certain you wrote a good song if the assignment was reversed?"

"For one thing, it would groove."

"I don't like the Macarena, but it grooves. Why can't I call it bad?"

"What's the Macarena?"

"Am I that old?"

"Yes."

"So what's the point of writing a good song?"

"We're not studying music so we can be bad at doing it."

"Good point. The thing is, what one person calls good another calls bad. We could also call the assignment write a good song, same problems."

"So it's a test."

"Maybe, maybe not, I thought there would be less baggage if we started with what's 'bad'; we can discuss later as a class. It's like eating celery, this is good for you, trust me."

shhhh

(to the drummer) How do you do that?

I can't tell you.

Why not?

Because you wouldn't believe me.

Try me.

Better to stay silent about what you know, like you're growing a plant and talking about it is pulling it out of the soil to show people proof that there's roots. Then you killed it.

I see. Well, what you did is incredible.

It isn't me.

It looked like you.

I turn the key in the ignition, but I'm not responsible for the belts and pistons. That's what you want to know about — truth is, it isn't me.

Is that what you didn't think I would believe?

We've said too much.

Tell me more.

I don't want to be taken away by men in white coats.

What men in white coats?

The ones I'll see if I talk about it. Certain things you don't talk about when you want to preserve them.

mind fail

Why can't I take lessons with you?
I didn't say you couldn't take lessons, I said I couldn't teach you.
Why can't you teach me?
Because you don't practise.
I'm just being real. I don't have time to practise.
I'm being real too.
Can't you just show me how you do that thing?
It requires practice.
Why is it so hard?
It isn't.
Yes it is.
What do you mean?
Playing something over and over, coordinating your hands, remembering details, that's hard.
You know, I can recommend someone else, I know a classical teacher.
But I like you.
But you don't hear me.
No, you're the one not listening.
How is that?
I just want you to show me how you do that thing and you want me to make a commitment to practise.
Right.
Right.
Okay, I'll show you how to do that thing.
Thanks.
You go like this.
How did you do that?
Like this.
That's hard.
Do it slow.
It's crazy.
Do it very, very slow.

Why can't I do it like you?
You can, but it doesn't start by being able to do it exactly like me.
Why not?
Hey, are we in a tape loop?
You think?
Is it starting over again?
Why can't I take lessons with you?
Shit.
Wow, we did this already.
A bunch.
You think there is a way out? Or at least an interruption.
I don't know.
That's what you always say.
I don't know.
Say something different.
[...]
I don't want to study with you.
Perfect.
Just kidding, I do.
Do you want to escape eternity or not?
Then agree to teach me.
Unfair.
In the scheme of unfair possibilities, this isn't the worst.
Agreed.

20 years ago, detroit

Lineup of cars at the Canadian side of the Detroit border. Inside a clunker van the driver is carefully rehearsing.
Canadian. Toronto. 101 Major Street. Chicago . . . my friend Matt. 1631 Henderson. For free . . . for promotion . . . no cds. Just two days.
Canadian. Toronto. 101 Major Street. Chicago . . . my friend Matt. 1631 Henderson. For free . . . for promotion . . . no cds. Just two days.
Canadian. Toronto. 101 Major Street. Chicago . . . my friend Matt. 1631 Henderson. For free . . . for promotion . . . no cds. Just two days.
His car pulls up.

Burly US border guard, brush-cut and sparkly mirror sunglasses, expressionlessly observes young Canadian rolling down window.

BG: Citizenship?
YC: Canadian.
BG: (slightly annoyed) Where.
YC: Toronto.
BG: What's your address?
YC: 101 Major Street. The postal code is M—
BG: (raises voice) Did I ask you for that?
YC: No.
BG: Where you going today?
YC: Chicago.
BG: What's the purpose of your trip?
YC: I'm a musician and —
BG: Have a visa?
YC: No, I . . . because I'm not making any money.
BG: (matter-of-fact) So you are working in America.
YC: No, I'm playing for free at a publicity event for my friend.
BG: What's your friend's name?
YC: Matt Suhar.
BG: Where is Matt Suhar? (he starts to type on his computer)
YC: Chicago.
BG: Where you staying in Chicago?
YC: 1631 Henderson.
Border guard leans into the van, notices something very suspicious on rear seat.
BG: What's that!
YC: My accordion.
Border guard pauses.
BG: Your what?
YC: I play accordion, that's what I'm doing, playing accordion at this music event.
BG: (pitying tone of voice) People actually come to hear you . . . (starts giggling) on accordion?
YC: Yeah.
BG: (sighs and waves him through) Just go, just go.

telling children to look closer

I miss the days when my daughter asked me questions like who made everything? Why do we die? Are you going to die? Am I going to die? How did Jim Keltner get all those gigs? Why did Dylan go Christian? Why did Joni Mitchell stop playing the dulcimer? I was confident I knew it all and then she asked what is the difference between primitive accumulation and accumulation by dispossession? Turns out I wasn't monitoring as many Paw Patrol episodes as I should have but all right, I'm modern, I can tell her the truth.

The Earth made everything and everything dies, I can't tell you why, but probably it is the same answer as why we are alive, I will die, you will too, Keltner obviously made a deal with an evil magician, Dylan believed in those ideas, Joni got into modern jazz and the dulcimer was locked into a diatonic sequence, she might yet play it again. Marx was trying to sort out the big historical picture of who had wealth and how did they get it, generally it was from stealing, robbing and murder. Harvey is talking about the same thing, but updating the term because Marx was writing 150 years ago, language changes.

It's a pity, in your father's humble opinion, that some Marxists might fight too long over these differences because the larger issue is the plight of the poor or the possession of power by a few, regardless of everything else. Musicians used to waste hours like this too over analog vs. digital. Have you noticed Ryder is always telling Skye, Chase, Zuma and Rocky what to do and where to go? For every rescue completed by the little pups, they never acquire the positionality of Ryder despite the fact that they perform the work. Look closer, see how the workers perpetuate themselves as workers and the capitalists as capitalists?

Three songs

Teacher: Try to figure out why these three songs are grouped together. (Teacher projects lyrics onto screen and plays songs)
Pusherman by Curtis Mayfield

Free Man in Paris by Joni Mitchell
Lonely at the Top by Randy Newman

Student 1: They're in the same key?

Teacher: Nope.

Student 2: They're all about people on drugs.

Teacher: How did you get that?

Student 2: Just a wild guess.

Teacher: Listen a little harder, please, and tell me what's similar?

Student 3: They happen in different cities.

Teacher: Maybe . . . but still not what I was trying to point you to hear in this course. It's about songwriting, remember?

Student 4: The songwriter isn't the actual person telling the story.

Teacher: Then what are they?

Student 5: Characters.

Teacher: Right. They're someone else.

Student 5: Why do that?

Teacher: Because you can do anything you want in a song. Because it allows you to say something in a different way than if you are saying it as yourself. Because maybe they're bored with the usual ways they write? Let's make an assignment — write something from a character's point of view.

Student 6: That's too hard.

Teacher: That's too hard?

Student 6: I always write from my point of view.

Teacher: Then that's a reason to try this.

Student 6: I only know myself.

Teacher: Take someone else you know. You think I'm unfair sometimes, right?

Student 6: You're always unfair.

Teacher: Thanks, okay, write a song as though you're me being the unfair person I am.

Student 6: Do I get a bad mark if I make you look bad?

(Insert *Planet of the Apes* soundtrack while teacher ponders answer)

trick or treat

Two best parts of the AGO Halloween kids' party.

First — realizing on the dance floor when YMCA came on that it was one of the greatest examples ever of songs that had an effect on power and culture.

Other best part — when my five-year-old asked me (told me) to stand over by the wall, far away from her dance space.

open stage part 1

Teacher: You should go play your songs in front of people.

Student: Why?

Teacher: It's like an invisible part of writing, doing it in front of people reveals something else about the song. Go do it at an open stage.

Student: But I'm scared.

Teacher: What are you scared of?

Student: Stage fright.

Teacher: The audience is probably just three people and they're trying to watch a baseball game while you sing your serious little song.

Student: I still get nervous.

Teacher: About what?

Student: I might forget my words.

Teacher: Then put your words on a music stand.

Student: I might forget the chords.

Teacher: Uh huh.

Student: You don't understand.

Teacher: Think you might look stupid?

Student: Yes that's it.

Teacher: It's a convention of people looking stupid . . . and not looking stupid — that's exactly why you should play it. Nobody is so uncool as to be seen at an open stage, thus it the *coolest* place to get your shit together.

Student: Do you play them?

Teacher: My favourite place.

Student: Why?

Teacher: I like being wrong about what's going to happen next.

Student: Why do I get nervous?

Teacher: The more you actually "fail" the quicker you figure it out. Looking foolish isn't something anyone wants to do, but why not look foolish in front of nobody rather than later if you get that big break from Breakfast Television?

open stage part 2: oz

Student: You like not knowing?

Teacher: I'm usually wrong about what's going to happen next and I like that.

Student: Why?

Teacher: Keeps the assumptions in check.

Student: Which assumptions?

Teacher: When someone takes the stage, one gets a sense that they might be this way or that way and many times these assumptions are wrong. That's the best part of an open stage. No — I take that back — the best part is when I think someone is something I've seen a million times before but they turn out to be so original I'm destroyed.

Student: I think it's about entertainment.

Teacher: Entertainment is part of it but the artists I like the most aren't primarily entertainment.

Student: What are they?

Teacher: Dangerous.

Student: What's that mean?

Teacher: They're not entertainers. They take the stage and pretty soon we're not in Kansas anymore.

job interview

Bossman: do you know much about us?

Applicant: I know someone who studied here years ago.

Bossman: who?

Applicant: Don Noyse.

Bossman: I remember him. he managed a band called change my chakras.

Applicant: right.

Bossman: I told him, do you have a signed contract? he said no. and then the band got a lot of attention and I said to him again do you have a signed contract and he said no. And then they left him for another manager, a girl named jamie something, and then it all went to hell.

Applicant: you think you should always have a contract?

Bossman: a piece of paper makes everyone understand better what's going on and keeps people straighter.

Applicant: what about all the people married who fall out of it? isn't divorce like 50% even though they have a piece of paper?

Bossman: the paper is an incentive to stay together.

Applicant: but there are bands that remained loyal to someone with just a handshake.

Bossman: we teach people about how to make money.

Applicant: okay. I can orient what I know to illuminate the probabilities of money.

Bossman: why don't you write it up for me in an email along with some . . . do you have some . . .

Applicant: a cv of my activities and awards?

Bossman: yeah.

Applicant: I'll send you that and I'll write up the kind of course I could offer. see if it works for you.

Bossman: good one. so what does Don do now?

Applicant: he has a yoga studio, maybe two, and he owns a building.

Bossman: isn't that something.

Applicant: probably signed a lease.

Bossman: probably.

the bus

In the mornings when I walk my daughter to the bus, five- and six-year-old kids return my look with stone expressions. I make a contest out of it, but they don't blink. Adults would never do this without looking away or getting hostile, but for these guys I am just another bush or fence. I like this more than a good play, wonder if I'm the audience or an actor.

memory

If I hold up seven fingers, my daughter doesn't yet know it is seven. She will count internally to get to seven. If I said, go to the part of O Canada with the lyric "we see thee rise," probably you have to sing the song to yourself from the beginning in order to find the moment in question. I never thought much about that before and wonder now if musical memories are actually time-lapse memories or if it's like the fingers on my hand and if you play the song a zillion times maybe you can intersect any moment without thinking twice.

when

When I actually get uninterrupted sleep I feel like I did whatever people hope to accomplish from pilates.

When I pitch another podcast I'll resume my rejection-letter-wallpaper art project.

When the interview started I was relieved the numbers were advancing, previously screwed up recording, my imaginary reputation ruined.

When the mother of the boy my daughter ambush-hugs said they were going for ice cream I thought she meant across the street but 30 minutes later at the library I noticed them eating ice cream across that street and avoided eye contact so it was clear I wasn't following them.

When the body shop guy said at least $2,000 I know then it's actually $500 tops.

When listening to the lecture about what the mind can't do, I couldn't.

When giving lessons via skype feels like starring in a tv series.

When sitting down at the piano, start a variation on a theme and regularly end up somewhere new and exciting all the while trying to keep a little piece of attention on remembering how I got there.

When I think one part of me is completely committed to playing and another part of me is trying to remember how this piece developed I realize I am more than one thing calling myself "I" but then I realize I am I — how can I be more than one of me?

countering monster music

Went to *Hotel Transylvania 3* with my daughter. (Spoiler alert.) The climax of the movie is the unleashing of a monster to destroy all other monsters and the way to give life to that most evil of evil monsters is through playing a dance beat. I was amused by that plot development. To counter it, the good guy monsters played three songs to destroy the capacity of the evil thing to be moved by the dance music. They played Good Vibrations followed by Don't Worry Be Happy followed by the Macarena.
Yawn. I would have used Helen Reddy or Moxy Früvous for igniting the villain. Then to counter it, sticking with the producer's template of three songs building in musical-goodness-intensity, I'm thinking Breezin' by George Benson followed by Cissy Houston's version of Bridge Over Troubled Water followed by The Champs doing Tequila.

touring italy (pt. 1)

I am very pleased with my situation now as I sit upstairs from the "video-bar" owned by generous Natalino — my brother.
"Buono sera, my brudder," he said for good night.
Centobuchi, the city of Natalino's video-bar, is east of Rome and the coolest show of the tour. Better still, the next day will be our day off here. We arrived around 8:30 to a full house, kind of an odd piece of theatre to set up the show in front of the crowd. A scrunched tiny space that doesn't accommodate my video screen, but we make makeshift solutions.
Coolest part is the French guy asking if I parlez-vous and realizing I

can communicate more things in French than in Italian and successfully inform him about the lights, about being vegetarian and about the draft from the door. He's on the case.

The audience freaks out, the Italian subtitles are working, they laugh, they cry. I do two encores — we're definitely not in Hamilton. When it is over and I'm packing up, some people buy cds, each asks same question — "weach juan ease bitter?" Natalino waits patiently to ask, "Can I ug you, Bob?" Sure you can hug me, Natalino . . . brudder.

types of teaching

Skating with five-year-old who clings to plastic support thing, which I am pulling on the ice to help her move forward. Briefly stop the teenage ice patrol for her opinion, probably she is a pro. What moves do you recommend for teaching this little girl the basics of skating? She says getting up on one knee is a good start because there are always falls. I realize I have interrupted or rescued all falls. I start to let it happen and let her get up using one knee for support. She is having a good time. It was wise and falling on your ass is part of it. I have had teachers put me in a position to be shocked or humiliated, falling on my ass in front of everyone. I resented it and thought they were assholes. Hard to tell now if when it happened it was because they truly were assholes or sincerely trying to position me somewhere uncomfortable to learn how to get up and start again. Don't know. Cut to: music conference 25 years ago, Saskatoon. A panel of "industry experts" rate demo tapes by local musicians. They complained and made lists of reasons each song failed. Everybody endured some criticism about what was "wrong." I wondered how to assure them that being in this line and dignifying the opinions of people who once tried to make it but failed is another wrong — maybe the only one worth thinking about.

touring italy pt. 2

Natalino can't speak very much English but makes it clear he is opening a special bottle of wine. Italians take pride in wine knowledge and this one he explains is a locally made combination of two grapes, red and white. It's beautiful, we sit and drink and eat bread drizzled in olive oil. Gino enters with trays of breaded zucchini, carrots, onions and polenta made by his mother. We talk about movies and his video store and Natalino and Sylvia's upcoming marriage. The fear I felt while Stefano was driving fades away.

He heard political ideas in some of my songs and he's eager to ask me questions and Sylvia and Gino try to translate for us.

Why did you start making movies?

Why do you write songs with political messages?

How do people in Canada react to it?

Will you get into trouble?

I explain some trouble I already got into and how I wrote a play called *Actionable* about lawyers and lawsuits (and me). They want me to translate the play into Italian, not sure that will ever happen. I explain that in Canada people either like me or hate me, generally no in-between. As for making films that I accompany it's because the extent to which people feel entertained relates highly to how far I can go saying something that's simultaneously humorous and serious.

Answering why I write whatever I write is the hardest to translate. In the world of song you can repair things that probably never will be repaired, about the heart or about politics.

everybody knows

leonard cohen at the junos in vancouver 25 years ago. just a handshake by the back door as he was leaving. wished a handshake could be a long conversation but so it goes. certain songs other people wrote, wish i wrote. everything is broken by bob dylan or everybody knows by leonard cohen. at the show yesterday, one performer said, "this is my last song . . . or is it okay if i do more? who is the time keeper?" annoying when people talk like someone else is responsible for their set length, like it is up to the audience to stop them. so manipulative and hambone. about as legitimate as a police union. have to persuade my big mouth to stay zipped up, later maybe in song, release opinions even if it doesn't make me friends. read about assassination of journalist daphne caruana galizia, like reading about assassination of anna politkovskaya like reading about murder of artist pippa bacca. leonard

cohen hit many nails on the head, maybe best was when he wrote
i've seen the future and it's murder. i feel kinship to those murdered
people whose crime in dark rooms was turning on the light switch. i
keep reassuring my four-year-old daughter that there are no monsters
but i'm lying.

dreams, talent and loss

Cheamer managed one artist, Reg Wood, who as a teenager imitated
Lenny Breau, or at least he could do The Claw the way Lenny Breau
recorded it. I would be surprised if anyone else for a thousand miles
could do that, and he was 16. Seemed a no-brainer: with the right
management, Reg should be a star. Cheamer's skills at buying and selling cars didn't train him for the peculiarities of the music business,
swag, bullshitting and payola. It knocked him off his game and he lost
everything after striking up a friendship with Jerry Weintraub, which
was clever considering Weintraub was in a powerful position booking
Elvis Presley during the previous decade and now grooming/market-
ing John Denver to massive success. Weintraub understood the math
behind advertising. Ultimately, you could sell anything if you could
afford to have it repeated on radio and tv and in print. Doesn't matter
what the music sounds like, people just absorb advertising. Like those
signs in the subway, "A funny thing happens when you don't advertise
. . . nothing." The formula holds true 50 years later. If you spend at
least 65 thousand dollars, you make back more than three times that
in units sold or concert seat admission. Thank God, he thought to
himself, hardly anyone understands this principle; less competition.

But he didn't have any reason to help Cheamer, so he gave him
misdirections, sticking to his motto (less competition). It was a stock
tip, encouraging the out-of-towner to believe it would provide the
gains needed to make his future investments. Cheamer not only
assumed Jerry Weintraub was sincere, he mortgaged his house and
put everything into Steep Rock Mines, whose only steepness was how
fast his net worth declined. In the first month 60% and the following
month even lower. Cheamer's music management career ended before
it started and young Reg Wood moved to Vancouver where he got into
heroin like his hero, died like him too. That was on Lasqueti Island

where he was a momentary star at a jazz festival backing up and falling in love with Anzuba Marseilles, a singer from Nigeria whose claim to fame was singing on Fela Kuti's classic Zombie, and her very original vocals. Her interpretations had that high delicate swirling Billie Holiday presence and an unexpected aggression in her delivery which was of course not like Billie Holiday at all, not like anyone. She found Cheamer in the water, she saw it as a curse, as proof there was something wrong with leaving Nigeria and so she left British Columbia, nobody heard of her again.

There was a tv show in Winnipeg hosted by Ray St. Germain and there are recordings there of pre-drug-addicted Reg Wood accompanying some pretty boring country music except that he is simultaneously playing bass lines. As though his guitar is the future instrument known as The Stick. He was a novelty act. It was the only gig Cheamer successfully obtained. There is also some stuff from Channel 13, a cable access outlet, like a community centre tv station. Two older women, lovers who escaped Nazi Germany in their youth, had a show called *The Cosmopolitans*, where they played organ and drums. They played old folks' homes, they played to children, they were grateful to be alive in Canada and living a safe life since they knew so much more about death and torture than the average person walking down Corydon or Inkster. Teenagers would call in during their show and try to shock them by requesting Stairway to Heaven or Smoke on the Water not really suppressing their laughter but the Cosmopolitans weren't born yesterday, they survived Hitler, the joke was on the teens. They learned those songs the next week and played them, albeit a little wooden. Next week Reg guested and turned up the surrealism. Two middle-aged good-natured polka lovers were now propelled into Hendrixian stratospheres. Such a shame no one pushed to rename the swanky Tuxedo neighbourhood to Cosmopolitan. A fitting tribute it would be to all these wicked intersections of dreams, talent and loss.

hat trick

Went to the café to do some writing. The owner asked me about the strike at York. She said horrible how the world is changing and people are out of work, you can't foresee how future technologies will impact employment, people are stranded and so many jobs are discriminatory and unfair. She and her partner recently reconfigured the restaurant, now fewer workers do more work, same minimum wage.

Went to an open stage, the performers and the spirit of the place were awesome. Former student invited me and later introduced me to a guy he referred to as his mentor, who soon started explaining to me his perspective about the exploitation of Black people in the film *Black Panther* "didn't even use a real star like Denzel because he costs 20 million dollars, people don't realize those actors were not big stars and this is all because of the Jews. They own the comic magazines and are behind exploiting Black people . . . you're not a Jew, are you?"

Went to a play with Magali, heard great things about the play from a classmate, but we were disappointed, bored. Driving home we discussed the holes in the writing and in the characters. Later, read something by the writer, about how she can't know if men who don't like her play are not liking it just because it is bad or because they are unconsciously biased.

Went to YouTube and watched James Baldwin freak everyone out in a 1965 lecture at Cambridge, calling them out on refusing to live and breathe equity. Perpetuating prejudice by filtering what passes for reality, "One of the great things that the White world does not know, but I think I do know, is that Black people are just like everybody else."

Anyone can be a saint or an asshole.
Like the Dylan song, "Wouldn't know the difference between a real blonde and a fake."

touring italy pt. 3

I wake up the first day, which wisely was a planned day to adjust and not perform. I make my way to buy food after Stefano tells me he hasn't any. That is of course totally fine, it is best I take care of myself and not worry about whether things in his cupboards appeal to a vegetarian diet. The first store I find is run by an old man and an older woman dressed in black and they cannot speak any English. We speak sign language but he moves my hand away when I try to feel a pear. The rules are he gets to select whichever fruits or vegetables I want. I bought tomatoes, pears, a ready-made salad and pink lady apples because of their name. A little farther down the street there is a larger grocery store. I would rather buy from the little people but I would also rather feel the food and select it.

I forgot how much I love being in strange places watching locals do business. Way less interested in medieval churches, more keen on neighbourhood life. This food store is remarkable for at least two crazy vegetables, a small clover cluster which I bought (tasted spinach-like), and a crazy white lettuce with purple swirl patterns. I didn't try it but I might have bought it to frame it on the wall. The customers weigh everything in advance on scales that have miniature pictures of the items. It's a game where you put your item on the scale and after you punch the corresponding picture an automatic price is printed for you to stick to your bag.

It's so fortunate to have a booking agent. Fifty percent of the situation is an agent like Monica. If the work I do ever becomes larger and profitable I would reward her with loyalty and bonuses. I would send other artists I believe in to her.

I've approached at least 20 others in Britain, Germany, the Netherlands and Scandinavia. They tell me to get lost by not responding or bluntly pointing out if I have no major support go away and besides they don't like talking directly with artists, there are too many applicants. It's down to who can pay them the most. Not unusual in the mean, lean capitalist world but still heartbreaking. I try to alert them to why my background might make their job easier. Previous records on both major labels and indie labels. Is it not helpful that guests on my records include Daniel Lanois, Edie Brickell, Mary Margaret O'Hara, Jane Siberry, Eugene Chadbourne? Even though they don't know me, doesn't that give them something to talk about when they try to sell the show? Of course that's the wrong reason but they just want any reason, right?

More silence.

If there are still agents somewhere who might take a chance on me they are hiding really, really well.

two prince fans

Two music fans were fighting about Prince. One said everything he ever did was magic, the other said he only sang about his penis. Soon they rolled out of the bar and onto the street and fists were swinging. A police cruiser pulled over and broke it up, issuing $300 fines for believing music was worth fistfighting over. They challenged the tickets. Almost one year later they had their day in court. There was build-up, Christie Blatchford published a piece defending the cop who she said did everything right and now was being judged for the crime of breaking up a fight. She asked, what's next? Taking away tasers?

At the trial the prosecution was eager to show off their homework. They prepared expert witnesses to explain the basis of how these two broke the law. Their first witness was Rob Bowman from York University. He was set to prove (utilizing overhead projector diagrams) his interpretation on the only known song where Prince didn't sing about his penis, but the defendants surprised everyone with opening statements. They said people have the right to beat each other up for not agreeing over musical opinions, because don't we sanction murder and survival regularly when we conduct war? And it went viral. The prosecution was blindsided. Soon the Young Turks, Fox News, Pitchfork and an intern from Canadaland set up outside the courtroom. The judge didn't like any of it and called a two-week recess while hearing arguments in his chambers privately.

Busking musicians using battery-powered amplifiers started to assemble outside the court building and started playing renditions of Raspberry Beret or Nothing Compares 2 U. The cacophony was substantial and they were making more money than in the subway. People liked hearing music by the same composer simultaneously, overlapping, interjecting and occasionally harmonizing. David Dacks was inspired to make this into a Music Gallery event possibly for next winter but there was nobody to talk with who represented everyone. *NOW Magazine* approached the two fans to do a feature story (and cover) and Shaftesbury Films offered to buy the rights to their story. The two fans took the money, did the interviews, changed their minds about fighting the tickets and started a Tim Hortons franchise together in Brampton. Some years later they were asked by Jaymz Bee (sitting in for Carol Off) if they owed everything to Prince. They replied there is no such thing as a single event being responsible for all the events that follow it. There is always something else that happened earlier and one could argue that that influenced the situation. Do we credit Prince for this cruller (points to donut)? or do we credit Mark (Winnipeg friend) who introduced me to Prince's work years earlier at the Lithium Café? Jaymz wasn't sure exactly how to respond, so he took a picture of the three of them with a bottle of vodka which later ran on his wall as Absolut Preence Fights.

(alt ending)

In his chambers the judge said we can't have this even though I agree with you. Absolutely, we go to war for imaginary reasons. If you want to beat yourselves up over musical opinions, I say why not? Freedom's just another word for nothing left to lose. Nothing don't mean nothin' hon' if it ain't free.

sometimes

Sometimes I'm totally distracted by someone in the audience.

Sometimes it's tempting to do certain flourishes that audiences like even if I don't.

Sometimes I think it was great but the recording reveals it wasn't.

Sometimes I tell the same intro as if I never told it before.

Sometimes I think the performance wasn't very good but the recording reveals in fact it was.

Sometimes I'm impressed with what happened despite no confirmation elsewhere.

Sometimes I don't make a set list.

Sometimes I wish people were in the room when I'm getting somewhere unique while practising.

Sometimes I think it is all in my head but that's impossible.

trained monkey

Went to a comedy show featuring seven acts and liked one especially for self-effacing jokes, seemed off the cuff. Following week I went again and same comic was on the bill and told same jokes. Not as interesting the second time, maybe due to the realization that this is the 500th time they told these jokes. Realized part of what I liked in the first place was believing her thoughts were unrehearsed. The appeal of improvisation is the same in music. Those ancient arguments when I was a teenager — is Keith Jarrett making it up on the spot or not? No he's not! Yes he is! Could spontaneous composition be a thing?

Another comic on the bill indeed was improvising, Becky Johnson. She asks for a subject from the audience, then makes it up. As connected to her art form as the best musical improvisers, walking a high wire between buildings with no net. How natural or unnatural her reactions are is what I find myself listening for. A little scary how perfectly she crosses. When dealing with customs officers at the border, this is the person you want to have with you.

I wonder sometimes about stand-up. What subjects one would gab about. And if one said something funny, how much pressure might one feel to remember it for next time and avoid improvising.

ai weiwei

I didn't understand the piece where he is smashing an ancient vase. Felt offended until I saw what the cultural revolution destroyed in the name of being modern, plus the shoddy construction and the thousands of children who, less than ten years ago, died in collapsed buildings. I like everything about Ai Weiwei. There is a line connecting those stories and music software coming with prefab loops which people drag to their DAW and call it a song they wrote.

touring italy pt. 4

The first show was at a club in Milan called Tourné and I forgot to put away the power supply for my video projector which is a unique cable, too many things to remember. I check my passport and wallet maybe three times an hour plus try to confirm all my cables, instruments, accessories and bag of clothes. I'm so disappointed I forgot the projector cable, freaks me out — such a basic mistake on the very first show. Stefano had a hard time, people didn't stop talking during his set, in fact they spoke even louder in order to hear themselves over him. He started to give them shit at one point but telling off an audience is sort of like being on the Titanic and cursing the water as a strategy. Fuck you, water!

Before I started my set he took me aside and apologized for the crowd, he thought I was going to receive the same treatment. He didn't know I have a secret weapon — movies, and I subtitle them. Actually movies and experience. The audience laughed/cried exactly in the spots I hope all audiences do. It was like the best of shows anywhere. Made friends afterward with a young musical couple. I asked the woman what kind of music she makes. "Eat ease dark soul," she said.

zen koan piano

Cecil Taylor, the man in the driver's seat of modernity for decades, who is 89, I heard today is ill. First heard him at music school. Hard to believe there was a course on piano improvisation, thought it was only my secret hobby. The course was awesome, stayed after class to practise, lived and breathed it, slept in piano cubicles. The pieces and assignments were melodic but I had another secret, playing clusters and abandoning melody or the usual ideas of melody. It started one time when my parents were out of town. Definitely not something to do within earshot of my mother. When I found clusters I found a huge cavity of freedom, the kind of freedom you fantasize about reaching when doing the melodic work. Yesterday while teaching a student blues, someone struggling with patterns, I said you can also suspend all the melodic ideas and play free. Keep the rhythm internalized then return to it, and I demonstrated. He immediately understood. It changed his excitement for the work of what was going on in the first place. One night at York while working on my assignments, in the room with painful fluorescent lights and a Petrof baby grand, where there was a record collection for students to peruse, I put on a Cecil Taylor record, probably because of the groovy name, Cecil. Had no idea who he was. Wasn't expecting my life to change but it did for a couple reasons. First, he was only playing clusters. There was no polite entry point, no melodic stairs to lead everyone up to a departure point. Pow. Started in the new land and didn't leave. These were pieces, and not easy-to-follow pieces, many listeners would dismiss if they weren't prepared to listen actively. Zen Koan piano. An even more extraordinary thing happened next, didn't realize but it was a live recording. He stopped playing and a decent-sized audience applauded. This whole recording had happened in public! Some involuntary tears, like realizing all my life I could speak Cantonese but never knowing it was an actual language with real people speaking, singing, living it.

hey ya

It's cool when a song is in 5 or even 7, but who puts a pop song in 11? Outkast, that's who. Hey Ya still kills me.

even zeus the god can't think straight

More than one student writes songs about betrayal and revenge. More than one tells me they're afraid they will cause a ruckus in present relationships or with friends. I suggest, hide behind Zeus. Many people write about something they appear to be interested in but there are other reasons for their interest. Zeus wanted to have an affair with a mortal woman named Io, but his wife Hera knew what was up. She surprised them in a cloud where they were meeting alone. As Zeus realized Hera would find them out, he changed Io into a cow. Hera made her dramatic entrance and Zeus acted like, "What's going on, I'm just hanging out with this cow. Beautiful cow, eh?" Hera, knowing he was lying, shared admiration for the cow and said she could use it. Zeus couldn't deny her. She took the cow, put it in a field with her most faithful servant, Argos the 100-eyed giant, to stand guard against anyone trying to steal her back. He kept many eyes trained 24/7. Things looked grim for Io ever being anything other than a cow. Zeus was guilt-ridden and sent Hermes to distract Argos. Hermes told Argos a story that had no beginning, middle or end. It went on and on until Argos died (they say this is where "bored to death" started). To commemorate him, Hera had Argus's 100 eyes planted on peacock plumage.

Some student submissions:

(J.)

The girl doesn't know he's leading her on (2 times), what does he care, why should he feel wrong

Ruined her life, his wife got fussy (2 times), even Zeus the god can't think straight when there's pussy

Don't cry, Io, not cow for long (2 times), tricked one time sad, if twice make song

(K.)

beware the betrayal
beware the hundred eyes
beware the long story
beware telling lies

(V.)

Wonder what waits for you there, should you go the distance
Will I have answers if I surprise you, remember your wife can be proud
I have my doubt about your love, I'm watching you from distance
Your heart seems less like it knows me, more distracted by clouds
Have you seen my anger, my love has this other side
Don't go being all wishy-washy, fat chance you are in fog
I'll damage your innocent lover, I can hurt you too
I didn't marry you just because you were a god

mother's day

Kid: Why is there a Mother's Day?
Dad: Because people thought it would be a good idea to have a day to

celebrate all that your mother does. There's a Father's Day too if you're worried about my feelings.

Kid: Why isn't there a kid's day?

Dad: There is a Family Day.

Kid: But that's not a kid's day.

Dad: You're right.

Kid: Is there a piano day?

Dad: The whole month of April is piano month.

Kid: Are you joking?

Dad: Maybe it is just three weeks and not the entire month.

Kid: Do people make cards for piano month?

Dad: No, they buy different pianists ice cream unless they're vegan, then they get them some wood chips.

Kid: Are you joking?

Dad: Not a good idea to play the piano and be vegan.

Kid: Unless you like wood chips.

Dad: Exactly. What would you like for kid's day?

Kid: A Hatchimal.

Dad: What's so great about a Hatchimal?

Kid: It's just that I don't have one.

Dad: You don't have a bowling alley, does that mean you need one?

Kid: You're not listening to me.

Dad: Okay, Hatchimal; next kid's day you want a Hatchimal. I'll speak with my board of directors and get back to you.

Kid: Don't forget.

held hostage

I stood outside the Asian market on Spadina and wondered about that crazy exotic fruit that polarizes so many, durian. Eventually one woman bought a small one. I asked the guy how much she spent. It was $40 but he said there are cheaper pre-cut pieces in the freezer. I bought $10 worth of durian and took it home. After it thawed I ate half of it; incredible, like a cheese that is called a fruit. Very strong smell. People will know next week that a durian was in my home today. Wonder whether Keith Jarrett would like it or be repelled. Earlier I attended a Summerworks play that bored me very much, the music too. Score was one instrument, an electronic keyboard playing meandering whole-tone intervals which never resolved. The play had no resolution either, maybe that was why they chose this music. Wondered many times why don't I stand up and leave since after the first five seconds clearly I was being held hostage. Am I too afraid of committing a social crime to get up and leave a play that has no meaning for me? Yes, I am. Remained in my seat and spent the time enjoying what I didn't like about the play and the music. This led my memory to an interview with Keith Jarrett years ago when he explained why he doesn't like electronic music: "For me it's like being in a room with a smoker."

whoever is producing

whoever is producing the record has to be the song's best friend.

- surround yourself with collaborators who don't make a hissy fit if you disagree.
- listen to every vocal take as if you were the singer, same goes for all the other contributors' parts, especially the drummer's.
- consider every fill, every cymbal ping or bash, and why they felt it that way — even if you later mute it, you have to be interested in understanding how each contributor tries to sculpt their part.
- lie reassuringly to anyone connected to the project who speaks negatively about the artist or speaks manipulatively about what should be on the record because producing a record is either about you helping the artist make a great work of art or it's about helping yourself be part of that club of power brokers.
- review the songs so many times people avoid asking you what you're working on.
- mix it with intense attention to detail or with someone who is even more insane about attention to detail.
- when it's over, as long as the artist is impressed, don't cry if it doesn't become the next big big deal. the reward is the work and it has its own lifespan. Bach and Van Gogh both died with

nobody sitting them down to say what you do changed my life.
it's amazing. don't stop doing this. and the future figured it out.

- time is much longer than our little ride on the subway.

the grant pt. 1

four middle-aged white guys sit at a work table at a grant meeting to
evaluate classical music submissions. one is the editor of a music paper.
one is an engineer. two are composers. they are handed photocopied
notes about each piece they will judge — title of the piece, name of
composers, duration, instrumentation, the company's recording and
marketing plans.
the seasoned employee from the granting body starts playback of first
submission. the photocopied notes before the judges indicate this
piece is 12 minutes long.
"okay, heard enough? shall we go to the next one?" she says, pausing
the playback after only 20 seconds have elapsed.
all nod their heads affirmatively.

robert lepage

I was on an airplane last year searching for a film to watch, eventually
settled on something about Salvador Allende, but as the film started
in French with English subtitles it became clear there had been a
mix-up indexing. This was not about Allende, but it was mesmerizing.
Seemed to be about the FLQ crisis and then about Québécois actors
during Expo '67 performing in Japan. Layers and layers of symbolism
and hilarity and drama. When it ended the credits came up, it was by
Robert Lepage. Couldn't believe it. The last Canadian film that killed
me this much was also by him, *Le Confessionnal*. The other night in
Stratford my brother took me out to see *Coriolanus*. Killed me. In the
beginning I wondered if the music for *Coriolanus* was live, it sounded
echoey like real instruments. I couldn't figure out where those musicians might be located and it turned out to be pre-recorded, but like
everything by Robert Lepage I wouldn't be surprised if he pulled off

another challenge for whatever I assume can or can't happen on stage. At the end after the actors took a bow I walked up to the guy doing the sound and light cues, asked why he wasn't on stage too.

superhero

My daughter invited seven kids from down the street over to play tonight. Girls between seven and ten. They all went downstairs to her room and put on costumes. One seven-year-old then came upstairs dressed as a superhero and slowly approached the piano, asked if she could play. Sure, I said. Then she started Mary Had a Little Lamb in F# with just the index finger of her left hand. I have never seen a kid do that except in C and with their right hand. I asked are you left-handed? Yes, she answered. So cool to watch a little kid play in F# left-handed. Totally correct costume.

art mum

While recently in Winnipeg my mother said she is grateful for art in her life and the useful role it plays in her aging; soon she will be 90. I think that is hitting the nail on the head. Engaged with art, self-generated practice, whispers something pumping hearts yearn to keep hearing.

playlist

Found a piece of paper someone left on the seat before me on the subway, a playlist. Took me a couple seconds to realize I almost met Jordan Peterson.

1/ My Way
2/ Never Gonna Give You Up
3/ Ballad of a Thin Man
4/ Theme to *Roseanne*
5/ Cortez the Killer

6/ You Ain't Seen Nothing Yet
7/ We Are the Champions
8/ Cherish
9/ Baby You're a Rich Man
10/ Macarena
11/ Thus Spoke Zarathustra

the grant pt. 2

"I think it could have been recorded differently," says Engineer.

"This grant is just to get money to record it properly, right?" says Composer #1.

"But even for a demo I would use a different set-up. You hear how tinny the upper register is and how brittle the percussion was? Sucks," complains Engineer.

"Excuse me, this is for the $20,000 grant, right?" asks Composer #2.

"Yes," answers Seasoned Staff, who's simultaneously texting someone about a party tonight.

"Well," continues Composer #2, "I wanted to apply for this category last year but they said I couldn't because it wasn't written 100% by Canadians, but neither is this one! It says they wrote it with Sven Puteånfjord in Scandinavia — that's not fair!"

"For the record, I would not vote to approve this. They should know how to record properly," adds Engineer.

"I'm confused," says Composer #1, looking at Seasoned Staff Person for direction, but they're off in text-land.

"They played last winter at a benefit for the Church of the Holy Trinity," says Editor. "We were supposed to interview Albert Schmegelski, the first violinist, and he never showed up. Some excuse about his cousin and chemotherapy . . . basically wasted our time . . . just saying, they're not the most professional people."

Seasoned Staff Person: "So we'll pass on this one and move on? Everyone good?"

Everyone nods in the affirmative.

touring italy pt. 5

In 1999 I started making short films that I could accompany live. I've made about 30 but didn't think of using words like "director" to describe myself until 2005 when Roberto Ariganello, the president of the Liaison of Independent Filmmakers of Toronto (LIFT), said, "We should make a retrospective of your films sometime." I felt drunk with this unexpected compliment and soon was imagining my retrospective.

Unfortunately a year later Roberto died in an accident, a horrible shock to all who knew him. Within weeks after that I was at a party and found myself talking to a filmmaker about his death. I wasn't a fan of this particular filmmaker's work, but then she leaned in and sniffed, "You know, he wanted to do a retrospective of my work." Suddenly I got the joke and felt more admiration for him. What a guy.

overheard on subway or instant anger gonna get you

1/ The Grateful Dead weren't really a band.

2/ Morrissey knows what he's talking about.

3/ You can get better music at Walmart.

4/ John Coltrane influenced Pharoah Sanders.

5/ Yoko broke up the Beatles.

6/ New Order is better than Joy Division.

7/ Prince could only write one kind of song.

identi-key

Sometimes people talk about different keys of music as if they are distinct emotions. Sister Rosetta Tharpe said B is the sad key, in an interview once. Dylan said E minor is the mystical key. Where do people get this? And maybe it is true, but they seem equally sad or mystical to me. I've tried checking this out, paying attention to whether I have an emotional response, is there something I can articulate about this key or that key? And there is something emotional, but isn't that the potential for all music in any key? Plus each instrument affects the player by the unique ways they are laid out physically. To play in E is different for the hands than to play in F etc. and that has a certain emotional response, for me anyway. I do like the idea of this, maybe because I like the idea of music having superpowers because it does. The humans play 3 notes to the aliens in *Close Encounters of the Third Kind* and then the alien ship responds with two notes that complete the phrase.

back at bias

Kimchi failure, very sad but even worse, on the same day I dropped the glass blender and now it is unfixable. I love blenders, wish I could get the hardcore Vitamix or Blendtec but can't justify it. Always thought the pro models might be life-changing. York subway station up and running now, and very life-changing. Watched *Triumph of the Will* in my new art class, also life-changing. Whole room of students interpreted Leni Riefenstahl differently than me. That's a lot of differently-than-me's. I don't want to fight with them, not yet anyway. So many music teachers insist there is only one way to play and they know it and you are not allowed to question their authority. Met a political science teacher, works in Barrie, shared similar views about how bias is taught despite people patting themselves on backs for excellence in objectivity.

the grant pt. 3

Seasoned Staff: Thank you all for being jurors. Here's your own thank-you baseball hat and are any of you interested in being on the next juries, which are September 14 and October 2? Coming up is Aboriginal music and children's music.

Engineer: I could do it.

Composer #2: I can do it.

Publisher: I can do it.

Composer #1: Don't you need people who have an Aboriginal background or who make children's music?

Seasoned Staff: No, that's okay. Are you available? There'll be coffee and danishes again.

Composer #1: Sure, let's do it.

touring italy pt. 6

We arrive on time, sleep-deprived after a 1:30 a.m. wakeup, and park in front of the club, the one that wanted us there for 6:00 p.m., the soundcheck Stefano lectured me about, here we are on time — they're closed. Stefano starts cursing and calls Paolo, the club owner. There's a grocery store across the street. I buy tomatoes, carrots, pink ladies, zucchini, garlic and ginger. Paolo arrives at seven. He's a little surprised we came for soundcheck. We start to set up and I have a shock — my video cable is nowhere! (Touring Italy pt. 4) We doubled back this morning and got the screen I forgot at Stefano's apartment, but I didn't grasp until now the cable from two days before was never put away. It's not common like the universal video cables.

I brought two audio adapters

two video adapters
two extra quarter-inch cables
two sets of Casio batteries.
But I should have also brought two of these power supplies. I lose. I
have come so far and now cannot show what makes my show different than a zillion other singer-songwriters. I'm humiliated. I generally
never have screw-ups, and now I have had two screw-ups in two days.
I show the owner the kind of cable, and he thinks he may have one
upstairs. It would blow my mind if he did. He returns with the exact
type of interface for the projector but for European power. We plug it
in, and I wonder if it doesn't work will I in fact fry my North American
projector with this experiment?

It doesn't work. He goes back to his closets to search for another;
meanwhile, with Stefano's help, we retrieve the club's ceiling-mounted
video projector and it will work so at least I can present my work
tonight.

Small crowd of 20 people, many are musician friends of Paolo, at whose
place we will sleep. I enjoy talking with the musicians, especially a
skinny guy named Dario who also plays accordion, we talk of perhaps
future touring together. Paolo's place is from the 4th century. It is tall,
stone and shaped weirdly, cavernously and twisty like naturally the
4th century would be. It gives one pause, beholding the discord of
human activity in this ancient place, modern advertisements for Pepsi
or the many broken bottles of alcohol on the street. Then again, lovely
public water taps and archways of beautiful stone, you wonder about
the generations who lived in and built these places.

The smell of cigarette smoke and booze follows Stefano each night
in each room we share. My partner Magali will FedEx the projector cable to Perugia — the smartest destination because we will be
there for a day and a half. Better odds. Nonetheless, I check electronic stores in case the same cable exists here. They're all closed, it
is Saturday, shrug.

best bio

Some of the artists I admire most coincidentally supplied promoters with the best bios.

SAM LARKIN

Sam Larkin milked the cow morning and evening when he was six years old. And continued at that till he was over 12. His little girlfriend at school told him, "You smell like a cow." Sam was shattered and went home and wrote a song. He was seven at the time. And has never stopped writing them. He has been playing harp since the age of three, and guitar since the age of nine. Everything he has ever written in his life has been well received. Often with great cheering.

Because he did not grow up with television, and has never owned a television, he missed many pieces of popular culture. This unintentional withdrawal from that world has had the effect of rendering his view of the world unique. He often has the experience of not realizing what he has said till well after he has written it.

SUN RA

I'm really not a man, I'm an angel. If I was a man I couldn't do anything, because man always fails, he's limited, he doesn't have the right to do things to make a better world. Angels are not under the same code as a man. As an angel I can do a lot of things, I move into the world of celestial communication. I don't have French connections, I have celestial connections. I prove to the world that this is an exit out of their problems, I supply the exit and I use it in my music and my music is a sound bridge, more than psychic, more than spiritual. I call it spirit sound.

JOSEPH BEUYS

Had it not been for the Tartars I would not be alive today. They were the nomads of the Crimea, in what was then no-man's-land between the Russian and German fronts, and favoured neither side. I had already struck up a good relationship with them, and often wandered off to sit with them. "Du nix njemcky," they would say, "du Tartar," and try to persuade me to join their clan. Their nomadic ways attracted me of course, although by that time their movements had been restricted. Yet, it was they who discovered me in the snow after the crash, when the German search parties had given up. I was still unconscious then and only came round completely after 12 days or so, and by then I was back in a German field hospital. So the memories I have of that time are images that penetrated my consciousness. The last thing I remember was that it was too late to jump, too late for the parachutes to open. That must have been a couple of seconds before hitting the ground. Luckily I was not strapped in — I always preferred free movement to safety belts . . . My friend was strapped in and he was atomized on impact — there was almost nothing to be found of him afterward. But I must have shot through the windscreen as it flew back at the same speed as the plane hit the ground and that saved me, though I had bad skull and jaw injuries. Then the tail flipped over and I was completely buried in the snow. That's how the Tartars found me days later. I remember voices saying "Voda" (water), then the felt of their tents, and the dense pungent smell of cheese, fat and milk. They covered my body in fat to help it regenerate warmth, and wrapped it in felt as an insulator to keep warmth in.

angry bob

Asked the stranger sitting near me to watch my computer when I went downstairs to pee, she said of course. Later steeled myself rounding the corner that maybe I will find her gone along with my computer. Similarly when my little girl hugs me for no reason, imagine a future version that screams she hates me because I bought the wrong sandwich. In recent weeks construction happening at many subway stations. Retrofitted for cards vs. tokens and the ticket collectors bored, distracted, often taking smoke breaks. People could just walk right by and if they play it confidently enter free. Some of these growlers testing that theory bear a striking resemblance to me. NFB, you rule. Became angry Bob while watching *Angry Inuk*. The Friday student is making a record though her generation does not buy records. I don't mind, I trained for this. The new Tranzac manager hears me record-ing/fixing/repeating phrases a million times. Fine-tuning small aspects of pitch or timing or harmony. As a result he sings back through the walls new nonsensical lyrics, turns "no jumping off this train" into "no gerbils on this train." I'm liking that version a lot. Yesterday realized I'm currently without callused fingertips, better make time to scrape them on sandpaper or else be accordion guy for my upcoming show.

two jobs

Today I made zucchini sticks with flour, oat milk and cornmeal. I recommend. Used jackfruit and cherries for latest kombucha. The trick with exotics is just like pomegranates — more expensive if bought prepared, or take five minutes and cut it up yourself for less. At the check-out counter the satellite radio played Joan Armatrading and when I sang along "down to the ground down to the ground" the cashier looked at me like I did a magic trick. Tried to understand the rabid story the old homeless guy on the bench was spewing despite our friendlier talk last time. Halfway through I realized the lack of respect I gave off by trying to encourage him to be different than how he is. I definitely am not an example of a listener, you would think a musician should be good at that. Raced home to teach the three six-year-olds a bit of a science experiment. Can I keep them interested in the piano without being the cliché authoritarian grown-up scaring the young about what is and what isn't music, as if anyone has the authority. We use a lot of freeze dance and whoever loses becomes the next pianist. Got a call to meet a director who has made some great films. Got another call from an agent lukewarm about future possibilities between us. I braided the little girl's hair into three as per her wishes. Made incremental efforts towards compiling my late tax return. Had my last lesson with college student who will stop for August, she is overwhelmed with doing a part-time job plus practising piano. Two jobs — isn't that called a vacation?

i don't believe in i ching

1: God by John Lennon
2: Gloria version by Patti Smith
3: Slow Train Coming by Bob Dylan

4: This Train version by Sister Rosetta Tharpe
5: That's the Way God Planned It by Billy Preston
6: It Ain't Necessarily So by George Gershwin
7: That's Why I Love Mankind by ???

Never knew for sure what John Lennon meant in his God song, "God is a concept by which we measure our pain." Like did he mean the more upset people become the more they turn to the idea of God as something to alleviate their struggle? And the less they have pain the less they identify with talk about God? Since the sentence contained an acknowledgement of God as a concept, probably accurate to say Lennon saw God as an idea. I like that Gershwin also had a reflective lyric in It Ain't Necessarily So. There has been no God talk with my daughter since she was born and now she is almost six, I'm sure it is coming and maybe when she does ask I'll offer a musical response featuring one song from that list, see where it goes from there.

switches

Garth Hudson walked over to me while we were rehearsing The Weight for their induction into the Juno Hall of Fame. I was expecting some sort of exchange since we were both keyboard players and this is The Band and he's the keyboard player. He waited for a moment when Greg, Jim, Robbie Robertson and Rick Danko were engaged in discussing something and nobody really noticed. He got up and walked over and I saw him coming. I had already thought I would play a simple, single note, just background, and not interfere with his expression. He had an absent-minded, old-professor drawl and spoke without looking you in the eye.
"What exactly are you going to do over here?"
"I thought I would just play in the mid-range, just chords, so you're heard very clearly."
"Uh huh . . . um, why don't you just not . . . play."
"Okay."
"Yeah, uh huh, that's good." He walked away. So that night I played the show like an actor with the keyboard mostly off. It was win-win. But the best part was hearing Rick Danko's magic voice in the rehearsal,

right in front of my face, and feeling his pain, wishing I could turn something off for him too.

ew&f

My daughter turned on her miniature radio during dinner and landed on a station playing Latin music. She started translating the lyrics, suggesting it was about a girl who should be allowed to watch more tv. Fortunately I also don't speak Spanish so I had the authority to explain it was actually about a girl who needs to stop eating ketchup on everything and whose father knows it's bedtime now.

My mind later wandered to the horn sections in this style and then I thought about the Earth, Wind & Fire horn sections that distinguish themselves with firecracker bursts that I can't figure out how to imitate, so smart and useful and original. Then I had a eureka moment that it's not a big leap between the embellishing shapes in Latin music to the EW&F structures. I should listen more to Latin music, then try my luck again because I make long pads that are boring and horrible. Sound like a guy playing sampled sounds through a keyboard (quelle surprise).

All I want is to not recognize myself when I hear things back.

touring italy pt. 7

A plan is hatched when Paolo's friend Benny, who purchased a vinyl copy of In Her Dream and loved last night's show, meets us. The plan — he has an old North American cable. He suggests we cut and splice it with a European cable and make a Frankenstein. I don't know enough to know whether or not I'm making a huge mistake and we're late for getting to Sorrento but we start the job.

The performance space in Sorrento is owned by a wonderful man named Nello, I like him immediately. He was an electrical engineer for years and saved his money and started this place as a coffee shop but now it's an upscale restaurant with occasional concerts. More importantly he puts together the two cables. In my mind an imaginary drum roll commences when we are ready to try it — *it works* — I'm back in business! Paolo also has a friend who owns a natural food store who offers me some free shopping. He is the doppelganger of a remarkable promoter friend in my Western Canadian tours named Jamie Elder. Jamie formerly had a vegetarian restaurant on the Sunshine Coast where he brought me to play many times starting in '94. Even had a juice named after me. I was between the Sven Robinson and the Terry Fox.

The show is perfect. One guy rushes me afterward and asks if I love Andy Kaufman. Occasionally, people think Andy Kaufman is my big love, and yes I did love him but I love a lot of artists and I think we're obviously from different worlds. What he did was more brave and talented than yours truly. The tools Benny used to cut the cables earlier in the evening he left in a plastic bag. At the end of the night he ask, "Do you still have my treasures?"

What an excellent translation for a utility knife and electrical tape.

beep bla beep bla beep bla beep bla

Another documentary, another Philip Glass–style sequence.
Everywhere you go.
beep bla beep bla beep bla beep bla woooo
beep bla beep bla beep bla beep bla woooo
beep bla beep bla beep bla beep bla
Scared to be different syndrome.
New music categories coming:
best cliché
best unadventuresome
best predictability

maracas

Played a cabaret featuring a Chilean singer-songwriter accompanied by a percussionist. When he played maracas the quality of his work left me spellbound. After, I complimented him, then he explained some details. I didn't know maracas are male and female, are weighted differently, can have little holes in them for resonance. Decided not to brag about my chickpeas in Tupperware.

hanging with bullies

Many times I was standing on stage and the leader of the band started screaming at a guy in the crew who was underpaid to do the heavy lifting and set up the equipment and tune guitars and later break it down until the wee hours and then get up early the next day to drive everyone to the next place. He yelled obscenities and called the crew guy worthless because the A string was not completely in tune on his guitar.

It wasn't so long ago the same guy screaming was a waiter in a restaurant at Front and University and I was a cook at a restaurant on Baldwin Street. Known so many bullies.

chrysalis

Once upon a time I was offered a publishing deal after playing a solo showcase at SXSW in the 90s. This first of all means you should try to always play those things, shit happens from showing up whether it's a conference or a party, go shake hands, meet people . . . things happen, not necessarily for the right reason, but that's how it is.

The deal changed. They offered it to me in March and reneged on their offer in April. My then-lawyer thought it was his fault, he felt terrible. This was great because over the next four years anything that came my way he did free because he had an ethical streak (which he has since successfully erased).

Back then he thought he dragged the process on unnecessarily and that's why they dropped the deal. Maybe so but I thought if they want me Monday but don't by Thursday then were they ever for real? Do I want to do business with people like that? Even more confusing was if I went through with signing a publishing deal, it meant about $25,000, which would have been awesome, but there were two other aspects that screwed me up. First there was the promise of great money if other things happened. Like if I cracked the Billboard Top 100 then they would release $75,000 to me. When I calculated everything I might earn a lot of money . . . might. What stopped me was the "ifs." You aren't too savvy if you think an if means something real.

But worse than anything was that signing this deal meant they owned all my music, including music I am yet to create. How can one write music, and occasionally music from a critical perspective of management, if one agrees to be on the same company payroll? Pondering this hurt my imaginary soul. I was more than fine when they dropped it because I never had to make a final decision. My lawyer was grateful I was forgiving, but he didn't understand my position; I felt relieved.

easy answer

My daughter spilled orange juice onto my MacBook last weekend. Whose fault could it be but mine, letting a five-year-old watch a program on a computer with a tall glass of orange juice in her hands. Trackpad soon became all whack-a-doodle, could not click on anything, and the longer the computer remained on, the more it started being controlled by invisible forces. Repair inquiries indicated $150–$300.

Decided to take the plunge after reviewing fix-it tutorials on YouTube, but more than one friend said

"I've never done that."

"Are you crazy?"

"Don't do it."

"Have you ever done it before?"

Chickens, all chickens, but the thing is, most of us (leaders of music projects) know we have to do everything ourselves — that's how it is, probably always will be. We book the shows, we pick up the band, sell the merch (nowadays I give it away), pay the gas, negotiate the door, negotiate the studio time, negotiate the schedules of others, (insert infinity).

Very unlikely anyone ever gets to be Ron Sexsmith: gigging around the world and doesn't know how to drive a car — astonishing. People drive him to and fro. It's unnatural, it's incredible. One in a million. If orange juice spills onto his computer, I bet someone swoops down from the clouds and fixes it free, maybe it would even be me, "Gimme that damn computer, lemme at it with my #oo Phillips. There, done, you're welcome."

Sometimes interviewers throw a certain question out to me as though they are asking something nobody ever thought of before.

"Let me ask you something, in a perfect world, what is it you want? A record deal? A movie deal? Produce a hit? Write a hit? A world tour?" I know the answer to this question, it's the easiest question ever invented in a world of difficult questions.

"Staff."

hecklers

Read about someone collecting retorts to hecklers. Reminds me of witnessing performers die on stage from heckling. Saw a solo musician enter into a nervous breakdown in Edinburgh many years ago. Had a bag of cassettes with him (was the early 90s), left them on stage screaming "you could all fuck off," stormed off crying and indicating the cassettes were something he had prepared for them.

Most amazing response to hecklers I ever saw was Sahara Spracklin at a coffee house in a church basement. Always a very visually interesting person, guitar covered in stick-on hardware store letters and numbers, a tallis around her neck, tall white leather boots, fishnet stockings, dramatic eye makeup, sleeveless red leather vest. Somebody yelled something incoherent at her, interrupting her song's opening verse, and instead of being shook up, insulted or scared, she stopped, looked out at the stranger and acted like his old aunt charmed to meet him again.

"Come here," she curled her index finger, "come here. What's your name?"

Guy looked around for support but there wasn't any. "Come come," Sahara again beckoned.

He walked over to her, she brought him on stage and into the mic said, "So what's your name?" and put the mic to his lips,

"Victor," he said, now shy.

"All right. Everyone, this is Victor. Victor, this is everyone."

He nodded. Maybe someone in the audience said helloooo Victor. "So did you want to tell the people anything, Victor?"

"No, I'm good."

"Okay, I'm going to go back to my song and maybe you can listen, okay?"

"Uh huh."

So satisfying, so amazing.

don van vlietstreet

Our routine when waking up in the morning is that my daughter wants to hear one of two Sesame Street vinyls we picked up a year ago in a secondhand store in Stratford. Christmas or Fairy Tales. She doesn't handle them with care, consequently I don't either — it's a lost cause and not a good turntable, one channel doesn't work.

As time passes there are more skips. The girl doesn't seem to notice or care, but for me it's more and more interesting each day, "Christmas merry we wish, wish, wish, wish, wish, wish, and a happy." Looking forward to how cacophonous it grows and whether she will ever be disappointed or just dig the journey to Captain Beefheartstreet.

the sounds inside

Yesterday's favourite food combination at street fair: mango with chili. Noticed eight policemen and thought the usual critical thoughts about bulletproof vests. Approached the oldest guy and asked if they used them when he started. "People used to buy their own," he said. Didn't feel like the right moment to reveal how much cooler I think it is in England without guns on the cops. Helped the young girl down the street, the one who often makes things up, try to find the cat she lost but she made it up. Thought more about the birthday present I will get my partner that will disappoint her. Must give up caring about whether it's right because among all the possibilities there is also one little, lonely, hiding-in-a-corner possibility that this could be right. Made a sandwich based on the latest thing I saw online. It was a better sandwich on YouTube. After agreeing to let my daughter watch Smurfs movie she put on the white shoes with heels, audience participation. Worst musical moment of the film was hearing Tutti Frutti in a candy store (somewhere a film executive thinks they are cool), a cover version that deboned Little Richard. Offensive like Madonna remaking *Swept Away*. Waited more than an hour for the opportunity to get my hands covered in grease and get oil spilled on my clothes at the co-op called Bike Pirates, totally worth it. Favourite band at the street party was six old guys who played drums, trumpet, accordion, accordion, accordion and accordion. They were my favourite before even making a sound.

stage fright

I know what I'm going to do and I know how to do it, including how to be okay with what I don't know. It's the fear of looking foolish; that's what stage fright is.

ayn rand, pastorius and professor advice

Listened to an older professor explain to students how to think about being on stage when presenting academic papers. He told them to take notes to the podium then walk away from it, to look at the audience while speaking; to never apologize, to think about the audience, to ask yourself what they want. Sounding more like things one might tell musical performing students, but these were academics ostensibly presenting papers on scientific subjects, not trying to sell cds and t-shirts. In another universe I had the courage to raise my hand and tell him they should practise their presentations at an open stage and ask their friends to come watch and/or videotape.

Yesterday, I drank the worst coffee ever, I knew it as I ordered it, no turning back. A little voice held hostage up until the cup reached the tongue, saying I told you so. Then looked for mind police to take me away. Doesn't first voice know if they take me away they take it away too? Thought more about a book idea, a situation in the north that intersects reality and fantasy, and wondered if it only remains a recurring idea. Listened to a recording sent to me from the Far East requesting my opinion. It was boring and missing elements that would excite, except the quality of the singer's voice. Exceptional voice. The kind of voice only glimpsed by people on psilocybin and later nobody believes them. She wants to know what I think. Bet I'll never hear from her again without first dipping my response in maple syrup, a frequent problem. The 50s continue to be a space distilling how much time is left. The pressure is on to become nothing quickly or suffer the consequences.

Would like to see a hidden camera on composers offered a lot of money to score with ridiculous directions. We have $18,000 in the budget, can you make it sound like a pomegranate or like you are riding on the subway wearing a turtleneck? Can you play anything like that? Bet they all say "for sure I can, done it many times." When I read Joe Zawinul and Joni Mitchell criticizing Pastorius, I was concerned. How could they say that when I was so blown away by his bass adventures? He could do no wrong. Then I read details about things he actually did to others. Got to the rehearsal last month before the students. Sitting in reception room, they didn't know I was the teacher. Listened to them talk about Rush, Lorde and Primus. Two of them particularly reverential about Neil Peart. Wonder if they know who Ayn Rand is and what might be her ideas. I read Neil distances himself now, 35 years later; congratulations, Neil. Still, Rush records printed dedications in liner notes to her and Neil was the lyricist. You students know any poor people pining for an Ayn Rand revolution? Am I offending you? I understand — how dare anybody criticize a hero.

Was told that my perceived reality is an illusion by a person who is also perceiving reality.

the mistake

people in concert play a "wrong" note while improvising or soloing, then a couple instant thoughts usually go through the brain. one is to correct the note but then you are confirming for the listeners that you made a mistake. two is to play the bum note again 200 more times as if to say i did it on purpose and insinuate the listener was at fault for assuming that first time was a mistake (very clever). a third choice is to not give a shit about being judged (by yourself or the audience, whose response ultimately is just in your imagination).

piano symmetry

At D or G#, the piano is a mirror. Take D or G# as a first note and you can play your hands symmetrically. Meaning if your right thumb plays A your left thumb plays G, if your right index finger plays B♭ your left index finger plays F#. There are a couple of engaging experiences that follow.

First of all whatever your dominant hand, you simply command the weaker hand to follow. Not the same effort as thinking about separate directions for left and right, playing symmetrically means one just has to follow — it's how our bodies are designed — a nice by-product is that the weaker hand, usually the left, will achieve more velocity but it works the other way too — if the pianist is a lefty, then their right hand will experience more freedom to play swiftly.

The other attractive aspect of playing this way is whatever harmony you know goes out the window and that's the place I personally enjoy the most. I like trying to improvise with this set of conditions and not sound like an exercise.

sportchek

I have the feeling sometimes that people like my writing but truth is often people don't want my advice, same with students. I was in a mall, in a store that might have been called Sportchek, I'm not sure. Buying swimming goggles for my daughter. The 19-year-old cashier rang it in and asked if I wanted to top up what I was spending to make a donation to such-and-such charity. I thought about it and asked if she could tell Sportchek I would like them to donate a significant part of their profits to this charity; since they rent this enormous space we are now standing in at the Yorkdale shopping mall, they must be very profitable. She started to laugh which encouraged me to further raise my offer, please tell Sportchek I would appreciate it if they would add benefits to your salary. If you like I could tell the manager, but she said it is okay.

deterrence

Trump pardons people convicted of crimes — first critical voice in his head has him on the run. He's trying to tell his opponents he controls the music. Lame. Lousy composer. When they remake *Little Caesar*, I know who should play the lead. Started new piano pieces yesterday, can feel the brain activity, like lighting up rooms that are waiting to be used. Arts education is still not mandatory in schools. This new piece is in B flat and when I started it, at first a critical inner voice thought it was too simple, then another voice became critical of being critical. Amazing how many times the first critical line of thought can get away with leading doubt and insecurity. Lame. If they remake *A Clockwork Orange*, Malcolm McDowell's character should be forced to view Sarah Huckabee Sanders's press conferences, nonstop.

some whens

when i hear muzak versions of hits, my ears fixate on how they did it.
when a piano string breaks, i don't expect to be blamed.
when bananas are spotty, i don't expect them to be perfect inside.
when people meet me and say i love your music, they mean blue rodeo.
when odetta kissed my hands after my set, i thought she might take me on the road.
when ani difranco threw her arms around me after my set, i thought she might take me on the road.
when the barenaked ladies did take me on the road, i didn't expect it to be so awkward.
when i tried the samsung, they left me regretting my iphone.
when i sent frank davies that commercial song, i didn't expect the mansplaining.

pianist arrives

Heard many times so-and-so was born with talent and figured that that was the way it worked. Whether it was amazing yo-yo tricks or amazing guitar playing, people said they were born with talent, they said it about me too but I knew it wasn't true. I could show anyone how to do what I do. I tested my theory but many times came up against people who can't get it no matter how hard I try to explain. It could then be easy to conclude the first explanation was right, but I still don't think so. Whether or not people do the work is a major part of it, whether they have the opportunity to do the work or whether the person explaining it has a talent for explaining or not. Talent then is someone inclined to do the learning and anyone can do that. It is about incentives more than randomly allocated mystical forces.

Up until now whenever I showed my young daughter how to play piano she was interested momentarily, but once she had to try distinguishing fingers and notes it was too much and she lost interest. That was fine, wasn't trying to force it, was trying to be sensitive to locating an incentive. Thought that showing her melodies that already delighted her would do it but it didn't. See, this is Happy Birthday. This is Yellow Submarine. This is Peppa Pig. Recently her best friend started to take piano lessons, they do a lot of things together and compare each others' lunches, clothes, scooters . . . now my girl declares she wants piano lessons and she's started improvising on her own. My daughter's attention is suddenly sustained. It's pretty beautiful to watch and whether or not she stays with it, it proves how these things work. Her talent is that she has the opportunity to play this thing (there is a piano in her house) and she has an incentive to sustain working at it (she wants to keep up with her pal).

birds of fire

Made best tomato sauce ever this morning, going to mark it in my calendar so I can celebrate every year. Still, my daughter won't like it compared to ketchup. YouTube tutorials — I follow at least six different cooks. Bet YouTube is an advantage to being a young musician today, consuming videos about how to do anything you can imagine. When I was a kid the idea of playing John McLaughlin's solo from Birds of Fire was absolutely impossible but one guy I knew could do it, Clayton — this made him a bona fide shaman. Maybe now even the esoteric is available in a simple search, I'm going to check right now, don't go away.

Yep. There were at least four different people playing it on guitar. Amazing.

Different rules. You would think it might mean one would be even more accomplished nowadays. Truth is, the bulk of the music students I have worked with the last five years at Centennial College have music software containing the equivalent of $70k worth of bells and whistles (if we went back in time to the 80s or 90s); and one might think that means they are positioned to make remarkable music, but most I've met focus on using it for very simple tasks like importing a factory-made loop. I bet it is an old story: living without the short-comings, one doesn't get the value of the improvement.

little streams

I have a little problem trying to position myself into teaching gigs. To quote a former president, to unclench the fist. I liked my dad's hands, how they looked and their shape and tone. And one day they became mine. I look down and there they are, his hands on my wrists. The view is different than when I was a kid.

He didn't play an instrument — he was the only one in our family of six who didn't — but he had an ace up his sleeve. According to his mother, we were cousins to Jascha Heifetz. In certain circles that would be like saying you were cousins with Drake. I grew up impressed with the mystical connection to a famous musician until we entered the age of YouTube and I could watch old footage of him giving abusive master classes. Beware the person who teaches by humiliation. My dad was a nice man, glad he didn't do weird numbers on my head like Jascha Heifetz or the father in the Parkdale Community Centre change room.

We were helping our daughters into bathing suits for swim class. His is a three-year-old. Everything she did — trying to befriend a new kid, sitting on the ground, playing with goggles — he would interrupt with warnings, buzzing around her ears. Poor kid has a mosquito for a father. In my memory banks, my father enjoyed me just being me.

It feels like both a long time ago and as close as the drive to Stratford yesterday. Picked up Ron's book to sell in Tranzac silent auction. He bought a nice old house 15 minutes from Shakespeare, likes mowing the lawn. Feels like only a moment ago we met downstairs at Sneaky Dees when it was across the street from Honest Ed's and he sang Ring of Fire and was instantly of interest to everybody.

Life whizzes by, poof we're dead and there is no point. Anguish for many when you say it out loud and matter-of-fact. They want somebody to answer the "why" but that's probably the wrong question. Like learning something complicated musically, "how" is more useful. Who cares "why" you can't play it, "why" you find it impossible. "How" gets you there. Had coffee with another professor who made the same warnings all the previous ones did, as if their degree is dependent on supplying negative hurdles to discourage people like me. I wear them down eventually. They don't understand, I'm not interested in explaining the "why," just the "how" of little problems.

jack layton

Jack Layton came to one of my Rivoli shows in 1994, stayed until the end, came to the dressing room to tell me he was there, that he was into it, that Olivia also liked my music. I was flattered and happy to meet him in person. I liked him especially as a Toronto councillor. In the 2000s I saw him one time at the Y on Grosvenor; I thought to myself, how cool is this, the leader of the opposition is working out at the Y like everyone else. There was a phone-in show in Quebec around the orange wave and more than one person voiced a complaint about the legitimacy of young NDP people running for parliament — he instantly responded something like, they're old enough for us to send overseas to die but not old enough to represent the people from their constituencies? I felt like Jack Layton's death was one of the most enabling things that happened for Harper. I think Jack would have been in the way of Harper's agenda or at least interfered better than the way most experienced, Harper treating democracy like it was a dog he could muzzle.

improvising

Like improvising in front of an audience. One musician plays something you don't like but you can't exactly stop, you keep going. Some instant choices, for instance restate your idea against the discord or change your stance to reflect what they are doing because at least for the moment you sound more like you're playing together. Like comments advancing contrary opinions, can't help themselves, and another percentage instead reflects the initial idea, still another offers something tangential, unrelated to what started the thread. The grown-up version of Spot It.

the scholarship list

Student showed up earlier than everyone else this morning — before I asked he volunteered, "I didn't sleep last night so I just came here." This is the same student who, for spring break, took a bus to a town 90 minutes north of Toronto that he had never been to and when I asked about his plan he said he had none, except to see what happens by showing up. Are you going overnight? I asked. No, for the week. There are structures in place for how I am supposed to mark these music students, but I wish I could give him an A right now just for having these instincts.

blues

Yesterday was several kinds of blue. The blue eyeglass frames on the woman on the subway, wondering how does one do that? How the homeless woman in the Bank of Nova Scotia lobby used her blue shoes to get the young businessman out of her seat. The darkening blue sky as puffs of snow floated down tall windows. Someone in class presented a talk about intuition, asked everyone to take three deep breaths and internally say "I am creative and intuitive," then doodle on paper for a minute, then share or interpret their doodles. My doodle was the words "this is stupid and a waste of time, I do not give a shit about this, creativity is not about taking deep breaths in order to be enabled." I considered sharing and imagined my explanation would simply be asking if anyone can guess what it means. Eventually I couldn't take it and piped up from a different angle, the one I know, and said when people listen to music they reserve special anticipation for the solo because it is like a demonstration of intuition and creativity. The how-much-should-I-say blues.

dear abby

>Bob, I'm playing with musicians I have a negative
>personal relationship with. Do you think continuing to play
>together is a good idea or not? The music is really good.

Have had to cancel sessions due to drugs, alcohol, forgetfulness or other mental health problems. Depending on how complicated it is for me to handle, if their actual talent destroyed me, I probably reschedule. It isn't like my own history is free from moments of being a total jerk.
But it is a different story if I have to travel with someone, hang out all day and night. I vote to work with people I enjoy being around instead of how well they play. Very depressing to be in a travelling band with people you are allergic to.

voice in head

My favourite voice in the head is the one that asks the other voices in the head who is talking then who is listening and if I am one guy then which one of you is lying?

who would serpico be?

>Bob, I liked a letter you posted and have a question too.
>How do I get a song that is a hit to the right people? Love
>all the posts by the way.

I'm reminded of a young person I am producing who marvelled to me how incredible it is that Sia has written so many hits. I told them that part of Sia's success is exploiting the powerful & privilege of her current situation or, to put it another way, if you are on the inside — then you are on the inside. Very different rules than the outside.

Me? Never got a song to someone I thought might like it, but I've tried. Just warning you, asking me this question is like asking me how to do a handstand — can't prove anything, just my instincts (first use the wall).

I think trying to approach someone who you think right for your song is a good idea even if they seem impenetrable. Most big shots when googled will turn up managers, agents, labels, all of whom have contact info. All of whom might not write you back but at least they supply mailing addresses. It helps to address a letter to the person you are seeking and add "care of" the secondary person; also add "personal." If for example I was trying to send it to Beyoncé I might address it to her and add "Care of Parkwood Entertainment" (three seconds of googling reveals) and somewhere else very visibly include "personal."

My friend Mendelson Joe is a painter/musician and his excitement for music he loves is uncontained. He writes to people and his letters are the best, there's paint on the envelope and it probably says "personal" in big colourful letters. Bobby McFerrin called him on the telephone because he loved the letter Joe sent him care of his record company. At that time Bobby McFerrin was huge so it was a wee bit interesting that Joe got through but then again maybe not. He also wrote Frank Serpico and Serpico wrote him back; in fact I think Serpico met up with Joe in Toronto as a result. In fact Al Pacino invited Serpico to stay with him at a house that Pacino had rented in Montauk, NY. When Pacino asked why he had stepped forward, Serpico replied, "Well, Al, I don't know. I guess I would have to say it would be because . . . if I didn't, who would I be when I listened to a piece of music?"

about hearing

There was a lawyer I worked with when I was in my 20s when many people called me Bobby. Hearing someone I didn't like call me that sounded too intimate. I didn't see us as friends, I didn't like the implication by virtue of this sound that we were close, even if only in his mind. I decided from then on when people meet me I'll introduce myself as Bob; it made me feel like I had a buffer. When people today call me Bobby it means either I knew them a long time ago or it means they are friends with someone who knew me a very long time ago; otherwise it's a dead giveaway they don't know me.

One time we played up north in Frobisher Bay. Pretty small place. Someone approached us and offered to take us to see the countryside like as if Frobisher Bay was a big city and maybe we want to have a break from those 12 cars "downtown" at rush hour. We agreed and he flew a single-engine airplane a few kilometres away, landing on a frozen lake within the frozen north. We got out and walked in different directions (not making a metaphor). Immediately smacked with unknown silence. In fact now the secret was out, all we previously took for silence wasn't. Haven't heard it since.

Sometimes people who are getting to know me develop a special tone of voice and pose to me a special question. Sounds nonchalant, as if just this very second it occurred to them for the first time. It's like a cross between the tone to bring up assisted suicide with a dying friend and the tone of kids going door-to-door to sell chocolates raising money for their sports team. It goes, "Can I ask you a question?"

I'm a musician. I have a good ear. I recognize unique sounds. This has happened 96,082 times before. I count to three and by two they go, "Why did you leave Blue Rodeo?"

grants

Strange facts about grants. The artist is supposed to explain what they will make before they have made it. Let's say Chopin comes back to life or

Jimi Hendrix or Billie Holiday. Bet a record company or 50 would materialize offering to release whatever they want to record. I wonder if they also need the new zombie to explain in advance what they haven't yet written. I wish they would just trust us and have the guts to let winning applicants proceed without having to bullshit about the content.

american beauty

Spoiler alert.
In the movie *American Beauty*, homophobic army guy makes a pass at straight neighbour, is rebuffed. Then, filled with shame, he murders the man who was the object of his desire. I thought that was too much to believe when I left the theatre, but many conversations with friends after contained remarks like "I sure saw that coming."
Since then have seen the truth of that. Many people who need to communicate how much they are not something are often fighting with an inner voice and it is that fight, or at least one side of it, that we are hearing.
Trump sure tweets a lot about how ashamed other people should feel about what they do.

heavyweights

If only it passed the kindergarten lunch test. Collard and rice paper rolls with tempeh, grated beet, carrot, some garlic and ginger, feeling proud. Some people sent me venom when I wrote how people can hold contrary views about art. I'm so mean and so wrong to imagine someone could love Bryan Adams while someone else is repelled by him. New idea for a play about my religious brother and how I might sneak the consideration of a different point of view into his cerebral cortex. I can see the ending and the beginning but not yet the middle. Ran into Ravi Naimpally and that chance encounter might lead to us playing together which might lead to who knows what, but if fantasies of being in the Mahavishnu Orchestra or Weather Report or Return to Forever ever could come true, it likely starts by exploring the expertise of heavyweights.

legacy

Never understood why they don't make benches available in the subway the length of the station for the waiting public like Parisians do. Is it just fear of poor people having an opportunity to lessen their suffering? Homeless might lie down? Everyone on their cell phones looking like they are in serious conversation, but when I sneak a closer view they're almost always playing games. Surprises me, very serious Tetris. I see ads sometimes for Indie 88. Heartbreaking that that radio dial location previously was CKLN, which was beautifully independent. I was on the panel that met with the Stephen Harper–appointed graduates of doublespeak who determined it was a positive thing to change the community station to a soulless corporate entity using slogan "Indie." Way to go, Harper legacy.

toss-up

Not sure what I enjoy more, the time Ramón Sender put a blank staff behind a fish tank and had the musicians play the movement of the single fish inside the tank or the moment Keith Jarrett told *New York Times Magazine*, "I've never heard anything Wynton played sound like it meant anything at all."

reading in the sauna

Yesterday at the Santa Claus Parade the first participant we noticed was a clown with a garbage can. Wonder if anyone besides me understood the planners' vision: Santa at the end and Rob Ford at the front. The sidewalk is filled with wet leaves, the new tree is now leafless, but when I gaze at it I see the future, how big and beautiful it will be and how unfortunate for my south-facing solar panel dream wall. Woke up and listened to the usual cacophony, same old internal issues, same station. Thought this is just like the external noise of disappointing human activity. Like how humans pollute and there is no appealing to them to recognize the future deaths, including themselves. Same emotional experience as appealing to inner tape loops. Change your own recording or else! Or else what? After the parade we took a sauna. I miss the sweat that the Y membership afforded, the conversations with random men about random issues, but especially the cat and mouse games between me and anal management types proud of the sign "rules for being in sauna." Threatened with being kicked out for reading in the dry sauna. Sometimes when my guard was down I would try appealing to them to think a little more realistically. As pointless as trying to change oneself and anyone else.

after the dog story

When he writes about the main issue after first writing about the quality of ketchup, everyone just wants to share ketchup stories. All of them miss the point. I told him the same thing happens to me and anything different is just fairy tales. He said he knows but the premise of people getting it is a big motivator. What was it Mark French said while hanging by one arm from one pipe at the Paddock? If 1988 had a best moment the Cartwrights nabbed it then and there. He said it didn't matter if people got it, what mattered was that you believed in telling them. Like it might change anything.

frosh week

One time at the University of Toronto during Frosh Week I watched the lead singer stage dive but first he warned them what he was going to do. At the critical moment the whole drunk college crowd parted and he crashed to the ground. He got hurt and crawled back onto the stage like a sequence out of the coyote and roadrunner and then he cussed out the audience. Then maybe we played Outskirts or Diamond Mine. I remember performing the actual songs less than beautiful in-between parts when the narrative he needed to control was disrupted.

in my blood like holy wine

Earlier this week I made a presentation to people studying food issues so I played them food songs that have affected me. Started with the blues and all those sex lyrics — used Molly Jones's "Anybody here want to try my cabbage."

I continued with Savoy Truffle. Who among us is not amazed that the lyrics are just the contents of a box of sweets?

Moved onto the layered A Case of You by Joni Mitchell: "And I would still be on my feet."

They didn't seem to really care about any of these choices but I was right about only one thing, ending with the 70s instrumental Popcorn.

birch trees in private

The thing about birch trees, besides occupying space in the book of fire-starting techniques, besides acting as paper in certain circumstances, besides having at least three vivid tonalities (white, pink and grey), is that they can play the banjo as fast as Eugene Chadbourne. It's like that damn Bugs Bunny frog singing "hello my baby hello my honey hello my ragtime doll" but acting like any other tree when I take it to record companies and introduce it. I end up looking foolish. I'm no good at keeping secrets. I've already said too much. I asked Eugene when we were touring together how he became so fast on the guitar. It was a crazy speed experience to hang with him and watch his show each night. I wasn't sure how he would receive my query, like asking Superman to talk about kryptonite. He had a blunt answer, Bluegrass.

Never considered that. I understood after how he took the ball and ran straight into the avant-garde. Like Nina Hagen took opera and ran straight to punk. Like Trump took bold egotistical traits, impaired empathy, celebration of the delusional and ran straight into the White House.

There is another chapter on pine needles. They light up and light out, just instantaneous. Like singing with Groucho Marx, "hello I must be going." First I build a little fort, maximize their duration before the show is over. Hope the balance is just right, prepare kindling dominos. My high school chemistry teacher should have explained chemistry by making fires or cooking food. I would have understood it all clearly. World would have had many more eager science students. I would never teach music by first playing Bach. I start by playing sound, by encouraging hearing what is musical about the world and exploring instruments as if we are cave people. Those who think the rules are what is important are all about the right way and the wrong way. Those guys are the last people I would share secrets with about birch and banjos.

harmonica

Lived with a dog that used to howl if I played a certain note on the harmonica. Like pressing a start button on his brain. Felt the same way about smoking, just couldn't stop it if a certain thought in my brain was pressed. Never subscribed to the line of thought that nicotine was the problem, for am I not my own master? No, apparently. There is no free will and there is. One of those things that can't be explained exactly with words. I tried to empathize with the dog and how it lived, especially being a creature that should be running free that found itself restricted by people and their important television-watching schedules. I promised the dog to be different and not contribute to unnecessary suffering. The dog promised not to judge me, which made me feel worse. I play a bit but have remained inadequate because I compare every note to Little Walter. And why not judge yourself against those who hit the mark? Maybe because judging yourself is like pressing a button on your brain, like starting a tape loop, like entering something that will end negatively, again. Maybe better than shaking a paw is to be disinterested in participating.

get out the door

Getting out the door with someone who is five can take about three hours. No sweat, you only live once, unless you are totally deluded and expect some sort of forever real estate waiting in some sort of imaginary world where just because you were born with the capacity to think thoughts you feel like that entitles you to some sort of never-ending existence. So, she floats, "We die?" Yes, but you'll first live for a long time. Will you die before me? Yes, I'll die before you. I'll miss you when you're dead. Don't worry, we'll know each other a long time but after I'm dead when you see the stars at night I'll be one of them looking down at you. That's good, you will be a star in the sky. Yep, the best kind of star. What other kinds of stars are there? Sometimes people call themselves stars but if someone calls themselves a star it is proof that they aren't. I know. How did you know? Because they aren't in the sky. Exactamungo, can we put your boots on?

24

Crazy fact I was clueless about before starting music school at York. Our Western system is based upon 12 notes that repeat in higher and lower positions. We call the distance between each of those 12 notes "semitones" but in South Asian music they play "quarter-tones" as well. They use 24 notes instead of 12.
That's like finding out people also can breathe underwater and nobody told you while growing up.

future stamp ideas for canada post

Over time as I hear my own habits, if I'm going left then I want to go right. I want to not recognize myself by the end of it and still like the song. Last year in between chasing cars when I'm off leash, wrote a song about Jian Ghomeshi but the arrangement wasn't satisfying. It'll get posted eventually. Actually it is about other characters too. Recently Marie took the case of women challenging Harvey Weinstein. Wonder if on some level she considers that a way to reframe herself? I wonder if taking a high-profile case of a victim proves something different than taking the high-profile case of an abuser? Hope it doesn't mean lawyers just do anything for money.

mystery words

Favourite expression I taught to a child: "close but no cigar." She knows it means almost not quite — but cigar remains a mystery word, perhaps one day she'll understand and it will make even less sense. The dream last night, Van Morrison and his love, 30 years ago acting in a musical and Kevin Spacey guest appearing as intoxicated extra. I don't invest too much into the interpretation department but love how many aspects of dreams I can't trace and just finishing a book called *Trace* by Lauret Savoy. Nature book/memoir. Stings when you read her account about old maps and racist names for many places. She's African-American and traces the terrain and offensive conditions her mother occupied as a younger nurse in Arizona. What is reflected about landscape and why, who decides what to call something, who is erased. Also conjures up Bach teachers, different insistences about the rules, though Monsieur Bach is dead and can't confirm or negate their authority as if they wrote it. Who to insert their tape loops into a young mind. Who allowed Glenn Gould to find his own way, to intersect it differently? Give them a cigar.

beached

At the fridge magnet workshop I was bored. The leader cut out slogans in advance to glue onto our awkwardly painted pieces of cardboard. Listening to Gord Downie's last record. My sense around him, especially in his 20s, was that he felt like an outsider and understood the place of privilege where the roulette wheel stopped for him. The trick is blending the tahini and lemon juice first before adding the chickpeas, if anyone is still wondering. There was a great improviser from Chan Shal Imi that said people have different temperaments and that isn't something that can be changed. Like genes for how tall you are and the colour of your hair; born with a disposition. I didn't think it true at first but I'm wearing different glasses now. Does it apply to musicality? Sam thought so. My favourite regular wrangling.

(him) I know you play the way you do because of past lives.

(me) There are no past lives.

(him) You don't know, but I do.

(me) Anyone can play like me.

(him) No they can't.

And that is what gets me beached because I'm right and he was too.

envy

Most of my life I liked knowing that as a man there wouldn't be a child coming through my body. The idea seemed way too painful. One day a woman I know said something about how cathartic childbirth was and now she didn't fear death.

Pardon me? What do you mean? I asked very seriously since fearing death was right up there among my favourite things to do. She said giving birth was, for her, like dying. She anticipated her actual death will be exhilarating as a result. That is the word she used, exhilarating. It occurred to me for the first time nature might set things up like that. Maybe many women have an experience with childbirth altering their state of mind forever also about dying. I'm envious.

fridge magnet man

Thinking on the children of my friend who died in a car accident and my fantasy of knowing them when they're old enough to appreciate me gushing about how much he meant and telling them stories, wanting to convey his sense of humour and intelligence and specialness. In that moment I might bring him back to life, or so goes my fantasy, but thinking harder it isn't likely. Plus they moved to California. Might try to write a song about it, perchance in song the goals are achieved. A superpower. DC Comics needs to explore "Making Stuff Man," a superhero who makes songs and fridge magnets.

listening to kenny g

People talk about their birthright as though to declare you are paleo or a blue bombers fan or someone who drives a prius is your birthright. Others would say the birthright is just needing to eat, to sleep, to have sex. Conditions often look like alvy singer's response to annie hall's brother, "excuse me dwayne I'm due back on earth." The thing about art is there is no objective measurement of good and bad. Everything is good or bad to someone and neither conclusion is wrong.

still waiting

There are so many good things online all over but radio stations are not designed for free-thinking adventurous music lovers. Amazing how stale radio music mostly is. Whoever selects what gets played has an agenda. And it is never hey everybody listen to this amazing shit.

In Germany opening for Bob Neuwirth we had one memorable conversation, I asked him about his tour-managing years with Bob Dylan. He told me when Like a Rolling Stone came out that the radio stations didn't know what to do with it because it was longer than their usual, but they had no choice but to play it because of the place Dylan occupied then in popular culture. I said I've never lived in a time where radio stations were held hostage; it must have been exciting. He said, Live long enough you'll see it come around again. Still waiting.

purple city

City cut down the enormous dead tree. No more imaginary crashes into the house during storms. Next day two big couches dumped in the night. Used to be offers from different recording studios for free but I no longer recall and now I have a use for them, trick or treat. Old high school people dying, others I never saw since grade eight but see Facebook photos, sometimes turn into grandparents.

The first band, Jim Clark, John Deamel and Danny Row drumming in his basement and Kurt Winter of the actual Guess Who upstairs playing poker with Danny's father. Being this close to such a famous person is too much to handle at 13. They're drinkers — I don't understand drinkers. Don't know anything yet about addiction or voices in the head, endless tape loops and self-medicating. At 13 it is just Johnny B. Goode every time all the time.

the juno for doublespeak

At some point a few years ago the head of A&R sent a letter to all the artists urging us to write the Government of Canada complaining about the unfairness of music copying and asking them to accelerate the creation of the blank tape levy. He framed his point as though Warner Music felt so disturbed about how unfairly exploited artists were by copying.

That was weird. Anyone who ever did the math on deals between record companies and artists would scratch their head reviewing the models they used for recoupment and concepts around "fairness." His letter was a Juno award–winning moment for doublespeak; bet he got a raise, probably the point all along.

Eventually the blank tape levy went through, more money for the corporations. There was lip service about artists getting some of it, which was great news for Bryan Adams. The assumption was that the rich and famous were copied the most but nobody could prove how often people copied anyone — maybe the most copied were Big Bill Broonzy and Yoko Ono. But the power brokers got to control the story, which surprisingly resulted in rewarding themselves.

The blank tape levy, a cash grab. If they had real sincerity that money would fund music in schools etc., something neutral that works for everyone.

music and flies

There are people you talk to who appear to be with you but you know they are not really present, drifting off somewhere, not listening, and other people can be so authentic and real. It is like the two different states of music playing. In one, the music seems mailed in, the person can execute it while daydreaming. In the other they are connected differently, undistracted and in the moment. Taking in all the cues and being present.

Sometimes when a fly gets in the room I try to catch it and "relocate it." This requires being in the more conscious state. You have to see where the fly is and consider whether it is watching you. Then you have to slink up to it super carefully and efficiently make your move. It is about showing a lot of sensitivity and selectivity about where to come in. If you don't listen, you can't get it.

never thought people would accept it

In the 80s I worked in social services and a charity bought passes to the Jackson Victory Tour for the residents of the group home and a couple staff people to chaperone. Nosebleed seats but the idea of being part of a mass of people viewing microscopic performers was pointless and made more insulting by the addition of large monitors. After all this we're just watching tv? Never thought people would accept that but they do.

In the 90s I noticed more and more records with lyrics calling women bitches or whores, which seemed impossible to imagine following the ways women countered language like that when I was growing up in the 70s. I thought any day now these men writing songs like that are going to get shamed and made accountable for their stupidity. Any day now. Any day now. Any . . . Never thought people would accept that but they do.

In the 2000s I played in a band that played a show in Montreal opening for Manitoba (Dan Snaith). The band had about a dozen people performing drums, bass, keyboards, accordion, cello, violin, saxophone, glockenspiel, vibes and dances. The show was packed, shoulder to shoulder maybe 300 people, tickets were about $25. Manitoba was the headlining act and after our set he took the stage with his laptop. He sat down and pressed play. He remained motionless at a chair on stage while the recording played, the capacity audience just watched. Never thought people would accept that but they do.

In the 2010s producers frequently added items to contracts wherein they owned all the music and eliminated the rights of the composer beyond the film they were composing for. So if A Spoonful of Sugar Helps the Medicine Go Down was written now the composer wouldn't see anything beyond their writing fee if it became a hit song despite the fact that hit songs result in performing rights societies (like SOCAN here in Canada) collecting money on behalf of the composer. Now they would collect that money for the film producer. Never thought people would accept that but they do.

wish list

People still alive I would kill to produce

Ray Davies	Dionne Warwick	Stanley Clarke
Joni Mitchell	*Cecil Taylor	Wayne Shorter
Bruce Cockburn	Bob Dylan	Randy Newman
Joan Armatrading	Emmylou Harris	Neil Young
Dolly Parton	Lucinda Williams	Patti LaBelle
Liz Phair	*Gershon Kingsley	

*died since this was originally written

scarlett's room

"What kind of music do you want?"
"I don't know, you're the composer."
If only that were true. Dancer/choreographer Yvonne NG Peck Wan approached me to compose music for a dance. So I made some music

and I added some whacked-out sections and played it to her, then counted the seconds before she would freak out.

"No no no I didn't mean like that. Could you do it more like . . ."

But she didn't do that. Did she really enjoy (or at least not mind) my using snippets from my answering machine along with sped-up whale cries mixed with harpsichord through a bass amplifier?

I called dancer/musician/friend John Oswald and explained my confusion. "The dance world is often run by women and it's not competitive the way men communicate in business," he said. "You're the composer; she just expects you to make the music, whatever that is — you're the composer, she means it."

Unique having that sort of freedom from Yvonne. Only once in 30 years did I work with someone like that, Susan Cavan, the producer of *Kids in the Hall*, who hired me to score a CBC sitcom because she liked one of my songs used in a film she saw by chance at the Bloor Cinema.

collaboration trick

When I was younger I thought in the studio I needed to control everything myself
not that drum sound,
yes that bass line,
not that vocal harmony,
yes flute in the bridge.
Thought my taste represented the smartest decisions possible and I always had a full tank of certainty.
Hence affronted when a fellow music producer told me this joke.
"How many producers does it take to screw in a light bulb?"
(pause) "I don't know, what do you think?"
Snickering, he expected a comrade-like slap on the shoulder but I thought to myself, you don't know what you want in the studio and you think everyone else feels just as insecure, that's a comment on you.
Then time passed and did what time does and something inside me opened up and a different picture came into focus. I noticed on some of my favourite works of art that behind the creation was more than one person at the wheel. I also noticed those pieces were stronger for

it, stronger for that opportunity to mash up the ideas of other people and that it's very unlikely those choices could have been predicted by just one person. To put it another way, what's predictable is that one person left alone all the time will probably make the same-tasting dish. On my recent records or recent records produced for other artists I try to keep that close. To consider the ideas I could quickly dismiss, that they might be worth taking a little longer to decide upon, especially if I sense more than one other person liked it. When I was younger I thought they just didn't know what was right and wrong but that I did. Now to consider a different idea over a little longer time is like a way to gain objectivity.

It's like when you're angry and you send that angry email and a day or two later you realize you might have played it differently if you'd lived with the facts a little longer.

When directors hire me to score a film, I do some time travel and I'm face-to-face with my younger self. Maybe twice in 30 years a director has asked me to just do what I do and didn't, upon hearing my work, respond in terms of what is right and wrong, what works and what doesn't work. I understand their response and they aren't "wrong," but it's rare that someone considers what I made and lives with it awhile if they don't like it immediately.

more testing needed

I asked my almost-five-year-old if she could imitate 4/4 time by clapping or tapping.

She couldn't do it. Wavered all over the place.

I asked her to try 3/4. Same thing happened.

Then I spoke it 1, 2, 3, 4, 1, 2, 3, 4, 1, 2, 3, 4; she tried but had exaggerated, uneven gaps.

Then I spoke it 1, 2, 3, 1, 2, 3, 1, 2, 3, and she could speak it back it reliably in time.

Either three is simpler on the brain or it was just a random experience (or chicks love a waltz.)

savasana

While living in Haldimand County some years ago, the Y in Hamilton was the most convenient place for a run, sauna and yoga. The teacher, Phil, was an inspiring lifelong martial arts aficionado who in his 40s developed a passion for yoga. He was in his 50s when I attended these classes and he looked 20 years younger. He brought a boyish excitement to all the sequences and his classes were attended by a diverse group of people. As a wind-down he would dim the lights and have people assume the corpse pose, savasana. People would grab a mat, lie on their back, and then he would turn on a recording of Pachelbel's Canon done on a synthesizer mixed with seagulls and ocean sounds. Unfortunately it put me in the "be not at peace" mood but I understood I was in the minority.

putting it off

I got an A+ when I studied piano at York and I never had good marks in high school. When I got that mark I remember thinking, oh so that's how those people in high school got top marks, they just studied and reviewed all the fucking time. I practised endlessly, I lived with the piano, sometimes I slept in the piano cubicles.

Some people tell me the day of our lessons that they just crammed the info today or last night. I explain to them the unlikelihood of progress with only working that day instead of every day, but it doesn't impact them.

Making the effort to do the work is something people have to teach themselves.

sacred music

Certain musicians in the course of their life have awakenings, then make music inspired by those ideas. For instance Robert Fripp and

J.G. Bennett, George Harrison and Hare Krishna, Tina Turner and Buddhism, Bob Dylan and Christianity, Santana and Sri Chinmoy.

Before he died a few years ago, Sri Chinmoy came at least two times to Toronto and put on free concerts at the Convention Centre. I bet he spent a lot of money renting the Toronto Convention Centre so a few thousand strangers could listen to flute and harmonium improvisations in exchange for inviting them to consider inner peace. Not a bad deal, I thought.

I invited an excellent musician and friend to come with me and he in turn invited another talented musician. Sri Chinmoy spoke about peace and love and then played slow-moving pieces. They were simple, childlike, and he smiled while he played. The two musicians with me slowly lost their minds, exploding like kindergarteners confronted with something they didn't understand and didn't know how to behave with, eventually they laughed uncontrollably. I think part of why they lost their cookies was because it made no sense that so many people were showing reverence for this music that sounded simple and didn't move at a hundred miles an hour.

I thought about the musicians they admired like John Coltrane and Ornette Coleman and if I was betting I would say their heroes would have had a different response, even interest in what Sri Chinmoy was playing/doing.

wary

In the 70s I was into Brian Eno with my pal Campbell. We were like a secret club listening to Another Green World, Before and After Science, Taking Tiger Mountain by Surprise. Eno was an underground artist then, not well known, then the ambient series emerged and it disappointed me, I found them only fit as a soundtrack for a documentary on torture.

Cut to 1994 and I'm living in the country, driving home down long country roads in the dark listening to the Canadian Broadcasting Corporation, and they announce they are about to premiere music produced by Brian Eno of a band from the Soviet Union, blah blah blah, it's a big deal, he found them so unique, behind the Iron Curtain is still a fresh thing more or less — then they start the music and it sounds like all the Eno albums from the 70s, the ones I liked, but strangely missing was whatever was supposed to be "unique" about these Russkies.

Realized then to be wary of things I produce sounding like me. My contribution should be realizing the artist's work before doing anything that exposes my own musical habits even if they ask me to play. Maybe Eno knows that too (?) but he sure coloured the whole thing like his other records. What a surprise when I realized George Martin was the producer on Blow by Blow by Jeff Beck. The only clue that the same person produced that and the Beatles catalogue is intense creativity, stimulating design and talent out the wazoo. What a great thing to be known for.

new age

Sensory deprivation was a thing people used to pay for. Flotation tanks. I signed up. Lying in a saltwater tank in absolute darkness. Maybe this would be an exploration of consciousness of weightless . . . sightless . . . soundless.

As I paid for the session and prepared to go to my chamber, the reception person asked if I wanted music. They offered a choice of five different New Age records to embellish the sensory deprivation experience.

To embellish the sensory d e p r i v a t i o n experience.

x-files

I worked on a song once with Daniel Lanois and Ron Sexsmith, 20 years ago, for *The X-Files*. That sounds surreal; it was, a little.

Lanois did something surprising as we developed improvising on the song. He turned to Ron and asked him to drum. Ron said he's not a drummer. Lanois said that's okay. And Ron tried drumming and it was unique.

Since then I've asked people many times, specifically singers, to play an instrument that they don't usually play. It often makes very interesting results because they're very aware of the groove and where the vocals are and their own limits.

security

Once in a while I'm in a lineup, probably in a grocery store, and a song is playing in the background and I am on it and I get the idea to tell the cashier, just to share the surrealism, but I know then probably the cashier will feel obligated to check where security is standing. So I take my change and go.

ronnie hawkins real estate

Ronnie Hawkins's place is for sale and some stars hung out there once, so goes the *Toronto Star* article like that's a reason to buy it, as if the creative thing that happened there is about that physical location. So many people in fact think that way, acquire that guitar so-and-so played, then you will write hits too. Misses the point because the ship isn't the cargo.

The great thing for pianists is they have to make do with whatever condition the piano is in when they get there. Have to make whatever piano sound good. Have to be ready to be creative wherever they end up. The story about good work is about the artist's inner world, not the socks they were wearing when they wrote it.

forgetting lyrics

Sometimes I forget my lyrics. Then I either make up new indecipherable lyrics or sing off mic as though I didn't realize I was singing off mic. Probably the audience gets annoyed that I don't realize I'm off mic. Sometimes you lie and get the job done.

musical toronto things

Twenty musical flashes in Toronto each time I pass by.

1/ St. Clair and Yonge, where Glenn Gould lived on the north side and the Fran's across the street that he must have gone to.

2/ The paved paradise of Yorkville and reading that Carole Pope had a job as a youth colouring Rocket Robin Hood panels somewhere around there.

3/ The [murmur] project in the Kensington Market where people listen to historic tales on lampposts.

4/ Live Peace in Toronto at Varsity Stadium — one stands in the spot and thinks about Little Richard's surreal performance that day (on YouTube now).

5/ Sherbourne and Parliament, George's Spaghetti House, seeing Moe Kaufman as a teenager with my dad.

6/ The Music Gallery's various locations, McCaul, Dovercourt, Richmond and St. George the Martyr.

7/ Isabella Street for the Neil Young reference in Ambulance Blues.

8/ Bathurst and Queen — the Holiday Tavern was my favourite place to play in the 80s and somewhere near that intersection Feist and Peaches shared an apartment.

9/ The Street Brothers recording studio by Park Lawn Road where while producing Andrew Cash my van was smashed in, all my stuff stolen. Once asked John why that name, he answered "because it's for guys (soft back slap) like you and me, street brothers."

10/ The Parasol Centre on Jarvis where Freddie Stone established a unique musical destination.

11/ 427 Bloor West, Trinity-St. Paul's, where Greenpeace was downstairs and I had keys to the building and regularly played the nine-foot Steinway all night long with various free improv friends from Mark Hundevad and Wayne Cass to Anne Bourne and Step Raptis.

12/ 300 Bloor West, Bloor Street United Church, which housed the Fat Albert's open stage on Wednesday nights where I learned craft with song friends from Kyp Harness, Tom St. Louis and Diane Barbarash to outsider performers like Anhai and Sahara Spracklin.

13/ The old CBC building that is now a Staples at Summerhill and Yonge where Glenn Gould had an office. I see his ghost behind the poster for what's on sale.

14/ The old McLear recording space previously RCA previously

CHUM where Blue Rodeo recorded in '86, large enough for an orchestra and a zillion U87s and heavy-duty mic stands on rollers, where Tom Cochrane made a mess overflowing the coffee machine by pouring too much water into it, I helped him clean it up, and where we later got the news Ned overdosed.

15/ Upstairs on Queen Street near Peter where the illegal after-hours club The Paper Door was in full swing when as a teen I visited and jammed with real Torontonians.

16/ The amazing green house on Huron where Mary Margaret lived.

17/ The rotating Ontario Place stage.

18/ The Cameron when Paul or Herb or Anne-Marie were behind the bar.

19/ Under the Michelin Tire sign like an advertisement for Mendelson Joe when he lived on Ossington.

20/ Around Again Records on Baldwin, obtaining bootlegs in the 70s, blowing minds back in Winnipeg.

listen to part of my cd

Guy: hi, I like your work.

Performer: thanks.

Guy: I'm a songwriter too. could I give you my cd?

Performer: sure.

Guy: we don't do a couple of the songs on this cd anymore.

Performer: I'll try to not to listen to those.

Guy: right.

Performer: you got it.

Guy: #2 and # 8.

Performer: any other conditions before accepting a cd I wasn't looking for?

Guy: well #5 is awkward because we broke up since so maybe you could skip that?

Me: totally skipping #5.

Guy: great, thanks.

methods of failure

Stay in the key of C
Use the sustain pedal
Only play slow bass notes in left hand
Never obtain a piano made of hammers-hitting-strings
Keep playing that music you already know how to play
Don't slow down if you make mistakes
. . . might state the obvious, to get good is to be the opposite.

2 nominations

Couple of my nominations for best stupid songs that were also bona fide hits.

24 Hours from Tulsa

A story told by a man who was almost home but damn it, he had an affair. He's confronted with the fact that there is more than one "self" responsible for his personality and one of these goddamned "selves" slept around — but the irony is he was almost home! Almost didn't have to deal with that particular bastard "self," the one that cheated on her . . . if only he had arrived sooner. He sees himself as the hero in all this and the blame goes to that damn attractive woman at the hotel who seduced him when he was almost home.

The other loser is Paul Anka's You're Having My Baby.

I wonder how much Paul laboured over the lyrics. He sure adds a sinister twist following the second chorus when a female voice representing the pregnant woman affirms his version thus qualifying Paul's hallucination. She's grateful to the man for impregnating her and for just being the amazing guy he is. We find out in the last verse she almost had an abortion but was either against abortion or else overwhelmed with the possibility this child was associated with Grammy award–winning sperm, either way it's got my nomination.

touring italy pt. 8

There was a big build-up to playing the Loop Caffè in Perugia mostly because the odds were best that the video cable couriered from Toronto had arrived, thereby making the remainder of the tour easy and then there was Stefano going on about an old communist I had to meet who hung out there (like it was a tourist attraction) and then there were two Gianlucas. Gianluca 1 the owner and Gianluca 2 the booker. I tried to communicate with the two Gianlucas how important retrieving this cable was but their English was like my Italian, we couldn't communicate.

No cable arrived.

The ups and downs, moment by moment, are really what doing this music work, touring/performing is about. If one finds that stimulating then it couldn't be more perfect but if you can't handle the pathetic and the humiliating you shouldn't be a touring artist. Anyone can handle compliments and good press but the work is never only about that. I think of the motor that died touring Western Canada in the mountains, the band house in Thunder Bay, practically a *Breaking Bad* set for meth-heads, or critics who might dismiss everything you do even if they attended a show that was successful to fans and new fans. Many times you feel like you're in jail waiting to get bail.

As it turned out the communist was an old man in a trenchcoat who called everyone comrade and drank too much but did some research about performers. Upon meeting me his first question was who do I love more, Céline Dion or Michael Bublé, which I answered with universal gestures of throwing up.

déjà vu

When I first walked into the classroom at Centennial College I noticed students on their computers while I was speaking. I spent time dreaming up these lectures but now they're on Facebook or Snapchat and not paying attention to the planned discussion — aren't they students enrolled in a course ostensibly to hear what the teacher has to say? Where do I know this problem from before? Oh right, live performance.

Audiences making noise is a real strange experience — aren't they an audience that paid an admission ostensibly to listen to the work you showed up to perform? Someone is loudly eating a bag of chips or arguing with their buddy the quality of the story from a movie last night. If you stop and address it directly, it might silence people but then there are new problems. You might seem like a prima donna, you might in fact be a prima donna, you might be sidetracked with regret for your emotional outburst and then feel more layers removed from what your work is about in the first place, the reason you are there, but you were also layers removed because of their noise making. Also they might resume their noise making soon after you return to your performance, making your request for consideration all the more impotent.

I improvise — after all, that's what I do. I'll ask a student a question they won't know the answer to because they were on their computer. It makes everyone look at them, it makes for some embarrassment, seems fair to me, like this is now the lesson. Same with the audience member who's loud. I'll musically imitate them or make up lyrics about them and sing it. This means a certain amount of audience or students will think I'm an asshole, maybe I am an asshole but maybe it's a creative response. Either way it's a distraction from why I'm there and it's not what I want to do. I just want to deliver the goods, dignity intact.

city of wood

After my first two records people complained to me that the major label didn't promote it. They told me this like I could/should do something about it, but what? Seemed lucky to be taken seriously by the machine that could otherwise be indifferent and corporate machines were the whole game then, distribution was all theirs.

If one were to listen to what became my next record they might notice many musicians credited on it and they might notice it sounds like only solo guitar or solo piano and voice. And one might notice the peculiar names of the guest musicians like Bjorn Mulroney, Gloria Duracell and Blind Loosa Bernstein, might even notice the unknown producer named Dame Julia Nesbelch and a unique chamber group known as the Altona String Quartet. One might just question the whole thing and ask is this bullshit? Are there really all these people on this record? Is this some type of test? Anyway I invoiced the label as usual and they didn't have any questions either.

Had one cool aspect to my record contract, by the way — $3,000 in guest performance fees that didn't have to be paid back from sales.

autotune

Didn't expect autotune to become an instrument but that's part of our now and maybe an attempt at technology being humanized. Whoever developed autotune was busy trying to improve its seamlessness, probably never imagined people wanting to use it in fact to call attention to its shortcomings and for that to be a desirable effect. I love the things I can't predict. The decline of video rental stores, no smoking in bars, people having pin numbers for their cash which they pretty much expose publicly in lineups while buying stuff.

taking direction

When someone hires me to play on their music, try my best, follow my instincts and check whether they feel it hit the mark. If they're happy, end of story. If they're not, try to help get what they want and if they aren't very articulate it's up to me to try ten million variations. Finding a version that makes them jump up and down and hopefully say "perfect." Then I feel like a pro.

This stems from the first times people hired me to play on their stuff and I threw a hissy fit when they weren't satisfied. Mostly an internal hissy fit, but still emotional. The fact that they didn't "get it," that what I did was perfect and they rejected it for something lesser, didn't compute. Now it stuns me that I was certain my choices were the best decisions for someone else's taste because it's their baby, not mine. So many layers of wrong about my attitude.

I never hire anyone who's that out of touch with reality, or at least never a second time.

jonius pt. 1

The greatest thing about dismissing The Hissing of Summer Lawns and Mingus when I was a teenager is that I get to have them now like brand-new Joni Mitchell records and vintage.

Great art isn't necessarily understood when it's released or maybe I needed 40 years to figure it out.

jonius pt. 2

I saw Joni Mitchell at a Live and Interactive concert at MuchMusic in the 90s. It was a dream to be so close to someone as important to me as Mr. Bach. She played a classic, Car on the Hill. I was about 20 feet away, got clobbered over the head with a whole other reason to admire her, the realization I incorrectly credited the arrangement to guys. Court and Spark is filled with guts and magic, like the moment in *The Fifth Element* when the Mondoshawans arrive at the pyramids and waddle over to save the universe.

For years I thought the first-person Free Man in Paris was her point of view until somewhere it was said it was about David Geffen which made a whole other clearer meaning. In Court and Spark so much is inspiring and beautiful that I avoid listening to it, best to keep exposure limited, then it can be savoured and occasionally might find a surprise. Like that time two years ago I heard trombones in the bass line of Hey Jude on the White Album, shoot me now.

There are two tricks in song design on Court and Spark that always play fresh. New melodies for background vocals and new instrumental motifs between verse sections. Usually in background vocals people harmonize with the lead, but she made new melodies as the background vocal then harmonized specifically to them. The results are like another singing group, more unique colour than a harmony in parallel motion to the lead voice. And the new instrumental motifs — after a verse ends, instead of starting the next verse on the next downbeat an electric guitar or a flute go off on a tangent, just a little bit of new chords felt organically before returning to start the next verse. The surprise of introducing new instrumental chords stands out — I assumed other musicians brought it to the party until I saw her solo at MuchMuzak and realized it was her arrangement all along. Her guitar was just mixed lower than the flute or horns, when in fact they were playing along to her part.

One small step for song, one giant leap for song-kind.

skydiving from the couch

Over the years as the Gerrard Street restaurants and other businesses increase I remember the wee house still standing on the north side and the small-town feel, arriving there weekly in 1985, studying with Darwyn Aitken, a big guy, a smoker, unimpressed with whatever I wanted to show him.

He focused on exercises to play thirds or sixths with a technique called the hop. He thought mastering the hop was quintessential for a pianist. There was an arpeggio exercise too he said Bill Evans was doing when heard practising for his last show in Toronto. That's all I remember pianistically and it wasn't life-changing but the cool thing being around him was he studied with David Sapperton who studied with Rafael Joseffy who studied with Franz Liszt.

That's Mr. Franz Liszt, thank you.

Liked imagining some of Liszt's fairy dust travelled to his students and then their students and then their students even though I know that's as reasonable as thinking we breathe the same air as Stephen Hawking so we might all be just as good at physics. (Or does that make sense?)

Anyway the Hungarian Rhapsody #6 — a pianistic nuclear bomb. Just adore the mind behind that crazy ten-minute death-defying sculpture, especially the last movement which feels about as close as I'll ever get to skydiving while being on a couch with headphones.

factory arpeggios

I get a kind of Tourrettes around men in toupées. I never have actually said anything, nonetheless there is an urge to ask them if they're okay or even what happened in their childhood?

Also gets activated when hearing music triggered by playing one key that makes a factory preset commence followed by people praising the "composer" followed by them accepting the praise as well earned.

I'm not sure if my reaction is for the musician taking credit for nothing or the fact that the world is like this.

World — did something happen to you in your childhood that makes you take this factory preset for real effort and creativity? Are you okay, world? World, do you know everyone in this room can tell that's not your hair?

critic

I know someone who started playing an instrument later in life who told me when they started they'd be practising in the kitchen and their partner, who played the same instrument and was accomplished, from the other room while they practised would raise his voice and yell "flat!" or "sharp!" The way she told the story it was like he wanted to insult her with each proclamation. Amazing to hear because I found his behaviour understandable, didn't see anything wrong with it because I also matter-of-factly have made judgments to other people about their accuracy, maybe about pitch, maybe about timing or design. Didn't think he had a clue she found it hurtful. I think it's a heightened problem for people in a relationship.

There's a certain amount of slogging through beginning musical studies that requires mechanical help, like what you get from a metronome or like holding a kid's hand while they balance on a bike, but my friend felt insulted and I don't think her perspective was completely unfair, I get why she felt hurt. I also get why her partner thought he was helping.

I once shared critical observations about the recorded music of a friend of mine and since then it feels like a wound between us and it's a little impossible to address at this point so now I'm reluctant to tell them what I think, if in fact I have any critical observations, when they make new material. I say it sounds great because life's short and I want to enjoy our relationship. Sometimes I pick and choose how honest to be about my opinion.

normal

The mainstream absorbs revolutionary ideas then sells them back as non-threatening. Can you imagine punk rockers in the 70s with fuchsia mohawks and ripped jeans? If you weren't there, it was radical and incomprehensible. How long did it take before the machine was selling ripped jeans and pink-mohawked people on the covers of popular magazines? It's like the Borg assimilating everything, whether a mohawk or bebop or electric Dylan or President Trump.

It might be better for one's relationship with their own art-making to avoid working with the mainstream, might help sustain a longer respect for your craft or, to put it another way, it's a slippery slope to have a corporate partner — it usually dilutes the thing that was concentrated in the first place, even if there are exceptions.

reeling in wretching out

In light of Walter's death, some songs that reel me in with just the first three seconds:

1/ reeling in the years (steely dan)
2/ birdland (weather report)
3/ don't you worry about a thing (mr. wonder)
4/ silly putty (stanley clarke)
5/ watermelon man (herbie hancock)

. . . and in light of Jian Ghomeshi's attempt at a comeback, five that repel me with just one bar:

1/ sunglasses at night (corey hart)
2/ crocodile rock (elton john)
3/ blurred lines (robin thicke)
4/ don't forget me (when i'm gone) (glass tiger)
5/ king of spain (moxy früvous)

5 f student excerpts

Freud: Can you teach me how to play Bohemian Rhapsody?

Wiseman: Probably.

Freud: How will you do it?

Wiseman: We'll do small parts then incrementally you'll know the whole.

Freud: Have you done this before?

Wiseman: Not this one, but other songs.

Freud: That worked out?

Wiseman: Yes and no.

Freud: Yes and no?

Wiseman: Sometimes people got what they wanted, sometimes more than what they wanted, sometimes they didn't or quit.

Freud: I'd like to know more about when they didn't or quit.

————————————————

Finkleman: Can you teach me how to play Bohemian Rhapsody?

Wiseman: Probably.

Finkleman: Well can you or can't you?

Wiseman: It depends on what it's like to work with you.

Finkleman: What do you mean by that? I got the money right here.

Wiseman: Because whether or not you will practise what I show you is an unknown.

Finkleman: Forget it, I'll call someone else.

————————————————

Fenster: An your tiach mi t;playimg Bheman apsody?

Wiseman: What?

Fenster: Grat, Sozey de kaiser.

Wiseman: Benicio?

Fenster: No poem jes won dater Bheman apsody.

Wiseman: I love your work man.

Fenster: Yamahm it'd kay me toonie.

Fetty: Can you teach me or reach me? Can you preach me Bohema Rhapsody?

Wiseman: Probably.

Fetty: Better try 'n do a right job I got a glock in my 'rari, Bob.

Wiseman: If you buy five lessons in advance, I make a discount.

Fetty: You think this deal something I need more than her ass and how I got the weed?

Wiseman: Up to you, but I do have one opening.

Fetty: So I sit my ass on this seat. I get my stove you bring the heat. We hit the strip clubs find a magic pole then we be cookin' piano it's how we roll.

Wiseman: I think you do the club yourself, it'll be like a break to help process some of what we're doing and then we'll move on.

Flash: I need to learn Bohemian Rhapsody fast.

Wiseman: Fast?

Flash: Fast.

Wiseman: You have to learn it slow before you can go fast.

Flash: You don't understand.

Wiseman: A lot of people try to play fast.

Flash: It's my superpower.

Wiseman: Is that why the track suit and mask?

Flash: Not a track suit.

Wiseman: It's my superpower too, yes I can show you, easy peasy.

Flash: I got your email from Cat Woman.

Wiseman: Say hi.

Flash: We don't talk.

Wiseman: Sorry.

Flash: But she loves that song.

Wiseman: I get it.

piano for real

1987, in the studio with Terry Brown and Juno award–winning engineer Mike Jones, Bruce Hornsby's song That's the Way It Is comes over the airwaves during a break. A popular song then and a conversation between the two studio veterans transpires regarding how good it sounds for a sampled instrument. Can't help overhearing some of their discussion, "You were saying the piano isn't real?" They answer yes it's a sample, absolutely not a real piano. I listen too and I'm a pianist — I decide they're nuts.

By then I was also prejudiced, had worked off and on for at least a year with Terry whose claim to fame was producing Rush and I was allergic to Rush. Who knows, maybe Terry wasn't into Rush either? The opinions of Terry and Mike lingered with me a long time because they were professionals and so confident, even arrogant, that the Bruce Hornsby piano wasn't natural. I realized a few years later, after many recordings of pianos myself that probably they were right. Your ears change from getting up close and personal with microphones and recording.

There was a time when people in music stores wanted to impress me with the latest imitation piano sound and it never did, until the day it did. Someone cracked the code and then it was perfect. Subsequently I used lots of sampled pianos. More than one knowledgeable musician complimented my piano recording when in fact it wasn't a real piano. The reasons I used the sampled sounds were convenience. No microphones, no labour to find the perfect spot, no inconsistent tuning or inconsistent piano quality, plus being a midi recording transpositions could be made with a click. Surreal levels of control.

In recent years I prefer to record the real upright over sampled Bösendorfer. Maybe because my studio is at the Tranzac and there are three pianos there. It's more work but it's more fun. I realize now when all is said and done there's an obvious problem using virtual reality. Part of me has to pretend I am not playing a sampled sound and another part of me has to pretend to not notice that I'm not supposed to notice. That's two parts pretending instead of all of me completing the task at hand. Quicker method to play notes made by hammers hitting strings and I can give 100% to that easy.

do re mi

I attended a Toronto film party and gabbed with people about what they're doing and what I'm doing, gave out business cards, mine feature the Warner Brothers logo reversed. Sometimes these conversations turn into little light bulbs going off and more jobs — sometimes even stimulating cool work. As a working artist, hustling is part of my personality, my default position, but the music students don't seem to get it. Maybe one can't appreciate that until enduring longer durations of brokeness.

I've known many artists who are better musicians than me who struggle with capitalism and don't have the personality to attend parties like this and shake hands with people and talk about nothing and practise looking interested.

Played Poland in 1994 soon after it was no longer behind the Iron Curtain, and when I got to Krakow I stayed with a couple who previously ran an art school. I asked the guy, who spoke more English than his partner, how life was different between then and now. He said before, each school year, the state provided him with all the papers, pencils and supplies for his students. Now he doesn't know whether they will manage month to month. He was being objective and it was the first time I discussed the inner workings of non-capitalistic structures with someone who lived in them. I was a little astonished imagining being supported with supplies to accommodate the interested students. Makes me think about the people I've seen in the gutter who would be included for their artistic interests instead of whether they had the do re mi.

understanding

1998, on an airplane flying to the Edmonton Folk Festival. Kate and Anna McGarrigle were seated near me. Couldn't help it, went over to tell Anna how much I liked her song Goin' Back to Harlan. She smiled and without blinking asked, "Do you know my version?"

I understood so much from that. Understood that she wondered if my compliment was about her or Emmylou Harris's version. Understood that she hears many people praising her song not knowing the original. Understood she's being polite but would rather hear I was drawn to her stuff not because a famous person put it on her famous record produced by a famous producer.

"No," I answered sheepishly and went back to my seat understanding I had research to do.

what's wrong with this picture?

2016. I pitched another show to CBC and they liked it and gave me a little money to try making a pilot. They ask is it a podcast or a radio show, I don't know I just have ideas, you guys can figure out where to put it if you like it. Working alone in and around everything else I do, it took three months to make it and a few weeks after I submitted the finished sketch, they told me it was reviewed (committee of about 60 people) and it wasn't liked so much but they liked my voice and think I should try again, pitch something else please.

Said if you like one song by Prince you realize he had nine others on the record? Why not invite me in to be part of a team, part of the program. I made this in a vacuum but if you think there's something you like about my voice, allow for the opportunity to work with all of you and get paid in a regular way so I can justify reorganizing my life. But they don't work like that. Probably reflects damage done by Harper or maybe there's a different explanation, but I prefer blaming Harper for everything. It's not like he didn't do things that encourage one to think this way.

The idea of the podcast (or radio show) was to look at people who left an established career, but the emphasis I wanted to place was with the frustrated feelings and opinions of friends and family, some of whom still don't understand years later why the subject changed their path. Strange this idea would resonate with me, huh?

To make it more unique I wrote songs about the storyline and used my students to perform and record them, bending towards their aesthetic instead of mine, which made a whole other unique layer to the storytelling.

Proposed title What's Wrong with This Picture?
Back to the dustbin.

mind reading, not

Would love to play a gesture for 10–15 minutes at the start of a performance and let waves of repetition wash over the ears of everyone. The purpose would be to listen to what emerges within the repeating sound, whether overtones or something else, but there is something else to hear when you consider something looped over a long time. When you continue to keep your attention on the sound within the sound, little extra bits present themselves, not everyone hears it.

I don't think minute #1 would be a stretch but by the end of minute #2 or #3 I bet there would be a feeling in the audience like, okay you did that, okay do something else, okay we get it, okay you're boring. And if that wasn't actually happening for them it definitely would be happening inside my mind, the mind that's supposed to be playing and listening to the piano. How does that happen? Maybe I'm right, maybe I'm not. My assumptions won't be right, but that won't stop me from getting sidetracked with distracting thoughts.

care of cell 44

Some songs are like a big old beautiful tree you come upon and marvel at the branches and the leaves, the bark and the fruit, the majesty.

First heard this Zombies song when I was a kid going through my older brother's records, it slayed me. No idea what the lyric was about until a few years later and then it confused me, it seemed like it was about a guy writing to his girlfriend who's in jail, reassuring her he still loves her and has romantic dreams for their future . . . made no sense. What could this actually be about? A few years later I figured it out. It's about a guy writing to his girlfriend who's in jail, reassuring her he still loves her and has romantic dreams for their future.

Makes me think about recent years where transgender issues are more in the news, making us think about gender roles and why whatever is considered ordinary is or isn't.

Especially kills me when they reduce everything to a capella sculptural moments then explode back to the pop with urgency — I guess because she's finally getting out of jail.

being fired

Being fired is a total shock. In 30 years it happened twice and I never saw it coming. It was in a way good but painful. Makes you think lots about what happened or what didn't happen. Both times when I viewed how the pictures were completed by my replacements I didn't hear something I couldn't have done. Both times the final music reflected a different direction than the previous style requested of me. There isn't a simple answer about how things work or don't work, it's about how people talk and relate. I try to hedge my bets by making more choices than too few.

I've also had to end sessions occasionally because the person I hired couldn't execute what I wanted. One time I hurt someone's feelings but I was paying for studio time and had to call it. It didn't sound in tune and there was no software to try altering the problem back then. I offered to pay them anyway and they ripped the money up, threw it on the ground.

muscle shoals

The film about Muscle Shoals is an amazing layered story but weird when the main man, Rick Hall, explains there was no racism there.

Nope, never, not one spec. Maybe true but would have been more powerful if Percy Sledge, Aretha Franklin or Wilson Pickett wanted to contribute such thoughts. Hearing a white guy assert this doesn't seem as vindicating.

It's like the guy in the hamburger store in Toronto at Major and College, October 1982, who started to explain to me how Jews were controlling the Canadian government and that explains all the problems in Canada . . . and when he realized (a little late) that I was Jewish and leaving for the exit, he ran for his wallet in the back room, returning to show me a Jewish dentist's business card, insisting this was proof he doesn't hate Jews because that's his dentist. This was his get-out-of-jail-free card but it wasn't, it was damage control, it was public relations, as meaningful as Jimmy Fallon criticizing Trump when anyone with a working memory saw how pleased he was to play with Trump and normalize him after everyone knew he was a fascist provocateur.

silence her

I don't care if my kid plays music or not but I want to make it easy to grab it if she so desires. I play in front of her and invite her to play with me, to jam in any fashion. The closest I come to outright manipulation is playing Twinkle Twinkle or something from *Moana* or *Frozen* on the piano and offering to show her how. What little person can pass that up?

But once the work of remembering the difference between pitches starts she soon finds it boring and gets the new idea to ride her bike, fair enough. Maybe I can teach her piano someday, for now I'm okay with the only other thing we've accomplished — knowing the difference between an ordinary fart and a silencer, (insert Maui voice) you're welcome.

veg stock old songs

Make room for the fresh, stop imagining the old is okay. I go through the fridge and grab everything that's dying, wilting, as well as some decent pieces and boil it up, then through a sieve. Presto, vegetable stock. I do the same thing with songs I've collected that have stayed a long time unfinished.

freakonomics email about soft porn

On Jul 10, 2013, at 2:35 p.m., Stephen Dubner wrote

nice idea, thnx, sjd

On Jul 7, 2013, at 9:23 a.m., Bob Wiseman wrote

Hi Freakonomics,
I have an idea for an episode (if you didn't explore it already).
Sometimes musicians say things to me such as "I'm going to write some hits because I just want the money."
It is a very weird statement; it assumes writing a hit is simple (maybe) but the bigger leap of faith is the assumption it travels somewhere by virtue of being good. I believe soft porn is even more responsible for hit songs than musicality. Otherwise how to explain what I observe, especially the last 30 years of the hit parade.
This combined with repetition (advertising) is how hits are made. Or not?
Here is a current "new music star" making my point.
And a flip side to this story, seems to me, is that "new artists" are almost always good-looking young people. Are there no new artists to discover who are older and fat?
Thanks
Bob

subway

Subway, Toronto, rush hour, for a moment there's one empty seat. Man with cane approaches but millennial takes it first and keeps her eyes down, convenient way to not acknowledge old man. Now she's ready with headphones to play time-killing games between stations.

More than one person, over the years, has remarked that they hope I don't get jaded by the bullshit in the music industry. They fear I'm innocent. Hardly. Appearing naive isn't necessarily being naive. Could be just a way to make rigid power structures feel awkward. There was a character in *The World According to Garp* who thought more change gets done in the world through embarrassment than trying to win anyone's respect.

With a loud voice, someone in front of millennial offers to hold the old guy's grocery bag, and she hears it and looks up and sees other people viewing her. Then she gets up and offers him the seat.

rejection letter

Rejection letter came today, so it goes.

PROJECT TITLE (MAXIMUM 15 WORDS)
10 String Quartets and an Accordion Walk into a Bar

Total You are Requesting
$15,220.00

TELL US ABOUT YOUR (OR YOUR GROUP'S) OVERALL ARTISTIC WORK, HISTORY AND ACHIEVEMENTS. WHAT IS IMPORTANT TO YOU IN YOUR WORK (CULTURAL INFLUENCES, YOUR IDENTITY, GEOGRAPHY, COMMUNITY, LANGUAGE, ETC.) AND WHY? IF YOU IDENTIFY WITH ONE OR MORE OF OAC'S PRIORITY GROUPS, OR IF YOUR AD HOC GROUP/COLLECTIVE OR ORGANIZATION IS MANDATED TO SERVE ONE OR MORE OF OAC'S PRIORITY GROUPS, YOU MAY CHOOSE TO REFER TO THIS HERE. (MAXIMUM 300 WORDS)
My overall artistic work is lengthy, the details are better understood by reviewing my Wikipedia entry (https://en.wikipedia.org/wiki/Bob_Wiseman), but pertaining to here and now my capacity to realize classical compositions has not yet been achieved with real people, only with sampled instruments. I've won Junos, Geminis and Lifetime Achievement Awards, but the greater reward would be realizing the

work and this body of compositions feels like a novel I've spent a lifetime trying to finish and publish. What's important to me in my work is authenticity and blending modern with old — dissonant with melodic — and the age-old question, why is something considered beautiful that someone else considers ugly?

WHAT ARE YOU PLANNING TO DO, AND WHAT DO YOU WANT TO ACHIEVE WITH THIS PROJECT? (MAXIMUM 425 WORDS)
I want to rehearse and record these ten pieces with the four members of the Madawaska String Quartet and later invite film colleagues to create cinematic interpretations before organizing a national tour. Through this we would achieve making a powerful performance of sight and sound that inspires awe as well as musical appreciation. In theory each piece ranges between three to nine minutes — the durations might change in rehearsal.

HOW WILL THIS PROJECT CONTRIBUTE TO YOUR DEVELOPMENT? (MAXIMUM 200 WORDS)
These pieces are done with a computer utilizing samples, but ultimately that's artificial. Many hopeful composers are impeded from realizing their goals due to economic realities and nothing can facilitate achieving the real target like real people, real rehearsal and real performance.

Rejection notification letter came today, so it goes.

tiger

In the dream I re-entered the house where all the activity was for the tour and didn't see anyone when suddenly a 250-pound tiger approached me. At first I thought it was a joke, two people inside a huge animal costume, until it jumped in the air and with the thud of its weight and the way its eyes seemed to be breathing I realized it was real and unamused. Unlikely I can spar with a killing expert plus when I was 11 I never finished my judo training with Tug Wilson. I whispered Grant's name a little urgently.

He was in the next room on the phone confirming a show for Jerry Jerry at the Opera House in Ashcroft, British Columbia. The place that was run by a charming guy named Martin who in a previous life was with the Hare Krishnas in Los Angeles trying to turn on people he approached in airports. I played there the year before and stayed up a long while, fascinated by Martin's life stories. BC, always the centre of magical touring. No surprise there was a tiger in my booking agent's kitchen. A few years earlier the first time we played the Sunshine Coast, when we disembarked from the ferry we encountered large handwritten signs put up on telephone poles by Jamie, the promoter. These signs were brief encouragements every three or four kilometres. "Welcome Bob," "This way Bob," "Almost there, Bob."

Grant entered, oblivious about the tiger. Wanted to know if I would play Victoria. I pointed at the tiger and he looked annoyed at me. "Are you going to play Steamers or what?"

I changed the subject. "What do you think of comments?" He rolled his eyes like it didn't mean anything. "But they missed the point."

He paused a long time and then smiled, "About being jaded and the subway?"

"Yes," I said.

"Okay, look, I don't like trying to explain this because most people can't follow it, plus you're not even paying me for this information but here's the thing — people are like machines on autopilot and if you try to change them you're just like them. To get angry or upset when someone is jumping up and down angry and upset with you, that's pointless. They just want to hear their own voice bragging about what kind of guy they are. As if it were something other than a mechanical experience — so don't be the same, now where's the tiger?" I looked around didn't see it.

"How did you do that? Where is it?"

"We're good for Steamers?"

"Yes, sure, but where's the tiger?"

"I dunno, it was your tiger, not mine."

13-month-old baby

Stevie Wonder did something unheard of a few years ago. Made accessible his original tracks for Superstition so people could study it. So glad Doug set me up to check it out.

How many clavinet tracks are on Superstition? (Clavinet being the funky electric piano that drives the song.) Answer: about nine tracks just clavinet. Crazy and perfect.

How many tracks of drums? Answer: kick, snare and overhead (just one overhead mic). Crazy and perfect.

What strikes me most is that anyone who gets all authoritarian about recording methods insisting this or that is the right way to record is by virtue of talking like that proving themself a fool.

voodoo child (slight return)

The best ringtone I ever used was Voodoo Child (Slight Return) by Jimi Hendrix because the opening is just random chunky electric guitar sorta out of time and atmospheric — never felt embarrassed if the first ten seconds interrupts my surroundings. It isn't intrusive like many ringtones, but even if it goes long enough to the entry of the band it never results in strangers sending me irritable looks, just admiration.

evan parker and prince hamlet

Saw a Shakespeare play last spring in Toronto, *Prince Hamlet*. Doris offered me a ticket. Separate from great acting, staging and lighting, the audience was sort of put into an altered state. Hamlet was played by a woman, Ophelia by a man, and most of the actors had to learn sign language and deliver some lines signing. Some of the lines weren't understood by us in the audience unless we knew sign language.

When I took my seat at the start I noticed some audience members who were signing and I thought about them during the play. Thought those people will understand these signed parts and are probably excited about this, assuming they're deaf, they never get to experience theatre where they are included. I enjoyed thinking about this and the effort that went into the many dimensions of this creation. Some people left after the intermission. I didn't anticipate that, thought everyone was having the same experience I was. Just like Evan Parker.

There is a radical technique in wind playing called circular breathing. The player, on flute, saxophone, etc., appears to endlessly exhale — the sound can last longer than the length of an ordinary breath. The technique is to inhale a little air into the lungs while the air already pushing through the mouth continues uninterrupted. It's accomplished using one's cheeks to push during the moments when the nose is inhaling; at least that's how I can do it, but not strongly enough to do with an instrument. In the 80s John Oswald invited me to play with him, opening for Evan Parker, whose circular breathing was so effortless, more than anyone I've ever seen. He came on stage and musically went straight into fourth gear, his body and face relaxed, and he played for 45 minutes straight. Not one rest note for 45 minutes. Like being on hallucinogenic drugs.

After 15 minutes people started to leave; a steady trickle continued to exit for the rest of the show. I think some of them, maybe all of them, were oblivious to the mind-blowing virtuosity happening then and there. I bet instead they were frustrated, like when one doesn't understand why certain art is as it is. Why are they communicating in sign language when most of us don't understand sign language!

Is the flip side thousands lined up, dropping hundreds of dollars to share the same air as some latest pop thing?

assholiness

One time someone hired me to play for their record. Could I come Saturday and Sunday afternoon? Yes I could. They didn't offer to pay anything and so I expected to do it for free; I liked their music, thought they had some great compositions. It was a band of about five people. The composer wanted me to play without knowing anything about the music. I understand that sort of thinking but the music wasn't simple, had key changes and rhythmic changes which everyone else knew and had rehearsed, I felt like my improvising was uninteresting and clashing. Tried to honour the request but we did it over and over, couldn't improvise well, wasn't working for anyone (also not my main instrument, was asked to play this on melodica). Last effort to improve things, asked questions again about where the changes were but the composer stuck to their concept, didn't want me to know what's coming when.

The composer smoked more hash with his buddy the engineer and insisted I continue in a vacuum. The air was tense until sheepishly one of the other musicians whispered the changes to me. I played it better. The composer got into barking at the members of his band. I didn't like any of this and decided if I'm doing this free the least you can do is not be an asshole. He walked me to the door downstairs at the end of the day and double-checked starting times for tomorrow. I said no, I'm not returning. He grasped what had happened and then became a little boy trying to get permission to stay up later than bedtime, that tonality. Please please come, I'm sorry, I'm really sorry, please!

Said bye, didn't return. That's one of the ways I acquire enemies but I care more about feeling honest with myself than being okay with assholiness.

brain: who's in charge here?

From is the knee scab properly healing to paying the cell phone bill on time to getting the calories from a good source to changing its tone of voice when necessary, "Hello officer, was I going too fast?" The brain is mission control, biologically driven to monitor how everything is working.

Then walk into a pharmacy for three seconds, buy a bar of soap and on background speakers is I Wear My Sunglasses at Night. Forget about wondering why that would still be heard in 2017 — what is the brain up to if it repeats that melody for the next two hours no matter where I travel?

It isn't because the melody is special, ten zillion other melodies are as special, it's not the lyrics, it's not Corey's voice. It's all annoying. What does the brain get out of it? Maybe it wants to have a laugh on the part of consciousness that thinks it's in charge.

lubicon mulroney

At the Calgary Winter Olympics 30 years ago. The Lubicon protest to ban the event. Realized standing backstage my accidental power by virtue of position as entertainment: access to Prime Minister. Hello security, yes I'm in the band. What could a 24-year-old do? Only previous experience challenging authority was in junior high. Immediately it paid off. The seat of the carriage built for Mulroney's grand entrance now camouflaged a lone thumb tack. Hope it didn't get Mila, but then again she married him, right? Also left flyer about Lubicon issues, "Personal for Brian," placed under the armrest, unless some security dweeb intercepted and foiled my coup.

prepared

One day as a teen, put paper over the piano strings, sounded awesome. Couple seconds later mother freaked out, demanded it stop, piano will be wrecked. After that if parents went out of town it meant new chance to stick things between the strings. Many subsequent concerts with string alterations to imaginary audiences gathered on the living room couch. Bowing at the end. Beautiful shock arriving at Toronto music school, discovering history of people preparing/altering instruments. One night accidentally heard live album of Cecil Taylor. Applause at the end. Started to tremble like all your life knowing French but never did an actual person *dit bonjour*. There was a place found improvising. Made more special with lights turned out. Simply to make it all up. All I've ever wanted to achieve. Developing a way to locate that space where one returns to creating music that's unplanned and tries to sustain the unknown. Where the more easily it can be repeated, the less useful it is. That's still the target, but it doesn't matter now if the lights are on or off.

listening

Listening is a big deal, obviously, yet listening to each other is rare. If I start to imitate anyone in the band, in a subtle way, like what the drummer is doing on the ride, or the rhythm of the bass player — they will start to jerk their heads like dogs trying to pinpoint the whereabouts of a hiding bird. When they locate who's doing it (me) they smile because we will have this in common now.

With singers it's the same but opposite. It's not playing where they are singing. Singers realize when you give them room to be heard; or, put another way, showing how good you can play during most of their part ruins their space and they hear how you're listening only to yourself.

5 syllables

she explained again
i couldn't follow
said come direct me
she said I don't play
made many choices
like biofeedback
pleased with the results
now what would be fair
split the publishing
she said don't worry
i still own my film

mod-a-go-go stretch-a-lastic pants

Frank Zappa's We're Only in It for the Money is a cutting-edge musical masterstroke and it's 50 years old. Relistening to it destroys me. He was about 27 years old when he made it.

Police brutality, body shaming, fantasy, flower power, electronics, backwards samples, whole-tone scales, jazz, spoken word, harpsichord, not to mention the greatest cover spoof of the 60s.

ttt

Dame Julia Nesbelch, the producer of City of Wood, once made a remark when we were discussing a hissy fit thrown by an electric guitarist whose claim to fame was owning an expensive guitar instead the ability to play it. "Classic Tiny Talent Time" is what she called it. I liked that expression.

The first tv serial I scored arrived without any sound design. Nobody told me it comes later. I thought it was an enormous vacuum so I filled it wall to wall. When later I heard it back on television I realized what I did was unredeemable. I hid under the mattress. One of many classic tiny talent time moments for me. At that time many people patted me on the back because I was well known, they thought that in itself made the music good, but truly it was unlistenable. I only deserved fame if there was a Gemini category for worst music in a sitcom.

And some directors don't understand a sketch isn't the final music. It's a sketch. It's louder so they can "hear" the musical details, not because the music has an evil plan to obliterate important things like dialogue. Certain directors react to sketches precisely like that, they forget the sketch is controllable for them later, in any way they can imagine. It's like having an actor read lines and getting upset that lighting cues, costumes and make up didn't simultaneously exist in the audition. Classic ttt.

omar

If you have a straight job, a way to make a living that isn't based on the thing you love, it's better it not be compromised. If you love food and then open a grocery store it gets in the way of your love that you now have to sell food that is going bad etc. You have to do business, pressure to pay the rent, probably start lying and encouraging people to purchase things you don't believe in in order to pay your bills on time. Probably would keep your love of food in a different light if you didn't enter the business of selling thing you love.

There was a musician who took his life a few years ago who played in a band that he didn't believe in but the band did well and he was making more money than he did from anything else so he stayed, but he wasn't into the music and he didn't like the people he played with. Everybody knew that and said he was depressed. Maybe it's just that depression is a thing you can't do anything about or maybe he would have been better if the thing he loved wasn't what he was twisting into a form he didn't like contorting it into. He's missed by everyone who knew him in his earlier incarnation.

don't know what you're doing

You keep track of press, especially flattering press, because it's like currency and gets traded into more work. I've had a leg up with quotable responses about my music occasionally from the famous (Odetta, David Byrne, Guy Maddin), which were awesome and unexpected. But the best compliment ever wasn't something I could use to impress any magazine or publicist. It was when songwriter Sam Larkin, whose hundreds of songs are always in the key of G, said to me after hearing me play improvised piano music with many clusters, "I don't know what you're doing, but I like it a lot."

speed fantasy

Sometimes students describe a state of almost getting it and frustration surrounding them as though there's a missing piece of information hindering their accomplishment. But what's not as simple to relay is that the part of them complaining is more in their way than imaginary ideas about what's missing. Their personal tape loop of disappointment is what maintains the slower speed vs. the speed they should be playing in their fantasy.

fans

When I asked the guy in the long rush-hour line about whether the express bus would arrive soon, it was clear he couldn't speak much English. He's visiting from Mexico, doing research at the Osgoode

Library (I can't help talking to strangers), and soon though we couldn't communicate much we found out the love of Nina Rota was common between us. That's all I need to know. When later a seat opened up I had to insist he take it.

watch comedy

Another way to get over performance fear is go to comedy, especially comedy open mics. They have no song to hide behind and no instrument. It's about whether they know themselves or not and there's a lesson in there for people who have fears about performing music on stage or fears about talking into the microphone.

The best are comfortable with who they are. The real thing to practise is being yourself in front of people. One way to do that might be to pretend there's an audience present when you do the ordinary things you do. Flush the toilet (thank you very much). Boil water for tea (thanks). Burp (thank you, thank you). Empty cat litter (thank you and good night).

song plugging

There's song plugging. Trying to market songs directly. Song pluggers. People hired claiming they will get your song heard by the Taylor Swifts of the world. Some call it payola but then maybe all advertising is payola but then yes. Lot of "How To" books. But can a book reveal a secret? The secret is access and presumably, if the song is worthy, that could fly. How did Shirley Eikhard get to Bonnie Raitt? Once I read it was a song plugger; her investment paid off if that's true. I have songs I'd like to get to people like Michael Bublé but his manager is that fucking fuckhead who everyone knows is a fucking fuckhead. How can you ask a fucking fuckhead to let you play your song to "their" artist when you know they act as gatekeeper — it's up to their artistic choice not the artist that employs them (and at that level they convince artists that they are the manager's employee). When is Robert Munsch going to debut a new book about this labour dystopia and warn the children of the world?

Anne Murray apparently wanted to record Let's Give Them Something to Talk About but her producers, David Foster, Jack White and Keith Diamond, dissuaded her because it wasn't a hit. Artist defeated by the entitlement and arrogance of producers but then again if she doesn't stick to her guns, hard to cry for her. How can one get directly to the artist? Probably can't, unless there's an accident. Ron Sexsmith once told me that when he was a courier delivering letters downtown he found himself in an elevator with Gordon Lightfoot. He started whistling something from East of Midnight. Gordon was trying to not be noticed but he had to turn to Ron and point to him and smile. That would have been the perfect moment to pitch a song or at least ask for his email and pitch later.

neil young

I was in Winnipeg a few years ago touring a play called *Actionable* about lawsuits and songwriting. Neil Young was going to play the next night. I could guess which hotel he would be staying at, not too difficult to figure out. I left him a package with my new cd. A couple years earlier I did the same for David Byrne and he later added three of my songs to his playlist. The package to Neil came back in the mail a month later unopened. Neil has a different set of rules he travels by, likely based on legal advice. Congratulations to the firm protecting the musician from listening to unexpected musical gifts.

often

Often financial obstacles to touring at the level most of us work at. Often few free things promoters include, a place to stay, dinner, guarantee vs. percentage, rider. Often you bust your ass and arrive late afternoon, set up, check and eat perhaps very near the time you take the stage. Often while singing (maybe something very serious) you have to hide the need to burp.

every time

Every time I hear the two notes of certain Samsung texts I hear Bemsha Swing by Thelonious Monk.
Every time I hear the opening tone of my iPhone I hear Care of Cell 44 by the Zombies.
Every time I hear a perfect fourth I hear Here Comes the Bride.
Every time the Toronto subway plays three notes designating the next station I hear the theme song from Jesus Christ Superstar.

kindness of strangers

Access to a car or van and affording gas, insurance, upkeep are regular economic hurdles of touring.

I don't recall how I obtained the email addresses for the Ghost Bees but somehow I did and they lived in Halifax. It was around 2002 and I had nine Nova Scotia dates and asked if they had a vehicle they would consider renting to me. They got back to me, lent me their van for free and hardly knew me. I want to believe I am from the same planet as them.

Last I heard they changed the name of their band to Tasseomancy. They tour Europe. Does anyone give them vehicles to use for free? Hope so. I would do anything free for them anytime.

feel for them

New year, new crop of students. We go around the room, among my questions — what's your favourite music?

They are slowly freaking out when the teacher's response reveals he doesn't listen to or know much Ed Sheeran or Green Day or Harry Styles or Hosier or Sia.

How are they going to learn anything about playing together if they're trapped with someone not also amazed by their fave artists? I feel for them.

errol morris

I attended a tiff premiere for *Fog of War* by Errol Morris. So exciting to be up close and personal with a director of such accomplishment and outstanding legacy. Predictably I asked the only question not about Robert McNamara and the Vietnam war. I said what's it like working with Philip Glass? His answer was awesome. He talked about how they fight and freak out at each other. I was thrilled, left me feeling like when I have problems it's not necessarily weird or different, maybe sometimes just part of the process.

the yellers

People sometimes don't speak English well and certain people think the way to respond to that is to speak English back louder! Even more distressing when the fluent English speaker displays that behaviour in foreign countries.

Couldn't understand time signatures when a teenager, nobody explained it efficiently despite my ability to play fast or complex. Could imitate what I put my mind to. Other kids already musically trained tried giving me the lowdown on time signatures. They heard whatever rhythm I played, tried to explain it, they would start with quarter-notes — what the hell they were talking about? Boom, I was lost.

What does it mean to say a note is a quarter-note? Isn't it an entire note? Shouldn't that be a whole note? Didn't we just play it? Why then call it a quarter-note? They would say there were four quarter-notes. What does that mean? Exactly where are these four quarter-notes and why aren't they 100% a note, never mind being 25% of a note.

Once I got to music school the idea was explained again. Finally understood; like being given the key to a sports car. They meant how many beats repeat and you could even manipulate that. Pow — I was in 5, 7, 3, 9 or 4. I wrote a song later called Bhopal trying to play a blues form in five just because now it was possible to imagine time signatures. Made a new song from the rhythm of Train in Vain by the Clash because I loved that rhythm and now could manipulate it. Pow pow pow.

Teachers have to love trying to find a way into the mind of the student, have to have the humility to reconsider how they themselves talk about things; that is if they get something special out of teaching. Otherwise they should stick to tried and true methods of yelling meaningless equations.

guilty feelings

Friend overseas wrote to say she streamed my cd three times. According to her I probably earned a dollar in revenue. She is appreciative, not stealing music, prefers streaming, wants to convey her pleasure and no guilty feelings and likes knowing I make money. That's fine, making money is making money, but it doesn't have anything to do with making music. Awkward when people project onto me I am about being a cash register and just as awkward when judged for having made a dumb financial move, choosing to be an artist. Neither opinion has anything to do with the real point of it. Would the world really be pleased if Van Gogh and Bach quit earlier because sales didn't prove their worth?

unaligned chakras

The chummy filmmaker asked me and the sound designer for our opinions on a newly cut three-minute scene. We both noticed the same thing, the quality of the storytelling confusing. We expressed it differently but we were making the same point following the invitation "I really want to know what you guys think of this."
After we relayed our thoughts, she stopped being friendly, said we weren't viewing it correctly, parts were missing. Turning to the editor and sounding resentful said something about how he better get that

missing part before they show it again. Note to self: try to psychically know when asked for truthful opinions to not supply any truthful opinions unless they're flattering.

killer outros

At the end of *Silence of the Lambs*, after the serial killer is killed, after the story is finished, there is a final scene, Anthony Hopkins on the run, surprises Jodie Foster with a telephone call from a foreign land. He is following the former psychiatrist who made his life hell. Jody Foster is freaked out to hear from him and asks where he is and his answer alters the ending of the story: "I do wish we could chat longer but I'm having an old friend for dinner." He hangs up.

Songs with outros that start new ideas. I love that the most. At the end of Raindrops Keep Falling on My Head, B.J. Thomas sings a phrase, sounds like he's tossing it off, and then caramba! The band embraces that whole gesture plus, in case anyone thought it was just fooling around, it's in 9, doesn't get much better. The Beatles — heyla heba helloa or I'm Only Sleeping, too many to list, or the outro to Stevie Wonder's I Believe When I Fall in Love.

blips of blips wishing me happy new year

Loud large guy on the streetcar chose the seat next to me, soon told me he had been drinking but reassured me he gets mellow when he drinks. Said "it's smoking pot that gets me fucked up." So relieved. Then Craigslist brought forth someone from the burbs with accessories in pristine condition for $60. My 90s Moulinex has seen better days but this time I'll give attention to cleaning parts I previously neglected. Amazed to finally find vintage replacements; as you get older you don't waste second chances. Don't know why actors get so giddy about songwriters but it's a thing, or at least seems those in my orbit identify that way, as if someone playing a song is more significant than a powerful actor. Don't they know all of us are imposters, equally? Seems like every group wants to align themselves with the idea that God is something that cares about their group uniquely. Irish setters, springer spaniels, terriers can't get anywhere without the first order of business, an acknowledgement they're all dogs; everything else is second and not as important. You're Jewish, you're Muslim, you're a Lions fan — we're all on the streetcar talking to strangers looking for a magical Craigslist deal and equally pretending to be here when in fact our lifetimes are less than the blip of a blip.

dumb things some singers say

I just want to tell you before I play this song that it isn't finished and I shouldn't even be playing it.

Please don't judge me for the lyrics; I was stoned.

Hi, please sing with me in the chorus, it's easy, "you and I are travelling, far and wide, I like the tiny messages I receive inside," okay, goes like this, oh and any guys, can you take the last part and repeat it? "I receive inside" like do that twice, okay? Okay, here we go.

Don't blame me if you don't like the chorus.

Hi, this next song has a boring part in the verse, sorry about that, um, uh . . . I don't know how to fix it but just wait for the chorus. That's certainly the best part!

Hi, this song was written a long time ago and I don't know what I meant in the second verse or for that matter the third verse. Actually I don't know what it's about at all, so don't ask me later, okay? Here goes — and please don't judge me.

songwriters hall of fame

Fave moments at last night's Songwriters Hall of Fame.

Stéphane Venne talking about melodies, calling peaks or climaxes the money note, later k.d. lang demonstrating.

The arrangement of Lisa LeBlanc singing La Nouvelle Saison by Beau Dommage, like 60s classic revealed for the first time, the horn section reassembling at the front.

While Tom Power speaks he acknowledges he can't look in Neil's actual direction, it is too surreal to be in this space.

Synopsis video of Bruce Cockburn's career includes moment where Eddie Van Halen is asked what it's like to be the world's best guitarist. Answers "I don't know, why don't you ask Bruce Cockburn."

Buffy Sainte-Marie going off on a tangent.

Neil Young explaining songs are like animals, a rabbit hiding in a hole, it'll remain hidden and flighty, ignore it, sit far away.

Playing Beau Dommage video about applying for a grant five years ago and correctly referring to that government as the Harper Regime.

Don Ross's first attempts at Foxglove.

Randy Bachman referring to the old Winnipeg CJOB morning show Beefs & Bouquets and Neil Young's mother calling in to promote Neil.

The montage about Stéphane Venne's career and Neil Young's response later from the stage about charisma, pitch and fame.

Colleen Allen's classy presence on stage, especially her clarinet solo in Only Love Can Break Your Heart.

Turning to the music business lawyer next to me after a predictable version of a Neil hit, remarking it would be amazing if they did something from Tonight's the Night. Next Tom Wilson reads a piece on how Tonight's the Night changed his life.

So that's Elliot Roberts.

Neil Young imitating people: "So whatdya doin' nowadays?"

Doug Wilde leading arrangements on stage and just a guy I usually see playing the Tranzac.

Photographer before the show asking Magali and me to pose before the corporate backdrop just in case we are celebrities.

memory of a great man, not

Beethoven dedicated his 3rd symphony to Napoleon because Napoleon was associated with the French Revolution, which Beethoven believed to be about radical hope, about altering the previous power structures. But upon hearing that Napoleon ordained himself emperor, Beethoven changed the dedication to "In Memory of a Great Man." Since Napoleon decided he should be known as a king, Beethoven concluded the man he admired was dead. Like 200 years before the Sex Pistols wrote EMI.

trump's best part

I saw a big shot at the Hall of Fame thing from the world of music publishing so I wrote him since we knew each other years earlier. Reintroduced myself and told him about the young people I'm producing who I think worthy candidates blah blah blah. Said send me some so I sent him a couple songs I've produced. Then I was offline for five hours.

On my way home I imagined what a rejection email would sound like when I get back online.

"Hi Bob, I listened to the links you sent but they're not something we can work with at this time." Something like that.

It was good to remember to prepare for those feelings, painless to deal with when imagined in advance because it is easy to feel like a critical opinion means it's game over and you failed. That could be true, but there are so many examples of people in positions of power who don't belong there. That type of rejection letter is also a comment on him, not my dreams . . . and being an industry guy the things he is excited about probably bore the shit out of me.

That's the best part about living with Trump, the constant reminder how meaningless the person in charge can be. If you like your own work, it doesn't mean anything if people in charge don't also praise it.

And if by chance it's a letter of praise, that would be the easiest thing in the world and takes no emotional practice, but I might wake up the neighbours when I scream.

As it turns out, I was wrong on both counts when I got online. "Okay, give me a couple of days to get to them and I'll get back to you."

hola

I usually don't teach kids but I agreed recently. When the lesson started I asked what songs they liked and once they fessed up about something I could find on the computer, I listened to it, then played them back a fragment of it. They were on board and excited but once we started to coordinate their fingers to play the melody, previous excitement waned, the effort necessary to play this song turned playing the piano into pulling a tooth. Like you know how to say *hola* so you start to learn Spanish but then there's a bunch of other words to learn that aren't as easy. Then I said let's make something up. Kaboom, they were ready for the chase. Imitating each other, playing anything. I think then each lesson needs to regularly have sections of "let's make something up."

smile

Producing a record for a talented former student who happens to work at little restaurant called McDonald's. So far the songs she has written are about her heart and relationships and they are very good but while talking the other day she told me about getting flak at work

— not smiling enough. A male customer complained about it, apparently a thing she could be judged on by the boss. Sometimes I get a little wide-eyed and say you have to write about this or that. I hope she realizes it would be very amazing and interesting and compelling to go in this direction. It would also interrupt the bullshit of an asshole slinging mud at her. A music supervisor showed off her psychopath side recently because of something as significant as the colour of my shoelaces. Now my next record has a song about her.

short film

New York–based director just paid me for the music I worked on for his film. When I thanked him I remembered we never made a contract and it was all simple, thanked him for that as well. Being ordinary is pretty radical.

do it, jeff

At the intersection I looked up at the three-storey brick house and over the uppermost window was a blown-up photograph. Jeff Beck seated playing guitar, late 60s. I wonder if they think it is a generic cool guy playing guitar or if they know Jeff Beck well enough to appreciate how much closer he is to other galaxies than the rest of us? Guessing the latter.

Didn't tune in to Roy Buchanan until a few years after he died and when I did I realized Jeff Beck had a neighbour. And then there are the amazing artists who were never known widely, who achieved unspeakable heights in their work and died in obscurity. There will always be amazing artists who sometimes try to pass it on, but is it that simple? Can you teach what you know by offering to show how you do it? Nope. The student has to also be positioned in a certain way to catch the ball.

A teacher I worked with, who wasn't the kindest person I ever met, once paid me a compliment. While I was playing he turned to a colleague in the room and said, "You can't teach people how to do that."

My two favourite moments on Talking Book are in the same song, Looking' for Another Pure Love. The first moment is Stevie Wonder laughing out loud after hearing the first two notes of Jeff Beck's solo. Second favourite is later in the solo he can't help himself and goes, "Do it, Jeff."

banjo

a certain sought-after bluegrass banjo player from New Jersey
often gave internal dialogue advice
said people talk about what they don't do right
what they wish they had done
if they paid attention they would see it wasn't limited to studying music
how they wish to change their bodies
or their emotions
or their parenting
or their savings blah dee dee blah blah
you live with a horrible radio station in the corner and can't turn it off — trick is to ignore the station and do your work. Don't get hung up on stopping something that won't stop, like having tinnitus, learn to fuggedaboutit.

no wine before it's time

Among the people I teach there's always some who think one or two lessons and they will have it down.
Got storage locker while doing some cleaning up, reorganizing. Thought we might use it for two or three months, just got rid of it the other day, four years later.

smiling

Working with young musicians, rehearsing covers, my job to be concerned about everyone's part, to diligently listen to each perspective, like producing records.

Hard to not show any bias when the keyboard player becomes obliterated by bass, drums and guitar. Isn't this my area of expertise? Upstaging others using only what's on the right of middle C?

She's playing piano and I try explaining this dilemma of using piano "sounds" in a live rock ensemble and why choosing organ or synthesizers will make her contribution clearer even unique but playing a piano keyboard in a piano style is so easily made puny and voiceless.

She's sticking to her guns, she knows how to do it this way. If being wallpaper is okay with her then okay, my job is to let go of trying to prove how right I am.

two worlds

As above so below. There's two worlds all the time, the big world and the small world. The world of international stars and the world of local stars. For every truly amazing actor everyone knows a truly amazing unknown actor. True in every art form — painters, dancers, musicians, etc. My students love Bruno Mars but there's someone local just as good, maybe better, just not yet sponsored by Heineken or touring the world with a major-label 360 deal.

An artist from Toronto bemoaned to me once in the late 90s, "I'm just going to write some hits — I've had it." She isn't the first person to talk that way, yes she knew the ingredients common to hits in terms of melody, lyrics, structure and arrangement. Now it's about 20 years later and you've never heard of her. Maybe she changed her mind . . . or maybe there were some missing links to her plan — perhaps the interest of someone with a lot of money to back the project, advertise and promote it. Also maybe a little luck was needed. You can't plan luck but you can be smart enough to realize luck is in the room when it opens the door.

i believe when i fall in love it will be forever

When the records were on Warner Music Canada, I took a chance that the association with corporate might could be permission to dream. Went to the CNIB asked if they could print a letter in Braille and sent it to Stevie Wonder; would he consider producing me. Never heard back. Who knows if he ever got it and why should he give a shit but I still like my line of thought, follow my instincts and don't cry about whether it's possible.

At the same time I like to tell students the music business is like a building with a hole in the front door that ten million people are trying to squeeze into and the other side is standing room only. But if you must you must, nothing wrong with that.

Michelle McAdorey once said something complimentary to me along the lines of hoping I don't get jaded. She didn't understand I was already jaded and proceeding with my dreams anyway.

insomniac

I'm an insomniac, don't know why. Once in a while I have a long deep sleep and wake up refreshed. Like I won the lottery. Writing music also feels like I go to bat and go to bat and go to bat and once in a while feel like I knock it out of the ballpark.

accidentally acquired beliefs

Another reissue to Spotify. More than 20 years old. Was a long labour of love making this one. Alone in my new digs, middle of nowhere. Squirrels throwing parties at 3:00 a.m. in the ceiling. Evangelist neighbour children curious to talk to a stranger as weird as me. Ripped off when tried to hire contractor to install skylights. Beautiful willow, black walnut and wood stove. Time making this overlapped with Carmaig, Tangienne, Liz, Selina, Dave Lee, Willy Wisely. Don Kerr driving people up, checking in on me, the amazing moments with horns and the always friendly energy of Chris Brown.

pals

One time I showed up to a place where another artist was rehearsing who knew some of my work. He was excited to meet me and to show me his imitation of me. It was basically an imitation of a rotten singer which perhaps I am but even weirder was that the guy expected us to be pals because of that.

3 way

In the health food store earlier. Bob's Red Mill products always priced way more than same product with different packaging. A betrayal to Bobs everywhere. Then Billy Joel comes on the speakers. Now I can simultaneously dislike Bob's Red Mill and Billy Joel together, only thing missing is Christie Blatchford entering the store.

songs with synths

Three songs with synthesizers that get me every time.
Here Comes the Sun (because I heard it 500,000 times before noticing it was there and what it did)
Boho Dance (because it's obvious and primitive and unique for Joni Mitchell)
Black Market (because Joe Zawinul had some kinda mystery in his fingers/ears, like every time it is a unique lesson in harmony)

autopilot

A friend who studied states of consciousness said, "It's amazing when you play piano that your attention is divided."
"What's the big deal about that?" I didn't understand.
He clarified: "You do more than one thing at once so your mind is in more than one place simultaneously."
So what about people driving a car I thought? I think about this a lot. You can drive and not think about it and you can play music on autopilot too. I admire the opposite very much. Driving and think-ing about what you're doing, playing music and being present for each note:
At least trying to.

literature

Been wondering if there is a literature out there about music altering power, stories in history, then or now, where musical works did
something to power structures like governments or other. Like the
stories people sent me last month about Leadbelly getting out of jail
after writing music about the governor. Like Stevie Wonder writing
MLK birthday song and eventually a holiday was established. Like
Pussy Riot waking up Russia about its totalitarianism run amok. Are
there writers or thinkers associated with this? Christopher Small
maybe? Others?

5 points

Had a conversation with a musician crushed by an album review.
Reminds me of a theatre company in Atlanta where my friend Joe
King worked as an actor among many other thespians not arriving
from the usual channels. The director encouraged using pseudonyms
because critical reviews can hurt maybe less so when it isn't even the
real name you go by. (Joe King?)

That was interesting advice. It's not easy to hear rejection publicly
but at least if they are using not your real name it's like the joke's on
them. And if it was flipped and the reviews were flattering it's also
good, harder to get big-headed because again that's not you they're
writing about — they wrote about "joking."

anhai

At an open stage 30 years ago I heard a woman called Anhai
(pronounced an-eye); she played an acoustic guitar, strumming a
rhythmic loop more or less, and her guitar strings were tuned like
spaghetti. When she sang everyone changed what they were doing
like when you realize there's an ambulance behind you. Pull over,
this is an emergency. If you're into music, the kind of emergency you
hope to experience.

Everybody wondered what was the language, was shouts, was screams and yelps, long notes, angry dog sounds and high hawker cooing. More than one person certain she had Indigenous origins. I asked if she needed a producer, she said yes but had no funds. Said I would do it for free but free things can't do right away, jobs that pay take precedence. I predicted it might take a year for us to finish. That was disappointing for her, she said no thanks.

I got to know her better each week when she returned to play and further stun the audience. We would chat a little more. She had a horse, she had a family, place in North York, played in a band in the 60s. I asked her one time about the open tuning of her guitar, the strings that were so wobbly. I knew a few open tunings I admired from Bruce Cockburn's work. I asked her what her open tuning was. She sometimes had a disarming little-old-lady voice.

"I tune to nature, Bob."

(long pause) I said, "You keep tuning to nature, okay, great."

Then one night she made a reference to her lyrics. I didn't know what she meant, thought she was singing sculpted sound similar to avantgarde artists like Meredith Monk.

"Your lyrics?" I asked. "What language are they in?"

"It's English, Bob," she said.

I was confused. I asked her if she could bring some next time and she did, in very nice handwriting. This added a whole other dimension to my enjoyment.

Cut to 20 years later, we met again, some big life changes happened, she was living on the street, we applied for a grant and a few months later got it. Finally had the money to hire people and studios and get to work. There were some obstacles, very hard to arrange meeting with her, she regularly disappeared, sometimes for years. But I managed to capture her in a living room with a digital recorder somewhere she was house-sitting for two nights. I organized some favourite musicians to study each nuance and colour it accordingly. I had plans to help her release it and arranged for a photo shoot with a student friend. I fronted the money because I knew she had the grant money to reimburse me but by the time it was done, she was nowhere to be found.

Two years went by before she reappeared and she had some details about how the money was lost, another story. So for the time being it was my loss and the recording sat on the shelf. A year and a half later a friend with funds asked if I had anything happening he might contribute to. Can anyone hear such an offer and have an answer different than yes of course I do? So we mixed it professionally, mastered it as well, she returned to Toronto from somewhere on the east coast (?), heard the finished work, was excited and then vanished to somewhere unknown again. It sits on the shelf, last seen in 2013. Don't know anything more.

"heartsong (skyprayer or magic song)"
or
"we can dine in 2nite"
C u C me!
C u C me!
C u "seeing is be me"
shed the skies —
sing ur novas
recognize
recognize
concentration,
fascination,
that's a mutual
situation . . .
you know bay bay baby
going insane
who to blame
it's a shame!
but, i intend,
i will bend —
there's a goal now —
it's not my end . . .
i could never
be ur friend —
got 2 hold on!
got 2 hold on!
got 2 hold —
here's the wind —
do not-knot!
Do not!

do not-knot!
Do not!
do not-knot!
Do not!
ooh-boop-boop-bow-bow-ooh ba-da-ba-da-bop-ba-da-bop —
body be there!
C u C me!
C u C me!
C u "seeing is being"
be, be, be me!
shed the skies —
sing me no lies —
we can dine in —
we can dine out —
feed ur head
on LUV instead!
got 2 feel
really, Really, REAL!
when u r warm, yeah!
u won't be lonely!
when u r warm —
oom-bop-oom-bop-oom-ba-da-ba-da-bop —
body be there!
C u C me!
C u C me!
C u "seeing is being"
— be, be, be me!
shed the skies —
sing ur novas
(sing ur "no byes!")
we can dine in —
ah, ah, ah, ahhhhhh . . .
what?
get down!
uh oh . . .
what?
uh oh . . .
get down!

ooohhh —
now!
uh-ohhhh!
come down . . .
from the strange,
creature legs,
stand alone,
beside u
hold me!
we are here — yeah, yeah, yeah!
we are there — yeah, yeah, yeah!
we are here — yeah, yeah, yeah!
everywhere! yeah, yeah, yeah!
we are cumming,
but we're going . . .
we are dreaming,
it is showing . . .
visions come,
but they pass . . .
on a day,
in the vast-land
take my hand —
& hold my heart —
take my hand
& hold my heart —
& u do that —
u do that —
u do that —
u do that — bop!
u do that — bop!
u do that — bop!
bop-bop-um-bop — bop um bop ba-da-ba -bow-ba-da-bop —
body be there!
C u C me!
C u C me!
C u "seeing is being"
— be, be, be me!
shed the skies —

sing me no lies —
we can dine in 2nite —
we can dine in 2nite —
we can dine in —
na na na, na na
we can dine in —
yeah, yeah, yeah,
yeah, yeah, yeah, yeah, yeah, yeah, yeah . . .
(transcribed by m.e. grey)

prove it

Hate trying to prove something about what the future could bring for someone in the arts. Don't want to go there.

To clear the anxieties of parents who want to help their kids, I like explaining they're right, this could all be for nothing. Can even walk us through the work, but can't prove it'll pay off. Most of the time it won't. Too many people trying to get into the room. It's already standing room only.

If you are determined to find someone who comes with a very different spin, consider working with Mark Whatshisname (rhymed with scary), who CBC and *NOW Magazine* ran articles about when artists felt ripped off. Give him your credit card, good luck. (I just googled and looks like Drake joined the list of his insulted credit card holders.)

I can prove how the structure works. I can prove how the things they admire work. Maybe I can even prove they will be able to write.

I can't prove that any of these efforts will result in anything happening in the external world, but a very high probability for the internal one.

podcast songs

My favourite theme in a podcast is for *On the Media* because it's a whole-tone melody. Pretty amazing and it all comes down to the guts of the people who green-lit it. Naturally, anything that's repeated over and over will become familiar. People show little guts in choosing music, in allowing adventuresome music to be present in more mainstream places. They rely instead on what sounds like a nursery rhyme, like what most pop music sounds like.

The Moe Kaufman theme for *As It Happens* always made me pause; there's something Jumpin' Jack Flash about it, but I'll cut him some slack because I saw him at George's Spaghetti House with my dad. I was 12 and it was a pretty big deal, though lost on me that performing in a restaurant might not be so amazing for Moe as it was for a kid from Winnipeg. In recent years CBC added "modern" grooves to distance the 70s sound of the original and I suppose to stay hip. Did it work?

This American Life sometimes has original music, also has a library they repurpose lots. I hate hearing libraries. I understand the economics of it, but I hate it. It's like if Martin Scorsese tried to use the same tunes in each of his films (maybe that's actually an amusing problem).

I made a theme song recently for the *Raconteurs* podcast; they liked a pre-existing song so that sort of was simple but my favourite thing is writing lyrics, writing an actual song for a theme. I tried one time for Dan Savage when he was looking for a song but someone else beat me to it.

I tried four years ago to write a theme for Alan Park's podcast *Conspiracy Queries*; it didn't pass the audition but damn it was fun trying. I asked comedian Alison Hogg to sing the song I wrote after I saw her perform as Björk. So I asked her to sing as Björk, which felt like a good metaphor for a podcast ostensibly about getting to the truth beneath layers of deception. It exists on my original blog in April 2013.

imagine harper

Thinking about that time on YouTube Harper played Imagine with a kid next to him during the election that he won with a majority. One possibility was he was trying to reach people who are all about classic rock, another possibility was trying to reach people who didn't think he could be a non-robot, another possibility was that he was a fan of the song or a fan of John Lennon. I suspect that's true and isn't that weird? Guy whose energies went into disproportionately rewarding the wealthy while at the same time undermining the poor sings "no religion too" and smiles at the cameras and makes an aside about how he'll get into trouble for that because his base was filled with evangels. It was a moment of saying he wasn't so doctrinaire — but he was. He was a supremely biased, dictatorial poster boy for restriction. It surprised me that he played piano and had relationships with music because of my bias, that people playing music have a greater likelihood to not be assholes — I'll keep my bias, thank you very much.

everyone needs a pimp

Mendelson Joe had a song called Everyone Needs a Pimp, and he was quick to make statements like that when I met him 30 years ago, wanting to do an interview with him for *Nerve* magazine. I understood his point, that someone has to be selling an artist in order to move through the machinery of the world. I was reminded of it at the Hall of Fame ceremony I attended two weeks ago when I noticed that next to Neil Young was Elliot Roberts and next to Bruce Cockburn, Bernie Finkelstein. Invisible priority parts.

more banjo stories

That bluegrass banjo aficionado also said one time that when the song is over, if people applaud you should hold up the instrument and point at it, implying who deserves most of the credit.

one more letter

>Hi, I read your advice about getting songs out there but
>nobody agreed with you. Are you a dumb schmuck?
>No offence.

Depends if you ask Richard Flohil or David Byrne.

Some people didn't see it like me but I don't see it like them either — it
is a big world, no? I see it as being about payola, which is in like flint,
is everywhere you look, if you know how to look.

The businesspeople make deals with their pals, you put my act on
the road opening for your act and I do some other favour for you. So
being a loner, an actual independent voice means you have very little
power (in the ordinary music business sense). I recommended trying
to reach artists directly — partly because no way their business partners (publishers, record companies, management, agents, etc.) would
agree to them working with me. It doesn't offer them a way to add
another percentage for themselves.

Feist took me on the road as her opening act in Europe because I wrote
her directly, same for Barenaked Ladies. No surprise, they were ordinary people and I was talking to them straight up instead of through
middlemen. I have never been endorsed by any middleman.

If you want to write me again you know where to reach me. Years of
dumb schmuckness at my disposal to draw from.

recording movements

Amazing how wrong I can be about the future, but perhaps it is a
hopeful thing, when you usually think we are just a lost ship in the
universe, fowling the nest. Maybe I'm wrong and Kim Jong Il will
blow up Mar-a-Lago before the USA blows up North Korea before
Russia and the rest of world join the blow-up party.

But that's not where I was going. I am just bewildered to have not anticipated the surveillance society we entered. That people would use Interac, where very easily a secret code is not so secret to everyone around you, and there are ceiling-mounted cameras recording above you.

But that's still not where I was going. Spotify sent me a playlist and it is perfect. I don't like that. It means they followed everything I did in my searches and then algorithmed it back at me. No thanks, don't want them (or the police or my mother or you) to record my movements. I want the illusion that I am free. Get your own illusion.

earth wants this

Hard to believe how long it is taking to find a willing guitarist to play something funky on a demo for the young student who works at McDonald's. The first guitarist bailed the day of the session, the second one bailed two days before their session, the third one is always too busy — that is probably their way of saying they do not want to participate in the 30 minutes I seek — the fourth one, also former student, doesn't return my emails. This is so contrary to how life usually has gone for me. Could be the new norm. Heavens to Betsy. Come in Betsy, Betsy come in . . . can you play funky, a wee bit, for the demo? You would be doing something meaningful and we will show allegiance to you if anything financially flattering transpires ever. It is December. People are selling people as slaves in Libya and no doubt elsewhere. There has always been unspeakable pain in the world. The Earth that made everything, and planted each life with a mechanical plan, like to bark, to bloom, to chase, to fly, to buzz, to sting, to bite, made much humankind to act selfishly and unconcerned about damage done outside their immediate gratification. Also wired up some to yell about fucked-up shit. Can I hear myself yelling?

for every action

Republican child molester, then whackos attack the same news outlets, frame them using actors so they "prove" they found bias. Their message: despite so-and-so being a child molester, the greater crime is reporting it.

Lido Pimienta makes the performance space accessible for women who aren't white and gaggles of whackos pollute her threads online. Their message: if someone not white and not with a penis wants to challenge history, then they should be called a racist. Limelight comes with madness.

One time at Bloor Street festival, told Olivia Chow that Pat Martin said I should consider running. She said yes, you should. I looked at her screwy, to be at the centre comes with too much madness. I am attracted to making change but political office means being political, being nice to everyone, including whackos, and months or years to try moving the ball forward, if it even does.

And the defiant pointless psycho voices, always at the ready to scream and yell. Science-class soundbites from high school go off, an equal and opposite reaction for every other action, right Mr. Hawn? The sludge test.

Then again Nelson Mandela did blow everything out of the water. Never imagined political forces could set up truth and reconciliation instead of a national holiday to celebrate vengeance.

waves

The thing about music is, it isn't real. It isn't something you hold and inspect, like an object, like a painting. It is sound waves. What is a sound wave? It is what it is and it isn't something physical, which perhaps is why it is so awesome, because we aren't real either. We have bodies, but besides that our consciousness is . . . ? Are we anything more than a bunch of thoughts? Are thoughts real? Are they something other than thought waves?

chasing dorka

At the improv workshop, the teacher said his system regarded musicians as having two types of consciousness. One is attention, the all-over-the-place kind. Though you are supposedly engaged in playing music, that type is thinking about how long you should solo, how much better or worse you are than other players, why doesn't this piano have better action, the colour of the shirt of the person in the front row, what you did yesterday, what is for lunch — the all-over-the-place mind, like a fly in the room going everywhere.

The second mind listens while playing, has another experience, brings empathy. His point was that the second mind is a better musician, the one you should encourage and, by virtue of reaching it, the first one has less grip, disappears for a bit. Gets out of the way.

I think what he was getting at was that getting there is as simple as just listening.

lists

Ambrosia has knocked honeycrisp out of the running. Honeycrisp held first place a long time. I admit my bias was pink lady but mostly because of the name; you have to be objective.

When I record someone doing various takes I list my reactions. Once on a session with Danny Lanois, I noticed he did that after each take. Thought to myself that is a fairly low-tech method for such an entitled big shot. Okay, I can use a pen and paper too. A list ensues, best takes, mediocre takes. But if I do not write down what was what, I won't necessarily distinguish months later when I return to mixing this, what was best vs. what was imperfect.

Am I saving myself work by making these lists? Or should I listen as a blank slate, make notes and then compare with my fresh notes from the original session? A potential student sent me a sample of her music, a song which has the same melody for the verses and the chorus. Not sure if she is inexperienced or exceptional.

Alternate universes. One where songs have no changeable melodies. One where Mr. Spock uses logic for evil. One where Trump's son marries a Palestinian woman and she becomes his adviser. One where if Al Franken resigns, Trump does too.

perfectly

There's this funny thing that happens when you play a mistake and try to fix it. Often you play the mistake over and over and over, expecting to play it correctly. It isn't a good strategy for stopping the mistake. Instead one develops the mistake instead of the correction.

Like when people are upset about their behaviour and focus on what they did wrong and supply judgmental feelings. Telling themselves they are bad or wrong or guilty blah blah blah, over and over. Run the same action with the hope of new outcomes but it is also sort of predictable that if there aren't new elements introduced to the sequence of events, then probably the result is just the same sequence of events. I got this from Casey Sokal 30 years ago and maybe he said he got it from his teacher growing up in New York. Practise at the speed that you can do it perfectly.

It makes a lot of sense. Change the experience, practise doing it correctly. That it is a different speed is not a concern. I wonder if people can apply that to other problems? Probably no way that's possible. Nope.

what passes for thought

In the improvising world you work at listening (which changes what passes for thought). The extent to which you continue thinking is proportional to what is accomplished musically. That is probably a big part of the draw for those who can't stop, relief from the ping-pong of ordinary thinking. When is the bus going to arrive, what's the forecast, what kind of wallpaper should we get, I need a new shirt, what's for dinner. And anyone can get that by just tuning in to experiencing all sound unfolding with the same attention they might give when meditation leaders tell people to just concentrate on their breath, in and out, and let the thoughts just come and go like the current of a river. The attention of not being off in a fantasy, but experiencing now-ness.

objectivity

Lose all objectivity making a midi drum track. In isolation I might believe the kick or snare even a cymbal, but once I play it repetitiously it never holds up on playback. The peculiar thing is if I listen to anyone else doing it, there is a higher probability I am okay with it. Even when I hear horrible drum samples in popular music it doesn't annoy me half as much as if I do it. There is something about the difference of attention.

accompanying margaret

Six years ago I was asked to play at a benefit for Japan following the earthquake and tsunami and later asked if I would accompany Margaret Atwood reading a poem. I've been to a zillion open stages and many poets have asked me to accompany them. I don't think it works well, I don't like poetry readings in general — if I miss one word or phrase I've lost the whole thread. So I said sure, I'd be glad to.

We walked down the dark aisle out of sight of the audience, up to waiting chairs before being announced. She pulled out a small pocket mirror and checked her makeup or did her lipstick. It was a unique moment, I felt like a spy. Later on stage it was easy to play with her. She's a pro. I was pleased with myself for not bugging her about *The Blind Assassin*, *Alias Grace* or *The Robber Bride*. I had questions I really wanted to ask but so many other people kept gushing around her I thought better for all-around confidence she not know the piano player is another crazed fan.

Jian Ghomeshi was there. I don't think he liked me and I never liked him either. Had an imaginary electric buzzer in my hand waiting but he never shook it. Adrienne Clarkson wore a very cool delicately made batik jacket or dress, very folk art. Michael Ondaatje was there too. He liked my film for the song Separated, made me feel like I had made the right career choice in life.

beethoven, karma

Read on the back of an album of music by Beethoven that when the piece was first performed he had to do an encore of it, meaning the whole 40-minute piece again. At that time people couldn't hear it again unless it was live. I like rewinding, trying to see the before, would love to get a solid glimpse into my ancestors, generations back, where were they, who were they. Bet we're all connected to murderers, rapists, saints, maybe artists. Someone from 5,000 years ago is in a way still alive because we are. My ancestors obviously weren't very good at making cookies. That must be why it is a struggle for me, but then again, only tried once, a couple days ago. Maybe the instincts they passed to me were to judge too quickly or I got blogging genes. My dentist retired this year, he hated Beethoven. He was a bit of a classical music nerd and when he caught wind of my composition ambitions he said skip Beethoven, don't waste your time there. Didn't take his advice and fortunately the string quartets really kill me. Wonder if I'll get the quartets I wrote recorded by people instead of Logic Pro X. Karma is a nice idea but I don't believe in it. Too much that is evil goes to sleep at night pleased with itself and what it got away with.

stolen

First musical gear stolen was after a show at the Holiday Tavern. A bag of pedals and patch chords. There was a group of tough guys who used to do security there and they were considered the culprits, but I don't know. Never saw it again. I sure loved playing the Holiday Tavern, main floor, those two or three years that it was the new revamped modern place to be in deep purple splendour.

Second time was while producing Andrew Cash at Street Brothers. A big empty parking lot. Van window smashed in, two guitars and amp and rack-mount effects gone. After they were caught, cops said glue sniffers. It was too late for recovering the guitars. Between the capture and the theft everyone said "didn't you have insurance?" No, but I have ever since.

Third time New York. Everything was in the car of the guy who drove us, then his car was stolen. Nice young Canadian guy, Peter, drove us down and then when it was time to return . . . car was missing. But nine days later, it was found with everything intact in a tow truck lot. Too bad because meantime my insurance claim was about to reimburse me with a bunch of beautiful new replacements.

At least three times other people took me aside to say this person that person were stealing from me, imitating my song or my style. I didn't think so or if it was true I was left thinking they can't steal how I made it or my process, besides who exactly are you going to complain to? And what is more ludicrous, being upset about imitation or Arista issuing refunds when Milli Vanilli was exposed?

beehive state

Yesterday, coconut chickpea improvisation, worth it. Later added bass to Katasha's song, trying to do Vulcan mind meld with Kendrick Lamar production values, so far it is easier in my imagination. Successfully repurposed roti shell, masked old salad. Gave pep talk to winner of the low self-esteem award but didn't change anything, probably she'll clinch next year's nomination (again). Exchanged texts with anger management candidate, best to avoid telling the truth to those types. Duvet continues to confuse me, built to sag, look forward to marching on Ikea. How quickly it can all go by without returning to a country-based life, beware of that. Looking to record or obtain some solo dulcimer. Played back Beehive State and for maybe the millionth time enjoyed the piano with delay and Rhodes and then realized for the first time there is no chorus or bridge, love it just the same.

pool

Used to drive on the left and faster than the pack but experience altered me. Now the slow lane, no guarantee but better odds for longevity. Hard to not play fast when you know how to play fast, it often impresses everyone, except maybe you. Sitting with Jonnie Bakan yesterday discussing his thesis about café culture and Harlem and how politics and music intersect and that other more important school he graduated from, Freddie Stone school. He directed me towards spicy books I now need to eat: Adorno, Attali, Denning. Left music school in the 80s because of how much money I owed from having a student loan and what to do with my relationship to the piano. There is no substantial audience for what I'm drawn to do, freely improvised music, might as well pack it in, rethink what to do with life, and then I met John Oswald. Sometimes you have imaginary ideas about someone when you meet them. He hosted a jam session of improvisers in the back room of the Cameron and invited me to come. I agreed but internally imagined he wouldn't be up to my speed. Turns out I was the inferior one. Lucky about Blue Rodeo but luckier to befriend John. Those years I played with him every Saturday afternoon I could, often just us. Loved our molecules smashing round the space while trying to keep up, the free draft beer from Herb, Handsome Ned painting bandanas in the other room, an audience of maybe two people and other guest musicians. Changed my driving, golden lessons.

exceptional

The woman ahead of me at the 24-hour Sobey's had a $424.24 total. I was amazed. I asked the cashier after if that was exceptional; "Oh, no," she said. Over $500 is exceptional, need to call the manager to approve that. Overhead speakers playing Deodato's 2001 Space Odyssey, I thought that was exceptional. Next person after me, recognizing 2001 theme, starts explaining the ape scene to his girlfriend, the dramatic confrontation between different groups fighting for position. How the introduction of a weapon establishes power and dominance (not to mention murder). He wants to discuss whether the apes were real apes or actors. I want to call the manager to approve exceptional dumbness.

10 regrets of 2017

Trump is not yet in jail.
Criticizing Darren Frost's Rivoli set from many years ago without realizing the violent backstory.

Every time I fall for believing the answer lies outside.

Not writing certain stories for fear of complications, like being fired.

Still having no idea how Keith Jarrett played The Windup with two hands.

That the YouTube video of June Tyson speaking about improvising with Sun Ra has been taken down.

CBC never takes me up on my podcast/show ideas.

Offering new music demo to ancient music publisher.

My attempt at making snowball cookies.

Failing the contest to avoiding hearing McCartney's Wonderful Christmastime.

going slow

Saw *Coco* the other day, that's two children's movies in one week. Used to envy those Hollywood musicians, and who wouldn't want a shot like that, not to mention the orchestral budget. But it is as likely to come my way as Trump would be washing feet of homeless people. On way to the cinema, driver was too close to other highway cars. Snow and ice, plus we're in the fast lane. Wanted to say can you drive slower, can you leave more distance between yourself and the other cars — could I do that without being thought of as an asshole? Nope, there is no middle ground. If I say something critical they will think I'm a backseat driver and if I don't speak up and we have an accident the story will be why didn't you speak up? Like in bands with someone always blaring, trying to decide whether to speak up and ask could you turn down because I can't hear my thoughts, or stay silent, remaining friends, but all along asking yourself is being nice really worth getting tinnitus? The animated details in *Coco* were powerful, especially the rendering of the junk guitar with frets made of nails and tactile cartoon wood grain. If movies hit the right notes, I get teary. The last time I was outright bawling and not sitting in a theatre was after a hit and run took Matt's life, Matt who booked me in America. Matt whose place in Chicago I stayed at often and who supplied the faxes to help cross the border, referencing evil subjects from my songs as though they were studio collaborators. Customs requires evidence substantiating that I was on my way to spend money in America rather than make money (even though I was performing for nothing and spending $200 a day to keep up). "Douglas Christie is very excited to be producing your new work and we will have the electric zither in the studio by Wednesday." Matt was one in a million. In the Castaneda books Don Juan was recorded saying things like death is always present, just sitting on your left shoulder ready to be introduced. Animals understand that, they can smell death nearby, they're alert in a different way because of that. I'm in Winnipeg on icy roads, in the lane on the right, going slow.

kingston 1985

Being the youngest in the band, I was the recipient of a lot of advice in the early years of Blue Rodeo. Time to update something Bazil shared with me the first time we played out of town and I began to grasp our different views of life. Update: what goes on below middle C stays below middle C.

animal improvisers

Animals are already in that space improvisers are trying to sniff out. They're paying attention to every second, already living it. I used to think it was valuable to try seeing how long I can keep my consciousness tuned in to the present, like each step while walking, or each breath. People can't maintain that very long but animals already live there. They are showing the way all the time.

chances

In Winnipeg, frozen river. Once, under Donald Street bridge, took a one-time chance, walked slowly across it, there was a path in the snow of others who went before me. Same feeling as seeing clouds below, first time airborne. We took different kinds of one-time chances as kids, sneaking at night into the ballroom of the Fort Garry Hotel just to play the piano in the echoey dark. Played roulette this morning with

Mastercard, they put me on hold, I muted them at random intervals, hoping to catch the real person and avoid the pain of direct marketing messages. Worked. Heard the father of my childhood friend died, but didn't see an online obituary. Yesterday went to old folks' home. Explained my reason for being there to the security guard. After he heard the name he smiled, "He's alive, I see him every day." This was probably a one-time chance.

wake up, time to die

Airplane back from Winnipeg, *Blade Runner* playing. As it started I read the credits, Harrison Ford, Edward Olmos, Daryl Hannah, Rutger Hauer, and I thought how cool they got the old cast together. The film started with synth sounds, which were awesome, what guts for 2017, then I realized this isn't the new *Blade Runner*, it is the original. I watched anyway. Music so unlike what people settle for in big films. I also recently saw *Downsizing*, exactly the usual film score, usual use of strings and orchestra to say now you are sad, now it is suspenseful, now it is action. It works but it is in almost every film and there are a zillion other ways a creative musician could do things uniquely. Makes me want to scream, wake up, time to die.

vasili arkhipov

In the amazing doc about him, pianist Sviatoslav Richter spoke lots about Russian musicians who I knew nothing about. One that sounded curious was Maria Yudina who also was Stalin's favourite pianist, whatever that means. Richter told a story about her playing Chopin at a concert during WW2 and she played it very tough and staccato. He asked her after why she played Chopin so weird and she answered defiantly, "Because we are at war."

During the Cuban missile crisis, there was a Russian submarine near America armed with nuclear torpedoes. Protocol required three officers to agree before launching an attack. The only reason nuclear war wasn't initiated in 1962 was because of Vasili Arkhipov's decision; he voted against it, the other two voted to proceed. He's dead now but in a couple weeks it would have been his 92nd birthday. We live in a world that names significant landmarks after Putins or Trumps rather than honours and shows gratitude for the Arkhipovs.

for whom is it done

There was a musician who loved sorting through their habits and later played at avoiding them. Their favourite musical contributions were whatever didn't sound like them. This frustrated many people who wanted to hear them play things that sounded like the way they originally sounded. Those "fans" wrote pissed-off letters or showed up to the gigs to complain. Critics even wrote negatively about how much they didn't sound like who they were before. So the musician changed their name.

the applause for whom

There was a sax player from out of town who played solos that blew some minds. When finishing and receiving applause they pointed at their instrument like it should take a bow too.

hearing

My friend musician Sam Larkin developed hearing problems and in the last years, I asked him about it one time. I liked his explanation, "Hearing aids work terribly with music. And terribly in general. You have very little sense of the direction from which any sound is coming. And I'm sure our ears somehow naturally adjust volume for sounds — as the sounds are on the way in. Which seems impossible. But with hearing aids, the rattling of a paper bag can be as big as a brick dropping on the floor. Sometimes, not always. For music, especially when you're playing, it's the filtering you miss, again. You want to turn them up to get some things better, but everything goes up and it's not much help. On the other hand, they pretty well saved my life because I can hear now. Can't make the distinctions between sounds too well, and volume is a problem

— turn it up and it's all up. Just not a situation without them, with natural hearing. Most of what is said and sung onstage — even at Fat Albert's — I don't get. I hear the noise, but can't filter it finely enough. Movies are the same. Really don't know what they're saying. But in the end, if your natural hearing is disappearing, they're the next best thing."

surprises

Songs I heard a million times before noticing something unique happening all along

- Keyboard in Baba O'Riley was an effect not a tendonitis experiment.
- No cymbals in Do You Know the Way to San Jose.
- Lyrics to Savoy Truffle was just a box of chocolates.

electricity

More so they do it underground in Europe. Often I don't remember, but then I look up and I do. Many wires get the electricity into each home. Like if it didn't exist, if someone described what that would be like, I bet afterward nobody would agree to this visual pollution. So it is. Weaving through trees, century-old branches received chainsaw surgery, even empty spaces have some permanent blobs suspended between poles. What can't I stand more, this or popular songs based on loops? 25 years of looping pedals is, to me, more interesting than the music. I presume being broke is a major part of the story, the ease of working alone vs. with a group. That's a little bit interesting but hearing a voice go pow pow boom boom is only neat for six seconds, but the song is four minutes. People hooked on novelty, like celebrating an air guitarist instead of Charlie Christian's fingers on strings. So much American Idol aesthetic in music made with loops, bores me like all unvarying repetitions. And my students gush over these songs as though they represent top songwriting achievement. I guess it does for them but for me feels like awarding Monsanto's new red wine because it tastes great without using real grapes.

evil plans

What was really fun, once upon a time in my life, was playing in a band that had simple pop compositions where I was expected to solo indefinitely, until the guitarist gave me an urgent look to finish. Sometimes that took a very long time and that was fine. How much can you do with ordinary melodic ideas in a song in C for instance that is a loop of two or three chords? Eventually I would move into C#. It was unique and probably confusing to some, exciting to others, but that's okay; after all I just wanted to make it more interesting.

The comments on Facebook sometimes are confusing or, to put it another way, there are some confusing comments because they miss the point of the subject. I'm thinking it would be more fun to replace the thread with something unrelated, like how to play golf. Then the comments that make no sense to me would be so much more interesting. That's my new evil plan.

long-time listener

Voicemail: Dear Dan, first-time caller, long-time listener. I write the same song over and over. I'm ashamed and a failure.
Dan: You should be concerned not about writing the same song but about judging it over and over, getting depressed and allowing voices of doom to set the agenda, fuck that shit. Try writing about that — if you're upset your paintings have too much red, the problem isn't too much red, it is getting upset about too much red. All you need is a little pivot.

secret target

There was a woman who lived in a neighbourhood where there was a lot of prejudice and corruption. She learned to play guitar and started writing songs about what was unfair. People noticed and invited her to sing the songs at performance places. It was interesting and meaningful for some. They wrote about her, put her picture on the cover of magazines. Before long, lots of people wanted to be there when she performed. Soon she had a following but many also attended just because she was now famous. The content became secondary to seeing someone who was in the news. The reviews were about what she was wearing, how she styled her hair, about the difference in the sound of her voice between recordings. Occasionally they also wrote what her songs were about but mostly, now, that was far from the main issue. Many journalists tried to find out who she had sex with and photographers spied on her hoping to snap embarrassing pictures.

She started taking a correspondence course on phenomenology and soon after, she started wearing Christmas lights on her shoes and everyone lit up and wrote about it. Sometimes she used solid colours, sometimes multiple, sometimes she operated a strobe with remote wireless technology. *Rolling Stone* placed a close-up shot of her shoes on the cover of their back-to-school issue. *Pitchfork* designed a Trump hairpiece on top of her shoes for their disappointments issue. The *Economist* made a triptych of three famous shoes, Imelda Marcos's, Dorothy's from *The Wizard of Oz* and her's. The *Economist* measured the financial impact of each. When she started to sell her own brand of Christmas Shoelights at her performances and in fashion stores, people started to call her a crass capitalist, they wrote articles about what a sellout she was, and Errol Morris approached her wanting to film a documentary. Everyone wanted her to explain but she wouldn't. She completed her certificate in phenomenology and directed her profits to community groups that made a difference in the neighbourhood that originally inspired her songwriting.

astrology

Sometimes when I meet people into astrology, who ask me when I was born, I like making up different sun sign answers. I like the knowing recognition on their face. Something like "that makes so much sense." Of course this devilish behaviour is typical of a Cancer like me. I would try to do it with musical instruments too but I think that would be harder to fake. Maybe it just depends on what you identify with (another typical Cancerian view).

your cheating heart

There is a certain gesture I like using currently as a starting point in improvisations, like the way certain people have a usual chess opening. It positions me to consider a bunch of angles, then the piece proceeds — who knows in which direction. For some years, thought as an improviser one should make everything new always. That is still part of my thinking but now less interested in being so anal about it. It's like if a country singer does Your Cheatin' Heart tonight in Toronto it isn't the exact same tomorrow in Peterborough, because it isn't the same moment.

pressure drop

New semester. Students discuss which songs they will do over next months. I ask if this time they will consider writing original songs, luke-warm response. Still more eager to play covers. So we audition their collection of favourites. This always results in a couple interesting things.

1/ I learn what is currently popular.
2/ They learn the teacher doesn't know about songs they think significant and their inner doubt metre goes up re: why was this guy hired?

The song that stood out for me was When the Night Feels My Song by Bedouin Soundclash. It stood out as Juno contender for most obvious rip-off. In the chorus totally doing Pressure Drop by Toots and the Maytals. This rivals He's So Fine by The Chiffons or Taurus by Spirit.

cheap thrills

Trying to catch my bias and interrupt it, decent cheap thrill. If I didn't put effort into it, my right hand would just play piano same way over and over. Trying to practise it, tune in to preference, then reject it. A new shirt, which one looks ridiculous, buy it. Parking car, that's too far, park there. Which movie wouldn't I put on in Netflix, choose it. On the subway which seat would be uncomfortable (the middle), sit there.

Trying to interfere with habits leads to different musical experiences.

recent disappointments

- Overheard students discussing a speech about coalition building by Bernice Johnson Reagon (of Sweet Honey in the Rock). On the value of risking the involvement of people you do not necessarily identify with or you even dislike. The survival advantage of that vs. collecting people similar only to yourself. After realizing the speech was from 1981, they agreed the material was too old to take seriously in 2018.
- Sat on the subway and talked about 60s jazz with two musicians who aren't Jewish and one told a story about saxophonist Dave Liebman and how listening to him, it is like he's trying to avenge the Holocaust every time he plays.
- Read that Elton John is on a farewell tour but it will take three years.

why improv

There is a zone my five-year-old gets into where everything is a why question. Why is that blue? Why are there police? Why is Trump president? Why is it garbage day? Why can't I have more? Feels like sometimes she is compelled towards the interrogative regardless of the answer. The worst is when it can't be answered easily, and time elapses while I formulate what to say and by the time I start that answer, she's bored and has moved on. It is an improvisational opportunity; I win points less for accuracy and more for not letting silence transpire. We're jamming trying to keep up the tempo. Sometimes it might mean supplying answers that make no sense.

kikawa

When the massage therapist who was working on my back muscles asked me what I did and when I said I'm a musician and when she asked me if I liked the music that was playing in the background, the horrible electronic one-note-generated wash of chords that made crescendos and dissolves slowly, over and over and over — I said yes it's great because I didn't want to risk insulting the person who is giving me so much relief. I love it too, she said. Lying was the right thing to do.

buddy rich, patrick brown

There is a cruel musician joke about drummer Buddy Rich who despite a great musical reputation was equally known for throwing hissy fits at the musicians he employed. I think about that in light of the Ontario Conservative leader resigning for sexual assault accusations because I keep rewatching the news footage, and enjoying it.
Buddy Rich's house after he died. Telephone rings. Widow answers.
Hello?
Is Buddy there?
No, I'm sorry, Buddy died.
Okay, bye.
(moments later, phone rings)
Hello?
Hi, is Buddy there?
I just told you Buddy died.
Yes, I just like to hear it.

mickey smith

There was a time after high school when Linton Kwesi Johnson, The Specials and Dory Previn were mostly on my turntable, that was lucky. Last week, in one of my classes the teacher assigned us to read about the murder of Mickey Smith who I never heard of before. This has been my favourite assignment so far.

changing stations

Student cancelled lesson, disappointed in their progress. Some get defeated about practising or, rather, defeated about not practising. It is as if there is a tricky part of the mind that fuels mind loops, the kind that lead to ongoing disappointments and conclusions about what you can't do and why did you ever imagine that you could? If one could overlook the negative voices or just see them for their meaninglessness, if one could stay on track, and change the station from the negative voices to any other voices, the payoff happens, the positive kind. I bet it is the same for learning a new language or losing weight, etc. That one has to enjoy not caring for the negative affirmations because their interest is your loss.

at the rehearsal

At the rehearsal, the guitar was so loud that the three vocalists were obliterated. Instead of directing the guitarist to turn down, this time I tried to get the singers to ask. One was game to speak up, their frustration obvious, but one didn't care and the third felt like asking the guitarist to turn down would make them appear uncool. So only one voiced a concern about the disruption and no fellow player backed them up. And the guitarist remains not tuned in to thinking about their effect. Like watching the news.

tempo

There is a tempo to everything and you play with it, in time or not. When I'm out of time with someone or something it is obvious; no different with music.

boal

Looking at exercises in a book about Theatre of the Oppressed (Augusto Boal). Many make me think of musical counterparts, about attention

and imitation or leading and reflection, similar issues for an improviser.
Makes me wonder about titles like Music of the Oppressed but too late,
top 40 beat me to it.

questionnaire fail

Name one song that affected you in terms of relationships:
Happy Together (Zappa version)
Name one song that got you interested in a culture you weren't famil-
iar with:
Planet Claire (B52s)
Name one song that is a guilty pleasure:
Try (Blue Rodeo — the original ska version)
Name one song that affected you politically:
Never Gonna Give You Up (Rick Astley)
Name one song that returns you to childhood:
Windy (The Association)

my only friend the end

Did Bach walk around
patting himself on the back for what a genius he was or
did he think about the next mad puzzle
to engage himself with?
Does one ever arrive at
the mountaintop or just continually
recognize higher elevations? What does it mean
for ideas of the mountaintop?
The space we make for imagination is unlike the
space we actually live inside.

solo

seeking original solo for acoustic song. no clichés need apply. electronics
will be considered but we do have some reservations. effects are also

possible but if it's all about the effect, that won't do. acoustic could work but as stated at the front, no clichés please. no worries about experience or education, just an original sound that lifts this song up a few notches.

power

I played Ontario Place many times with Blue Rodeo. One time while walking down the laneway post-show, a couple in a car recognized me and offered me a lift; I said sure and got into their car. They were thrilled. They had just seen the show and they liked my style — "You're a wild man!" said the man — and the woman driving asked which street she should take to get me home. He was especially animated about how much fun it was to watch me on stage blah blah blah and how cool it was that they noticed me and could give me a ride.
Then I ruined everything.
I said, "What do you do for a living?" His smile ended and he looked off in the distance. "I'm a cop."
I wanted to laugh, it was an unexpected answer, but I knew this was probably not the best reaction (especially if I wanted to get to College and Spadina). "That's great," I said.
Until that moment I was a person of honour and privilege; now the rules had changed and I became careful. He knew it too and that was the most interesting part. He just wanted to be a fan and me to be a celebrity. Now we were in a class experiment.

mr. wonder

When I think about songs that punch me in the brain and position me to follow them, wherever they lead, Stevie Wonder wins the gold. Sitting somewhere at York University and suddenly "I Wish" came over the speakers and it hit me how amazing that opening is — every time. Too many others,
Superstition
Boogie on Reggae Woman
Don't You Worry About a Thing
Higher Ground

Living for the City
All Day Sucker . . . on and on
If the people who teach music in colleges and universities were smart
they would offer a course called Infectious Openings of Mr. Wonder.

me to me

Walking in the subway sometimes I try to walk in the same time as
other people's echoey steps and if I get that down then I try to walk in
between their steps. They're the 4th note, me the 8th note. It isn't as
easy as I expect it to be. Next I try to walk in triplets with the stranger
being the one. This means extra attention to not make my weirdness
obvious. Lots of people have earbuds and I am one more of them but
I'm paranoid. Had friends lose their hearing or get tinnitus or need
hearing aids. I don't know what to do except practise finding silence
and not turn up the volume of earbuds. I saw an art show one time
at Harbourfront that truly blew my mind and ears. Five or six video
monitors, each representing a different singer, all performing a score
that the conductor created from bird sounds. She studied and encoded
gestures, organizing them into patterns or randomness. I thought this
work would become huge but now, more than ten years after, I don't
think it travelled very far. She was from Estonia, her name was Külli
Kaats. I had a dream recently with new musical ideas in it and when I
woke up I thought about those sounds. Tried to decide, in my conscious
state, whether it was something to go learn on the piano or just something unique to the dream state. I learned it, it felt like a spooky present
from a mystery origin but is there anything to our lives besides our
experience of ourselves? So then just a present from me to me.

it's my nature

There is an old story, a Sufi story I think, about a frog that gives a
scorpion a ride on its back, to cross a body of water, but not until
the scorpion assures the frog it won't hurt it. Once they arrive the
scorpion stings the frog and while dying the frog asks why did you
do that and the scorpion says, I can't help it, it's my nature.

I've recorded more than one singer-songwriter who didn't understand time or how to reliably play in time. I'm not very interested in explaining time to someone who doesn't get it, plus they can't instantly fix themselves. Trying to get them to follow a metronome or click track, if they can, also distracts from them being present with their lyrics, which, for me, is much more important. Makes more sense for me to be the one adjusting to their sense of time, plus I don't mind the musicianship challenge.

Some musicians understand right away and accommodate. Others get pissed off and pontificate about how they are so much better than this and they would never have left any part of a recording with any time questions, pushing or pulling. They can't stop their own complaining even though I hired them. Doesn't occur to them I won't be calling them again; they can't help it, it's their nature.

filter

I like how my own sense of hearing has a built-in filter: while I sit on the subway or in a noisy café, I can by virtue of observing filter out other audio except my subject. How does the brain do that? Maybe the same way it monitors a heartbeat or white blood cells or heals a bruise. More and more it is obvious the I of me (that which calls itself I) is not nearly as in charge, or as smart, as the rest of what is called brain. The brain does various jobs without asking for any acknowledgement but actually it is the puppet master behind that which calls itself I. This might explain why I hate most popular music.
(trick ending)

hi how y'all doin?

There is a politeness thing I saw when in New Orleans many years ago, mixing our record at Danny Lanois's. This is what happened —
I would be walking down the street, a stranger would pass me and simultaneously they would say "Hi how y'all doin'?"
I totally knew this was bullshit and appropriately checked my wallet

and didn't respond, kept walking like nothing happened. After four or five of these encounters I put it together — these people were taught to do this when they pass strangers. At first I thought how phony, but later I got excited, before you knew it I was trying to beat the next stranger to the punchline.

Unexpected American gift. Compensation for their border guards. Since that time, back in Canada I've tried it out, lots. Sometimes people act just like I did, looking at me like they know I'm up to something. Some smile politely. Some naturally say hello back like it is an ordinary exchange.

But all that is simply to say, similar to the greeting between strangers, when you are making music with someone new, you feel out whether you have common ground or not.

geordie mcdonald

Any meeting with Geordie contained equal parts consciousness and gossip. So glad I saw him last fall, after not seeing him for many years, and gabbed about Paul Bley, Escalator over the Hill, marriage and how Claude Ranger was not willing to play ball with musicians who played too inside. He said back in the day he was called the Lone Ranger (French pronunciation). Geordie laughed a kid's laugh, wonderful laugh. He was nice and direct about various assholes and saints he knew first-hand. Gotta love someone who plays back their experiences unconcerned about editing. I didn't know much about his compositional life but I bet since his personality was intense the music was too. Once upon a time, being Neil Young's drummer, a pretty decent calling card.

I had a job with Greenpeace in 1984 and while I was there I created a fundraiser at Trinity-St. Paul's on the gorgeous nine-foot piano in the sanctuary. Myself and three other musicians playing new music. "Green Pieces," I named it. I asked great visual artist John Abrams if we could hang some of his endangered species paintings but I didn't know people need insurance for such things. The other solo performances were Malcolm Burn who worked security at the church, Anne Bourne and Geordie McDonald who died yesterday.

hanson

Heard an interview with Hanson on CBC, listened to them say things like this.
fame is really not impressive . . . the interesting thing is the future . . . we're celebrating 25 years for a reason, for us this is the journey . . . people say do you ever get tired of playing your songs, well it's part of the job
Didn't know I could throw up so many times in a row.

knots

When creating music, with others, mind is a little bit interfered with because to be good at it means positioning differently, like playing chess.

rip it up

When John Lennon released Rock 'n' Roll it threw me for a loop. I liked his solo records and his previous record, Walls and Bridges, was only a few months old — surprising another new record came out so fast. At that time in my younger life, I couldn't stand the sound of 50s music, it seemed hokey, but Rock 'n' Roll was a revelation. The horn sections, the unexpected percussion on every track melding with the Jim Keltner kit, José Feliciano on guitar and Lennon's voice in its best shape. Sort of ironic the record I admire most by him is just a bunch of covers but at the same time totally transformational. To this day I can't enjoy the original Stand By Me compared to the otherworldliness where John Lennon placed his version. The little chugging upstroke at the 5th fret does so much more for whatever part of my brain buzzes when happy.

Peggy Sue is as interesting as the best Buddy Holly work but that rendition has a psychedelic aspect that propels the idea of the singer's infatuation into surrealism. It made me think differently about the power of music. I could gush forever about each track. The cowbell on Bony Moronie, the nonchalant voiceover jokes to the intro of Just Because, the off-mic whisper at the end of Be-Bop-a-Lula, the crazy compressed piano sounds everywhere, the echo congas on You Can't Catch Me and the way the horns align themselves with the drum kit or with rhythm guitar tracks and still reserve moments to punctuate ends of phrases. Sometimes I think that whole record is a reference for how to think about using horns in popular music because they are so creatively placed whether supporting or soloing.

They brought such punch and insight and hilarity and respect to those songs and I think on some level this is part of what they hoped, that people like me who didn't get it would be awestruck and grasp something else, inspiration.

dark games at u of m

There was a music building at the University of Manitoba and sometimes I had my own winter Olympics there, arriving at night and not slipping on icy stairs. It was a white concrete building maybe from the 60s. The door wasn't locked. Piano sounds floating in the hallways. I could snoop. Mostly uprights but then I found one Baldwin grand and it was after 9:00 p.m. and no staff around, perfect. A bright-sounding Baldwin and the action was in that perfect zone of crispness, reacting super-fast but the weight of the keys light enough for swift end results of whatever ideas were going down. The light switch was reachable from the bench and so once seated I turned it off and played in pitch blackness. Making up compositional games about playing without seeing. How long can I play without knowing where I am and make a good sound? That was the first game. Eventually the second game starts, playing without seeing but know relatively where you are. The third game can I play in clusters and not have someone start banging on the door that I'm damaging the piano (which really means I'm injuring their taste). Fourth game is turning the lights back on and seeing what happens to my playing from playing in the dark so long.

freire

Some musicians try to control every detail, want credit for playing every instrument, deciding every fader level, judging every outside player's contribution, and others are pliable, unfazed to try supplying whatever they are asked to do. I'm thinking about this while reading Paulo Freire's Pedagogy of the Oppressed and the sides he articulates: oppressor and oppressed.

Reminds also of the different ways people control or submit to being controlled in music making. Still, the thing that is behind the art that most moves me, are people able to switch sides, on some level they get it — that to consider opinions that are not their own or not even necessarily likeable to them, is a frequent ingredient behind powerful pieces.

But more vividly, it is like the dialogue people have internally. The inner arguments between them and them or I and I, one can be the boss and the worker and forget that one is in neither, just a collection of belching synapses.

a good day to die

If they are going to discuss whether to sentence a youth as an adult or a youth — calls having rules into question. If they were a youth at the time, then they were a youth, that's how it is, but to say we'll do it differently because this one is worse than the last one, says something about the state. It says we can't adhere to our rules. Where have I heard that before, is the state just a mirror? Another old friend received a death sentence, Stage 3. If I'm in the second half of life, seems part of the tone is adjusting to knowing many players that are leaving the stage. It shouldn't be a surprise, have had a lifetime to register this, but that is the problem, one gets busy with plans and believing they can be finished. How did that story go? A certain kind of person greets each morning saying today is a good day to die. Sometimes I think I will get to finish every song I started, what nerve.

9 surprises recently discussed at dinner

that stevie wonder has the jackson five sing doo doo top on you
haven't done nothin'
that rita college's song, time, was stolen by eric clapton in layla
that martin scorsese used well well well in the departed
that in the big store chico says to young piano student "now you practise" and after door closes kid practises and it is all the same techniques
chico was known for
that gil scott-heron's first band was called black and blues
that zappa reconfigured beatles artwork
that john lennon reconfigured zappa artwork
that joni mitchell used cheech and chong in the bridge of my analyst
told me
that jemaine clement is the vain crab singing shiny in moana

falstaff

I have a box of old music, cassettes, cds, vinyl, and I was going through
it trying to justify why it takes up space. Many amazing things in the
box. Like a band in Chicago that my group found out by chance,
through the great Matt Suhar who took us to the store, Specimen
Products, the owner and creative guitar and amplifier designer, Ian
Schneller, had a band called Falstaff. Amazing compositions. Over the
years I've heard a few creative punk rock experimental sounds, nota-
bly Helicopter by Bloc Party, amazing — but much earlier Falstaff
raised that bar, radical ideas and making us laugh with the unexpected
hidden tracks with bass clarinet solos (was that even what it was?) in
Nothing Compares To U or the Melanie rollerskate song. Top drawer.

angry on stage

When I was little I saw Lightnin' Hopkins at the Playhouse in
Winnipeg, saw Muddy Waters too but Lightnin' Hopkins felt more
powerful or unique, seemed like we all were learning something

first-hand. Saw Sonny Terry and Brownie McGhee, loved his harp style, anyone who plays harp and does not sound like Sonny Terry (or Little Walter), doesn't keep my attention very long. I didn't know they weren't close during those years, that apparently they even stayed in separate hotels. I'm glad they didn't seem angry on stage. I was angry on stage once, for about a year. I stopped moving and tried to play everything with just my left hand, secret way of saying fuck you all, pretty sure it worked.

how i won the talent show

Sometimes I have been told by people that so-and-so is imitating you or ripping you off but truth is I started it. I crossed the line worse than anyone you know. I have no idea what ever happened to her, but at a United Synagogue Youth conclave between kids from Winnipeg and Minneapolis in the 70s, I impressed this one particular girl at a talent show where I destroyed all the wannabes by playing guitar and singing David Bromberg's You Got To Suffer (If You Want to Sing the Blues). Afterward, I sent her a bunch of songs written by Bromberg and other artists whom I thought obscure, like George Harrison, and claimed these were songs I wrote for her. I was 13. Wish I could hear that cassette today.

pause

Sometimes, back at school, I am in a position where I must endure stuff I am not into. In those moments a wee bit immobilized. Want to say things I should probably not say. A bit like watching a band and wanting to solo over what they are doing, I really could contribute, I am so absolutely certain it would add something valuable maybe even magical but I might be totally wrong. To jump in or not. For whom would I be doing it? How awkward if I'm totally wrong to think I'm welcome there or start a fight I don't want to have.

touring w carmaig

Driving on tour with Carmaig de Forest through Minnesota, 1990-something, there is a frightening wind storm, skies are grey or black, car feels like it is rocked, over the radio surprising news Jerry Garcia died and Carmaig needs to pause, I don't understand, but he's a Californian, a big part of his younger memories had the Grateful Dead's music in the background. Someone once told me people can barely remember details about their lives and I think about that lots, when I try to retrace things that happened and notice how much has gone to the void.

Carmaig and I did many shows, many people and places, only a few vivid memories have stayed with me, like his sadness that highway evening about Jerry. I didn't know much about the Dead or California but I remember the Binder Specialist van dying outside of Davis, California. A Dodge Ram, belonging formerly to a company with a fancy sign on the side — Binder Specialist, whatever that means — I appropriated the name for my band and we looked impressive, or at least the sign did. Lost so much money fixing cars, every musician does. Musicians should take an auto course or at least listen to car fixing podcasts and develop their understanding of how to trouble-shoot. Over the years rebuilt two motors, one transmission, repaired three ball joints, did rust work many times, probably stopped seven times by police and maybe six speeding tickets.

We had a sound guy that time in Davis, but the chemistry wasn't good between him and the band, that is a deal breaker. You are only on stage for an hour tops otherwise you are in each other's faces, if you don't enjoy the company it is torture. Trapped in a tornado with Carmaig, no problem.

cheating

After the piano lesson, we passed an old organ and the 19-year-old student said, "Wow, an organ, how does it work?" I plugged it in and told her to go ahead and try it. Then she pointed at the bass pedals and said, "What are those for?" I said that's for the bass. "That's cheating!" she said.

publishing

There is a strike at York University, one of my professors left me feeling confused about where she stands. I considered raising my arm in class and pointing it out but realized it might add an unwanted conflict to my eventual grade. Age-old problem of seeing and speaking up . . . or not. A musician wrote me to ask for advice about publishing between members of a band. Tread carefully, I advised, the person who gets to cut the pie might be offended by your sense of entitlement. Treat it like chess, make your moves by thinking through worst-case scenarios. Once found myself in a position where the leader of a band confided in me that other members might want part of the publishing, as if me being the older musician meant I would commiserate about how selfish side musicians could be. "But Joel," I said, "if you honour people for their contribution you get something most bands rarely achieve — respect and loyalty."

old neil young neil

Years ago, I watched an interview with Anne Murray and she talked about age discrimination in the music business. As time does its thing I see what she meant, the world treats the younger very differently than the older. Was thinking about different responses from audiences when Neil Young was young and sang "look at mother nature on the run in the 1970s" vs. older and sang "let's impeach the president." Not sure the second thing was noticed very much despite Neil arming his message for maximum exposure with videos and talk show interviews — so much more media on his side to utilize vs. the 70s, and yet I think he had less interest from that more recent public. Just taking him for an example, but maybe the point is the context . . . but then again there are lots of people who command a different attention from the world when they are young vs. when they are older — even if their message is more refined. Am I just a crazy old guy showing off his delusions?

hymie

My great-uncle, the brother of my grandmother, liked him a lot and he was different. His name was Hi (Chaim), the Hebrew word for life. Many Jews named their sons Chaim, often later nicknamed to the English, Hymie. He usually had a smirk and he was kind and playful. He was a travelling salesman, his living wasn't easy. Which adults treat you like an equal and which boss you around or are condescending stays in your memory when you're a kid. Didn't know until many years after he died that he was originally a sax player and used to gig in bands, probably in the 1930s. That explains it.

swap shop

The Stereo Swap Shop (Swap Shop for short) on Osborne across the street from greatest Winnipeg ice cream, Dutch Made. The Swap Shop allowed you to trade records for other records. They evaluated the records you brought and offered choice between cash or credit. Economic anarchy, my 14-year-old head exploding. Will Woolco, Eaton's and Radio Shack do this next? Certain records perpetually in the bins, New York Dolls, Pink Floyd, Marvin Gaye. Sometimes I made a major discovery, Speak to Me by Jackie Lomax (produced by George Harrison, orchestration by George Martin). Some places like that when I moved to Toronto, Around Again on Baldwin, but never a match for the vibe of the two women who owned/ran the Swap Shop and the joy they gave off being their own boss.

There was a musician I met looking through bins; we started a conversation about Billy Preston and his keyboard solo in Get Back by the Beatles. He thought it was hard but I thought I could do it. He was tickled by my confidence, Damian Turner, he wore a cape and a beret and played classical piano. Probably a smart move to hide away in Winnipeg, he was a draft dodger from the 60s who adjusted to his new Canadian identity though he travelled lots, to Bolivia. I wonder why a young man, not from South America, would make so many trips to Bolivia in the 70s?

The house he rented was funky, shag carpet, grand piano, stained glass. One of the first times I went there he said okay, play it, the Get Back solo. So I did. He freaked out, excited that I was a kid who could play the blues and other things by ear. He gave me a copy of the key to his house, nice to have a friend like that when you are a teenager. I could go play all night long in the empty house, even try on the cape and beret (not in public). His friends were into astrology, handwriting analysis, tarot cards, numerology and hookah pipes. Two journalists, one a professor at the University of Manitoba, one doctor, one middle-aged woman, Sharon, who took piano lessons from Damian and they were in a relationship or used to be, she funded some of his activities, it wasn't clear. She had a strange cackle of a laugh which was simultaneously fascinating and scary. There were two other regulars, musicians Barry and Michael, in rock bands and then there was Cheamer, his younger brother, a mechanic who frequently went to California to buy rust-free old cars, drive them back to Winnipeg and sell them for more money.

Cheamer also was on fire to be an entrepreneur, wanted to discover a hit song and manage whoever wrote it. He went to open mics on the lookout for the hit songwriter he might champion and get rich quick. I believed in him and wished I could be that person but I didn't understand yet how the song thing works, just how it worked on me. Cheamer loved the Supremes, he talked about the bass lines in their songs, this was years before people talked about James Jamerson's impact on the hits. Mendelson Joe also went on to me about the bass as key ingredient to pop music, maybe they know something I don't. No doubt Frank Davies knows all about this. Probably one of the first lessons when he got into Expert School was

What is the most important instrument in pop music?
i)   bass
ii) voice
iii) trombone

i'm so sick and tired

Musicians know something about brains. They know if they repeat something a whack of times, then go away, then try again, at some point the thing works on its own. Some people say muscle memory. I find that a wee banal because this is so much more mystical than that. I prefer to say magic, because magically the hands (or fingers or feet) can do that thing they couldn't do when you first tried.

And you imagine it a lot, especially while you are trying to reach that place you have not yet reached. Almost there ... part of the way ... more and more each time . . . and you keep repeating the effort, try again, let's try again, slower, faster, in a different chair, after a break, yada yada — the brain knows you want to do this. Even when you are away from the instrument you still run through the desire to master this thing you have not yet mastered.

So I'm thinking, if that happens (and it does), then perhaps worrying about whatever horrible thing one might worry about (ill health, rejection, etc.) constantly, is a way of replaying to the brain a certain picture, albeit undesirable, but we're imagining it over and over just as we do when practising. Like maybe that isn't so wise.

be here now

It is like playing music disrupts the thinking of ordinary thinking. Just like any new activity would. If you balance a ping-pong ball in one hand while walking down the street, your thoughts are mostly sucked into thinking about the balancing and it keeps you more involved in the present. All those mystical texts with directions essentially along the lines of "be here now," could just as easily be said "balance a ping-pong ball while walking down the street" or "play new music." I bet one might arrive in the same place.

dark horse

Anti-reincarnation lyrics, sure was cool to hear on the radio in a number one song, once upon a time
give me love
give me love
give me peace on earth
give me light

give me life
keep me free from birth

punt

The Grammy award–winning musician asked me to play something on the CBC grand piano; he reminded me of a pool shark, I recognized the tone or other non-verbal clues. So what he got was something slow, sans flash, and he was disappointed, could see it in how he looked mostly at his watch. But other musicians, later, fell hook, line and sinker and he complained about how inaccurate they were or how to do things right — meaning his way. He thrives on bossing and puncturing.

When you get conned, usually there is a moment where you thought you were gaining something. Maybe self-flattery is the downfall — I'm so smart I see where the pea is hidden among the three shells and I will make easy money — but as soon as you are congratulating yourself an alarm bell should go off, you have turned into a football. You have positioned yourself in a way that certain persons can punt you across the field, easy.

i can feel it coming in the air tonight oh lord

Still designing a zine syllabus inspired by Chris Cavanagh's example. Mine would be about popular music and how it can influence things, or so goes my theory. One part concerns itself with the difference between writing about things you don't know and things you do. Was looking online, could there be an example of someone making no bones about saying nothing? Poof, Phil Collins's interview about In the Air Tonight — "It wasn't about anything at all," says Phil. Would like to contrast that with the Kinks song The Money-Go-Round where every line speaks to Ray Davies knowing his sad and hilarious subject inside out, real experience about disappearing music publishing money. If there are voices in the head then who is it that is listening to them? Someone calls themselves "I," so are they the speaker or the listener? Started a book on art-based research and one chapter begins with a quote by Picasso, "I never made a painting as a work of art, it's all research."

beatles not so secret

If one wants to gain traction, maybe the secret is to liaise with the other. In a way bands are a microcosm of that because if one person is in charge of every detail, it isn't as powerful as when they consider other ideas that aren't necessarily to their liking . . . the Beatles vs. their solo records.

Many friends riled up about political assholes. That grips me too, but distrustful about preaching to the converted. An echo chamber is only an echo chamber. In one of my classes we read Bernice Johnson Reagon (of Sweet Honey in the Rock), and a speech she gave called "Coalition Politics: Turning the Century." Her experience was that political changes required coalition building, reaching out to people who are not like you.

ghosts

I really did it, best tomato sauce ever. The real test is if I can repeat this or it was just a fluke. Guy who was supposed to vacuum out the furnace cancelled at 8:30 this morning. He has no idea how many things I changed so that we could do this today. One more thing to add to the list of things to not complain about (and there it goes again). Wonder if there is such a thing as a booking agent who I couldn't complain about. Who could play a role in positioning me to do my little song + dance, in places that came with interested, sober people. Tried a recipe for cheese made of cashews with agar and tapioca flour. Worked and it melts and I will never open a restaurant because that would compromise the fun I have cooking what I like. I'm writing about music or cooking because I'm taking a break from the essay I am in the middle of, about ghosts and hauntings. Not the usual way we speak of it, more like the backstory of violence or trauma. As far as I'm concerned, there is no end to seeing this. Ghosts for every-thing, everywhere. Empty lot at Bathurst and Bloor, ghost of Honest

Ed's, Trump is in the news, ghost of democracy, dog barks at a bicycle, ghost of Daniel. But is the professor interested in me going off on a tangent? Doubt it. Ghost of confidence.

the 10th victim

There is a movie I like so much, seen it five times. Made in the mid-60s, called *La Decima Vittima*. About us, in the twenty-first century, and the state has sanctioned a reality tv show to help citizens work out their hostilities. Participants win a million dollars by murdering ten people and surviving ten attempts on their lives. Every time I watch it (starring Marcello Mastroianni and Ursula Andress) I wonder about the prescient mind of the writer. The soundtrack features one repeated weird futuristic song, on an organ, with female-choral-vowel-sounding accompaniment.

I thought about *La Decima Vittima* while reading about the pedestrian killed by Uber testing a self-driving car. The gist of the reporting was — too bad it happened and Uber feels bad for the victim's family, sniff, okay, everyone back to work and continue adjusting to robots in charge. If there is an increase in profit margins, then the death of this pedestrian or others is a small sacrifice, send flowers to the family and halt all testing (for up to an hour). The reporting focused on the car's camera failing.

Why isn't Uber, or the company who invented the "safe" robot car, charged with murder? In the 60s, the American trailers that advertised *La Decima Vittima* framed it as a wacky comedy, I'm too serious for the twenty-first century.

drawer boy

The Drawer Boy won last night at the Canadian Film Fest and I scored it. Fun to revise my CV this morning and add 2018 Best Feature Film. Best part is I wrote a whacked-out piece for the montage, which almost every director would politely reject; I'm used to that, but they kept it.

voices in the head

It is warming up. Only so many weeks before there will be out-of-control grapevine growth, now is the annual time to wonder if I can get it together and prune. Kombucha intervention, was about to pay for a course then remembered, everything has a YouTube tutorial ~ poof ~ started first batch, leave it alone for a week. People contend many benefits including clearer thinking, wonder if this can be tested on new piano pieces. At the check-out counter noticed recurring beep for each bar code scan. Did someone originally pick the key and if so why? Had to know, recorded it, turns out key of F. I have an old piano piece called Foster Child because it was an ostinado in the key of F. That morphed into Fost which became foster which became foster child. When George kills Lenny, it was a life-changing moment for me. Wonder how that morphed, if that was in John Steinbeck's mind the entire time writing or if it occurred to him much later? The story behind the story is the story. He was thinking pretty clearly, how did he manage to get kombucha 80 years before YouTube tutorials?

george

Watched music videos of artists I never saw as young people which led to viewing Lowell George whom I never got into, which led to discovering he played on Harry Nilsson's Son of Schmilsson and then finding his daughter Inara George's music. Never heard of her but now I feel like we're friends. My old cat was also a George, as in Madame George. About a thousand people met that cat, but hardly anyone ever asked, "like the Van Morrision song?" She was named by Sam Larkin while I was recording him in my old house (which coincidentally I bought from him). The recording equipment was on the top floor and the recording space below. Had to yell through the floor to command start! stop! The cat was then a no-name kitten. Sam yelled what's the cat's name? I yelled through the floor "no name yet" which he heard as "Madame George" and it stuck. George (favourite Beatle of the mystics) wrote at least two songs which I thought should be massive but never were. The first was Wah Wah. The musical hook is what impresses me there, strong as Satisfaction or Day Tripper. The other is That Is All, especially the Harry Nilsson version, the one without Lowell George.

only a flesh wound

Once upon a time, Amnesty International had a songwriting contest, I sent in a song with a metaphor about pirates, I lost to Bryan Adams. A few years ago Dan Savage was looking for a theme for his podcast, I wrote one, lost. Sent in a song when *Hockey Night in Canada* was looking for a new theme, something playful, not anthemic, lost. There is a scene from *Monty Python and the Holy Grail* where they confront the Black Knight who despite losing each of his limbs won't give up his essential identity — that he is an impassable guard. Me and the Black Knight, it's just flesh wounds, brothers from a different mother.

as you start to walk out of the way, the way appears

One of the earliest books I obtained that deeply "worked" was the *Tao Te Ching* by Lao Tzu. There are other titles for it and other names for the author, doesn't matter, the content is the thing. Everything there speaks to the improviser's mind, playing music (which is to say anybody in life, doing anything in life).

As you start to walk out of the way, the way appears.

dentist fills

I met an older guy on the subway platform last fall, I thought he looked like a professor I heard of at York. I asked him if he was that guy but he wasn't. We started a conversation, he told me he was a retired musician which led to a discussion about what he played, drums. Each name I dropped he had had meaningful relationships with, much earlier than most people I know. Herbie Spanier, Freddie Stone, Jim Blakley. He had a lot of details about the 70s and 80s for each of those people and he played in the Toronto Symphony. By the end of our shared subway ride he gave me his card, he's a dentist at Yonge and Lawrence. I was amused, he is probably a very successful dentist but still answers to a stranger that he is a musician, albeit a retired one.

dan from uic

Leonard Cohen said one of the best things I ever heard a dying man say. "I hope it isn't too painful." That's about right. Dan died, Dan whose surname as far as most were concerned was "from UIC." Dan from UIC died, yesterday. I hope it wasn't too painful.
https://www.dropbox.com/s/zbsqhcwzxx0zm97/Anything%20At%20All.mp3?dl=0

revolution

There is a great moment in John Lennon's song Revolution, the slower version, where he sings "but when you talk about destruction, don't you know that you can count me out . . . in."
Both "you can count me out" & "you can count me in." It's change-able. I like inserting duality there. Had not made up his mind or maybe his conclusion was both. All the more surreal it travelled so widely.

heart and soul

Five billion light years from Earth. The latest star, farthest ever seen, is apparently that far away. Yesterday showing niece how to play that horrible 1-6-4-5- song on the piano. The one everyone in the world always played, who couldn't play piano, at every public gathering since the Well-Tempered Clavier. Maybe it is called Heart and Soul. I know it was written long after Bach, still I bet the people of Vienna tried doing it when Bach left the room. My niece started it, not me. But I couldn't help myself, she played it wrong. Her ear is great, I showed her the correct fingering, she found it crazy. She went back and forth trying to remember, looks at me like do you know how insane your instructions are? But I know how it goes, she doesn't. She kept trying, I think she's a natural. Anytime I hear about how many light years away something is I have no idea what they are talking about. They mean if we were travelling at the speed of light, then one light year is how far we would have travelled given that velocity. Right, okay, thanks for that astronomers, simple, it is just five billion light years away.

drake snorting condoms

Best part about Tide Pod challenge or people snorting condoms up their noses is I feel less awkward admitting so much popular music doesn't have a draw for me.

problem solving

Wish I had the budgets to pay people whatever they wanted when I ask them to play on something I'm recording. For my own projects wish I could get paid what I wish I could get paid. Thinking the problem lies not with economics but with wishing.

party pooper

Money troubles, trying to find Waldo. The world is meaner and leaner, the bank doesn't care how many times I've been up. Have to look better on paper this year-end, have to look as though I am not in the arts. Lemon kombucha wins the first round and you better let out the carbonation each day or it can explode. I can prove this now, onward batch #2. A new film came my way, from America, how unusual someone wants to work remotely just like I always thought I could, and just like nobody hardly ever did. A good film, twists that make you laugh, don't see them coming. What to do musically, I have no idea. World inundated with people ready to bullshit. In film projects, admitting I don't have the answers is my second favourite place to be. Someone told me people in Toronto are always trying to prove how many things they are doing, I'm so guilty. My instant theory, that because it is hard to make a living that inclines one to prove themselves, listing a dense agenda of things in progress. After hearing someone point it out I felt like a dumb statistic so I started practising replying with dead ends. I recommend.

"Hey, what are you up to these days?"

"Nothing."

"What do you mean?"

"Nothing, I'm not doing anything."

They look back like I kicked their dog. Nobody really needs you to bullshit, except the bank and maybe whoever found Trump or Harper or Jacob Zuma or Margaret Thatcher or Vladimir Putin appealing. My first favourite place to be when composing is when I like my idea and the director does too. More meaningful to make everyone happy without telling lies.

ghost memories

An older trumpet player, an improviser, Herbie Spanier. Parachuted into some punk groups in the mid-80s. He was born in the 1920s. He was in his own world but an accomplished player (Paul Bley!), exciting for everyone and sometimes weird, good weird. There was an older musician from time to time playing for change on the street, playing vibes or a kit, playing makeshift reproductions or toys, very capable improviser with crazy white hair growing at symmetric 45° angles. I didn't know his backstory but I could tell there was a serious earlier jazz life in his technique. Another old guy, Jerry Lewis look-alike, thick glasses and a strange indent in the side of his head, used to hang out at Hart House playing the upright both to amuse and make friends. That upright is long gone; so is the lonely guy, aren't they all. An even stranger one used to play the open mic at 300 Bloor Street, called Lime, maybe because he was from England. His singing was incoherent, laughing to himself at the same time as trying to sing, but enjoyable precisely because it was like listening to another language, pretty sure it was English. I think about those old guys differently, being closer in age now. Wondering about questions

I never posed, and information they might have enjoyed delivering if anyone cared to ask . . . but those weren't the conditions. They were just being music people wherever a public shot presented itself, because in addition to knowing your craft alone in a room, there is something else achieved by doing it in front of people.

my way

Some people believe that what you think might manifest itself into physical reality, like the old friend of Blue Rodeo I met on the street recently, who is homeless, and while catching me up on his life explained his current method for studying winning lottery numbers. I wondered about this a long time when I was younger. Could it be possible? My religious brother found it amusing and frightening when I told him one time how I got over it by trying to think an airplane crash while we were in flight. He is in the camp of believing what you think can in fact make physical manifestations; after all he moved to Israel believing there is a God and that God wants Jews to live in Israel in order to return in person — singing My Way I guess. Can you imagine the royalties Paul Anka would get? I do appreciate the fact that since the plane remained airbound it doesn't make my telepathic impotence conclusive. There may have been other people on the plane simultaneously thinking the plane must remain in the air; nonetheless I doubt it and my thoughts to ruin our lives succeeded because they failed.

Thoughts affect us, but not outside us. Like maybe your cancer goes away or your difficult relationship changes but thinking some-one else's ill health away, no sir. Even if the Blue Rodeo guy does win the lottery (and I would love it if he does), it would just be a chance happening and not the result of the power of his fantasies. But the more you are thinking of something musically, the closer you get to it happening. Sometimes really big things, things that strike you as impossible before you apply effort to it. Thinking it over and over gets you there.

the student that came late

There was a student who came late, who missed a third of the classes, who was mostly on Facebook even when he was in class, who handed in assignments late, whose instrument was bass.

I knew some of the students came from difficult places, many of them did not have parents positioned to help as much as they did where I came from, many were holding minimum wage jobs simultaneously. Tried to keep my judgments in check. When the year ended, his final mark was a C, that was that.

Next year I worked with an ensemble of seven students comprised of four singers, a drummer, and two guitarists. He was one of the singers. I was surprised because last year he was a bass player, not a singer. I assumed his contribution wouldn't be too hot, might hold us back. True to the year before, in class he was often distracted, online and late.

Tried to organize things so that each member contributed one song of their own and when we worked on his, it was an improvised uncomplicated ditty with an A part and a B part. At one point while I was encouraging the other singers to add background vocals, he chimed in and told one of them to sing F# and not F. I became sarcastic — oh, you have perfect pitch? Yes I do, he said nonchalantly. I played a random note on the piano he couldn't see. What's that then? E♭ he said without looking up. It was E♭. I was even more taken aback when he started singing — he was brilliant. All my assumptions were ruined.

secret weapon

Don't recall what his final mark was but the marking system bugs me, flawed, suggests if you fail you aren't someone who could be successful or if you get a high mark you should be, but that isn't reality. Better to just be pass/fail or even just drop marking altogether. Pourquoi pas? You sign up to take the course, that's good enough. After that school year, I invited him to come sing on a record I was producing; he came and was like a secret weapon. Adding improvised parts, adding counterpoint I never asked for, riffing off the lyrics. Couldn't ask for more. Then he disappeared. Wrote him three times during the year to say hello and remind him I would help record or assist, whatever he wanted anytime, he had previously said he wanted that. He only wrote me back once acknowledging my position and offer, it was over a year ago. Another weird thing about that guy, seriously, he liked Elton John. He performed I'm Still Standing when they had to do a cover. Broke my heart but I tried to keep my mind on the bigger picture, his talent.

recent haiku death

Dan on bass, the weight
Cabinet of heavy woofers
A light smile, his face

Ben worked with uncle
They fixed and improved this house
Young man overdose

Sarah Sanders lies
Humility, she as if
Death by open mouth

bedtime

She plays white notes in the middle of the piano with both hands slowly, random spots. I join on the upper register at same speed, just different random white notes. Magali enters the room and gets what's left of the piano bench and adds bass notes. She wants to be able to play Mary Had a Little Lamb in front of an audience like her pal from school. Little does she know what's happening right now is also an amazing performance. Frankly, way heavier than Mary Had a Little Lamb and she's the composer. Wish I could convey to her that this is totally a viral YouTube performance consumed by a million or two but, you know, it's bedtime.

hat chair

On the subway last two months there is an advertisement for an upcoming financial expo. A conference with some expert millionaires, scheduled to share with participants how to get rich. Sylvester Stallone is the biggest name there. His picture at the centre of the poster punching fist into fist, caption "Knockout Strategies." What expert financial tips he will share for $49. The advertisement says the attendance fee of $149 is no longer true. There is a line drawn through the $149 — limited time offer — $49. All the posters were manufactured to include limited "new" offer, it was always $49.

At a music business conference there was a three-person panel responding to demos. One was a former lead guitarist in a band that went nowhere, one was a co-owner of a music publishing company whose biggest star was nobody and one was head of A&R at a major label in Toronto, a satellite office for the Los Angeles–based company who incorporated a Canadian version of their company to exploit lower taxation on their American product. All three are white guys in their 40s. One after the other, participants take turns playing their songs and the panellists respond with why the songs were not good enough, what was wrong with them and what they would have done if it was their song. They should have called this 45 Minutes of Music Industry Guys Complaining about You and Your Music.

Nobody Knows Anything, that's the course I would like to try teaching. First exercise, stand before the class and explain why any object is what it is. Then present an opposing explanation. Then have the class vote which was more true. This is a chair, it is designed for sitting in. No, this is a bad hat, you put it on over your head and it is too heavy but your hair stays dry in the rain.

we all want to change the world

For my final paper for the class Art in Crisis, have to write a ten-page essay about any of the people we reviewed or choose an artist from another time period and contrast them with someone we studied. I chose the latter and contrasted the Bed-In for peace with Ai Weiwei.

Never understood the ins and outs of John and Yoko staying in bed when I came upon it as a kid, I liked the song Give Peace a Chance, but why stay in bed? What did that mean? Now I see the hilarity and inspiration (and guts).

Beatlemania was still close. Predictably, the paparazzi would follow, spy or interrupt attempts at being private so they decided to exploit their positionality and announced where they would be. In light of successful civil rights sit-ins, like Greensboro, they blended their two major interests — love and peace. The paparazzi came, assumed this was going to be about sexual exhibitionism. Instead, they found the couple talking in bed about peacemaking. The room was dense with handmade posters that said "peace." Photographers couldn't shoot the couple without also advertising their message. Nixon felt threatened by Lennon messaging people to think anti-war and tried to get him deported. This only made Lennon more political. John Sinclair, Give Peace a Chance, Power to the People.

The Chinese government didn't want to acknowledge or bring attention to the 80,000 people who died in the Sichuan earthquake (mostly university students and schoolchildren); they censored and controlled all information about it. This was because schools built by the state are supposed to be very secure, they shouldn't have collapsed. Typical mistake of power that doesn't know true power. Control the narrative at all costs instead, for instance "I am a very stable genius." On his blog Ai Weiwei asked the public, who are the children that died? And people wrote back supplying over 5,000 accounts of who their dead children were. The public turned to his blog instead of the government. "The kind of authoritarian state we have in China cannot survive if it answers questions — if the truth is revealed, they are finished. So they started to think of me as the most dangerous person in China. That made me become an artist, but also an activist."

totally set up

My oatmeal, like my kasha, is generally perfect. Not bragging, there have been many misses, but the fact is the misses led to constantly perfect results (a few years in a row now). It's about the boil and the timing and the smell of something ready and the controlling of when to heat, when to remove heat. In high school, why did they never cook in chemistry class? Just a wee bit of popcorn, maybe melted butter — we would all get it. Would have understood the pop doesn't happen until the oil reaches a critical temperature, etc., etc. Would have been so simple: "Hey kids, everything is chemistry and chemistry is sexy and interesting." To start instead by memorizing the periodic table does not make sense. It's like starting a kid learning to memorize the lines and spaces of treble clef or bass clef . . . a no-brainer to get big ideas across to the beginner mind but first you don't start with complexity. If you do, you have a lot of disinterest, turn-off and inner conclusions that one isn't capable, it is too hard. Totally a set-up.

memories of stupid

I was reading Howard Kaylan's book (Flo & Eddie, Frank Zappa and the Turtles). When they were starting out they were approached by suits at a small label who wanted to record them. The suits suggested changing their name to the Turtles. Guys in the band said no way, that's stupid. The suits said the Beatles are big right now, they are also named after an animal and it ends in l-e-s. Nobody could argue with that logic, the Turtles were born.

In the lounge of McLear recording studios where we recorded Blue Rodeo's first record, someone from Warner Music came to discuss artwork. The album was going to be named after one of Greg's songs, Outskirts. "So there's a girl and she's wearing a skirt and the word 'out' is on it. What d'ya think?" I don't have many memories of Greg doing things I admire but this time he looked unsmilingly back and said no. Artwork guy, without missing a beat, acted like it was a joke all along, but it wasn't. He just knew part of his job was to be submissive instantly, whichever way the wind blows.

Customs stops us at the Detroit border, 1994. Selina on guitar, Liz on bass, Dave Lee on drums, on our way to tour America, even though we will lose money, both countries try to not let in foreign artists, because technically they are "working." We pretend to be on our way to a recording studio in Chicago. The customs agent smells something fishy. "Okay, lemme ask you one thing, you got recording studios in Canada too, why not record there?"

"Because our equipment is inferior to what exists in America."

Tense facial expression disappears, "Right," waves us through.

yesteryear

At a party, young award-winning musician is holding court and explaining why Bob Dylan is the worst artist in the world. "He can't sing, he's musically horrible," yada yada. Was a wee bit weird that they didn't see any value in the lengthy works and history of Dylan. I thought about some famous music people I can't stand but I'm less comfortable to brag about it, at this party anyway. I know people can lose their minds over meaningless things like artistic opinions, they can even murder over it. I bet people who are blind probably have some understanding of that because though they never have seen they have tried to understand what seeing is. And when sighted people explain racism to them, and it comes down to a willingness to hate based upon the pigment of skin, that must leave them feeling like the sighted are way more blind. Someday, somebody should try to write lyrics like that.

3d

One of them wants to have a meeting to discuss the performance after it is over, fine with me and yet I don't seem to be able to get it across that the mark is based on the rehearsals, not the 30 minutes on stage. Like picking musicians to tour with. I wouldn't ask someone primarily because of musicianship, the main factor would be personality: showing up, taking criticism, making suggestions, helping lift things. Yesterday, last class. I'm lax about the 9:00 a.m. start time. They live far away, Scarborough, Markham and Mississauga, using combinations of buses and subway. My job to oversee rehearsals. I let it reveal itself without trying to control much except for the fact

I tried to persuade them towards writing original songs, I failed, it is all covers. If the same songs are rehearsed 40 times, a lot happens from familiarity. They sound as good as anything on the Junos. The sequence reflects their mutual taste, as mutual as any randomly thrown together group of people can be. They perform tonight Saturday at ten at the Tranzac. Consider coming and experiencing these descriptions in 3D.

juggling trick

Everybody's mind contains a drunk heckler sitting in the front row. The stakes are heightened when one starts considering how inner thought can foil the whole thing, like juggling one ball more. Thought knows for the purpose of the music, it must turn itself off — that is why it grabs the microphone and starts screaming. Actual physical juggling with little beanbags should be part of a songwriting course.

beuys

When the customs agent asks what kind of music do you do, you could answer with a familiar category but for many artists it never feels right. Feels about as correct as talking to a dead rabbit. Last semester, I learned about a famous performance art moment. In 1965 Joseph Beuys performed How to Explain Pictures to a Dead Hare. He walks around a gallery, face covered in wax and gold leaf, accompanied by a dead hare who he is whispering to and all the while the audience (it was an art opening) are locked out and can only watch through windows. The explanations I read discuss the symbolism of a dead hare or gold leaf. Maybe that's more succinct but I couldn't find anyone explaining why did he call the piece How to Explain Pictures to a Dead Hare — but I think I know. At least I know what goes off in my brain, namely the pointlessness of explaining art to anybody. There is a primary relationship between you and what you make. That's why when they do ask at customs, I politely answer gangsta rap or easy listening.

playing w john

Many times distracted and so suffers the music. Maybe it is a maturity thing, but the last show with John Oswald was meaningful for all the right reasons, shooting for a certain focus and landing there. Same contest, whether I can maintain my focus or else cave to make it "nicer" for an imaginary idea of what the crowd likes.

the draw

Bad dream last night, best part is waking up and knowing none of it is true. Tempting to linger on hidden meanings behind imagination. Is there any difference between imaginary thoughts after sleeping and the ones throughout the day while awake? When we are awake are we not still asleep? Like if you were awake, wouldn't that mean you don't do the same stupid shit over and over and over? The heart never stops beating, the fingernails never stop growing, the brain keeps imagining even when technically you lie down and sleep, dreams are just more of the same. That's the draw for improvisers, the interruption, trading that for being in the actual present, active in a game of remaining awake to the sound of every moment.

lines i often return to

- But when he's gone me and those lonely blues collide, the bed's too big, the frying pan's too wide
- He hangs out down on Alvarado Street by the Pioneer Chicken Stand
- They say he rode in on the back of a pickup and he won't leave town till you remember his name
- A rat done bit my sister Nell, with Whitey on the moon, her arms and face began to swell and Whitey's on the moon
- Everybody knows that the dice are loaded, everybody rolls with their fingers crossed
- A bim beri glassala glandride, E glassala tuffm I zimbra

- A handful of thorns and you'll know you've missed it, you lose your love when you say the word mine

death and music

I visit the very old man, with body parts failing he describes his new medications and problems; he expressed confusion and disappointment that things aren't working the way they used to.

Sometimes at bedtime after I read her a story she will say things like I don't want to die. It is understood she wants me to do something.

While walking through Spadina station there was a guy playing a Chinese violin (I think that's what it is called); it has one string and he played so well I laughed out loud and then thought finally I can show my feelings in public.

r. murray schafer

While driving back from Stratford, Eye of the Tiger came on the radio and it occurred to me I never before heard the entire song. It was as unredeemable as one might assume. In R. Murray Schafer's book *The Thinking Ear*, a lot of great inspiring ideas. Like how pointless it is to judge music or call anything good vs. bad. Best part so far, when he gave students an exercise to try and find silence, that should keep them busy. I heard silence once, in Iqaluit. Only in the midst of it did I realize I never knew it. It is like seeing a new colour, feeling a new feeling, not something words in sentences can reveal.

r.i.s.e.

Last week I went to the open stage called R.I.S.E. in Scarborough for the second time. Unlike the other open stages I know, R.I.S.E. is predominantly hip hop youth, community messaging and a lot of standing ovations following performances. That part is awkward. I'm not disinclined to give a standing ovation if I'm blown away, but I've seen a lot of performances and my threshold seems different than most of the people sitting near me. I imagine the other people think I am an arrogant asshole for not standing, plus I'm older than most everyone, probably solidifies some suspicion — that seated arrogant asshole is a cop. I do have an appropriate dumb moustache too. Why is there a cop watching everyone jam over their beats? If they only knew. I'm a spy, plain and simple.

Best part of being in the music business, best part of any big performance, best part of attending the Junos is the fact that I don't identify with these places but I fooled them and now I can finish my can-do reconnaissance. For years my unchanged agenda — who's got talent and do they want to play with me? There was a woman performing poetry who stood out the first time I came. She said some surprising things about men and women, it was a long feminist piece. There were some lines about how pathetic it was that men can behave like shit to women when after all women gave birth to them and something else about how they (women) represent an opportunity for men to get to heaven (sex). I can't remember her exact phrases. I would enjoy recording her and seeing if I might contribute musically but I stopped myself because currently I have too much on my plate, plus she might not like cops.

million dollars

I played accordion on If I Had a Million Dollars. It was a fun session and there were a bunch of us singing background vocals. It is amusing when I'm somewhere public and it comes on the radio, I hear my line and know if I tell this fact to anyone else in this 7-Eleven they will think I am a crazy person. But when all is said and done, I prefer the older Beatles message: Money Can't Buy Me Love.

bruce cockburn joke

The best moment was everyone singing the background response "if I had a million dollars, if I had a million dollars, if I had a million dollars" and then someone exclaimed "some sonofabitch would die."

trying to reach everyone

At the end of the term when they had a public performance, his mother was one of the only parents who attended. I acknowledged his talent and made a joke about his predisposition for volume. She said, "Did he tell you he is on the spectrum?" I felt a little awkward, "Yes he did, but I didn't think he meant it." Thought about that when I assigned his mark. I wonder why I wasn't informed about that at the front end of the term, might then have had better ways to think about his needs and the needs of the other class members. Sometimes some of the singers complained like broken records and looked to me to police things. One week, I took him out into the hallway and relayed my confusion. It was then he told me that when he was younger he was a little bit autistic. He said it the way I've heard other people use expressions like that, "I was a little schizophrenic when I was younger." That was how I heard him even though he added, "You might have to tell me something many times in order for me to get it." I didn't think he meant he was actually autistic. I have no training around it but assumed people who are autistic don't refer to themselves as autistic. In all the following rehearsals the same problems persisted. I was annoyed. This had been addressed so many times and other students were contributing more, probably I will assign him a lower mark.

The job was to supply feedback and/or direct these young musicians to facilitate their own process. Wanted them to figure out what to do without being heavy-handed. Tried by asking questions: "Did everyone feel okay about that? Could anyone not hear themselves? How come?" Sometimes that would lead to a few voices identifying his volume and he would shrug and turn down, only to soon be back up. I started wearing earplugs and brought extras. The keyboardist thanked me for that.

He had some peculiarities for a guitarist. He was confused about how to set up the amplifier, the different knobs of treble, middle, bass, overdrive. He could play very well, his articulation was clean and reliable, but when I brought up time signatures he didn't know what they were. He also didn't read music and had perfect pitch. And yet, unlike anyone I ever met with perfect pitch, when I pointed out the out-of-tune-ness between his guitar and the digital keyboard, he said he liked it a little sharp. He played rhythm at a solo level and didn't understand when I asked him to turn down. Made this request often and so did the other students. He didn't change. I tried to be polite about it, he was tall, I asked him to try sitting instead of standing, then his ears would be closer to the speaker but he preferred to stand. Often I felt frustrated and annoyed and thought to get up, go to his amplifier and turn down the volume but it seemed hostile, like a little kid losing a game who decides to throw the pieces away. I wanted a real solution. This song isn't finished.

horrible string arrangement

at the tranzac auction to raise money to soundproof the place i offered an item — a horrible string arrangement of your song. bids started at $25 and it sold for $125. the winner left their telephone number on the bid sheet.

hi i'm bob wiseman you bid on the string arrangement friday night.
i won?
you did.
i was wondering what it meant.
it means i'll do a horrible string arrangement.
with notation or midi?
either or both.
this is great.
you mean this is horrible.
right, this is horrible or will be horrible, thanks.
don't thank me, thank the music business.
do i get my donation back if i like it?

oranges

george monbiot's book about re-wilding was inspiring, later pitched songs based on those ideas for an ontario arts council songwriting grant. won't get it but at the same time did submit, buying a lottery ticket without paying anything. there was a writer from georgia I liked who challenged readers to think something new. what he was getting at made sense, we think the same thoughts over and over just tape loops. my friends don't know what i'm talking about, seems i'm in a sufi story about a man who sees oranges in the corner and when he points it out people respond what oranges? where?

the tricky part about this re-wilding idea is that if removing man's influence allows nature to reposition itself and achieve some feral perfection what does it mean for man's purpose who is also a naturally occurring part of life. the thing about applying for a grant is that they expect an artist to explain what they are going to do. they need to explain and justify to funders why they gave this money to that person or that person. understandable, but at the same time kills what is wild about the artist or places them in a position to liberally lie in order to get funding in order to make art. the idea that an artist knows in advance what they will make is contrary to what artists do — play and experiment and discover. it would be enjoyable to answer their questions with "i don't know, trust me, we'll see." what oranges? where?

i shall be released

was looking through the richard manuel fan club page. liked him the most. there are theories about him taking his life when in rough shape. my theory is the uneven financial split led to uneven distribution of suffering. something rotten in the state of denmark if one person, who wasn't the lead singer, gets all the money for writing the songs when what we heard were lead voices of richard manuel, rick danko and levon helm.

let it fly by

Working on a rap song with former student, Akeem. Added new vocals to it today courtesy of another former student, Katasha, and her style lifts the production values significantly as did the drum ideas of Jake, yesterday. His drumming knocks me upside down any time I catch him playing the Tranzac. Also added myself playing flute, bass, electric guitar and piano. I want to get it into a place where it feels undeniably strong and then see what Akeem thinks. He might love it and want to do more, he might hate it and regret starting up with me. Either way it puts me in a position to try and grow some new parts and repurpose older parts.

fave rip-offs

other acts on the bill who play way longer than was agreed to.

the producer saying they had a technical problem with the take you preferred but fortunately the one they liked best they were able to use.

people who don't risk speaking personally about the show they just attended, but offer statements like "how was that for you?"

trying to survive sounds

Something else about sound that confounds me, that animals often make sounds when they sense predators, dogs bark, birds cry, snakes hiss, and yet if we were in the woods and a bear was walking by and the bear didn't notice us, probably we would not alert the bear to our location even though we too are capable of screaming. I wonder about this instinct to make a sound. Hate viewing birds who are threatened by cats and yet are revealing themselves with each song. There also are more than a few stories of tiny yapping dogs chasing away large predators. Confuses me about nature's programming. Maybe nature does this to help the predators be less hungry?

i in i

There was a musician at the college into mystical arts and she said to me there is no I inside you. Every time you say I it is just a thought thinking. You can pretend your face is I but it is just eyes, nose, chin.

You might as well say your toenail is I. The part of your mind where you are thinking I is in your brain. Maybe you should imagine a brain when you imagine the look of what you call I. I told her I understood but she said if I thought I understood then I missed the whole point. I might have understood that too but didn't bother to say so. She left the program without graduating. I bumped into her today, first time in three years. I asked if she is still playing music.

"If you were born to be a musician it isn't something you can turn off."

"How did you get so philosophical?" I asked.

"I ate a lot of Cheerios growing up."

"What does that mean?"

"You know," she said, "little circles, infinity, pointlessness."

"Think life is pointless?"

"Well, duh."

"You think the same about playing music?"

"Music isn't pointless, I mean maybe what's popular is but music has a point, it's the life that makes sense vs. the life we lead."

for the birds

Musicians seem like birds singing, sounding, listening, responding, jamming. Originally this was written as birds sure seem like musicians, then realized the error.

backwards

Sometimes I'm blown away by someone's music and that's a good enough reason to try working with them, this job is about music first. Sometimes I'm not blown away but other people I admire are, that can give me pause to take a chance. Reconsidering my bias does something valuable on a few levels at once. Seinfeld's series was rejected many times, the suits didn't get it. "It's a show about nothing? Get out of my office!" Amazing writing in CBC today about the NDP and how if they win they will have to face the cruel realities of government. The insinuation that taxing the wealthiest demonstrates unrealistic radical thinking. Don Pittis says everyone should be alarmed that the political party who might not smell like Doug Ford, Mike Harris, Kathleen Wynne and Dalton McGuinty won't know how to behave the way those guys have when they were in power, like that's something to be scared about.

digitaligentsia

Wonder when there will be a Margaret Atwood or Salman Rushdie filter for writing? A Scorsese filter or Lina Wertmüller plug-in for film treatments? Probably around the corner. I work a lot with digital samples. There was a 10-to-15-year span of heated arguments about this but it's history now and the digitaligentsia won. Met more than one film director happy to use the music that comes with software as themes for their film, tons of loops are credit- and copyright-free. Downside is they sound like loops, but most people don't care about the difference between Tom Cruise and Benicio Del Toro.

maybe some cbc

Had a meeting with CBC friend, possibly doing some segments based on what I'm doing at York — looking at music and power, how songs sometimes make the ruling class blink. Slowly making a list of work that had a measurable effect, like John Sinclair being released from jail because of Lennon song's embarrassing the establishment. Some of you made suggestions to me from Facebook or my website, thanks for that. The list of segments is now looking like this:
Joshua and the Horns
John Sinclair by John Lennon
YMCA by the Village People
Sylvia Robinson and Grandmaster Flash
The Rite of Spring by Stravinsky
The Singing Revolution in Estonia
Victor Jara
Fela Kuti and Zombie
Simon Bikindi
Ibrahim Qashoush

John Cage
Barbara Strozzi

secret method department

The old Russian conductor admired for musical surprises said in the final interview he owed everything to not thinking about it.

show us your hits

Sarah Harmer sang on one of my records in the 2000s (Theme and Variations). The session was inspiring; she is very creative and open, plus her groovy house was in the middle of the country somewhere near Kingston, many instruments and nicely organized spaces for doing the work of recording. I was also making a video then based on snippets of found poetry and she knew an Emily Dickinson piece by heart, "I Died For Beauty," eventually it started the video, not sure she ever saw the finished piece.

There was a showcase for her at Ultrasound in 1990-something, there was a buzz about her, enough that the president of Warner, Stan Kulin, was there. Other record company people too, one guy from Raw Energy Records was getting tipsy and during her third song yelled "Show us your tits!" Sarah didn't notice or just kept playing. He isn't around anymore but Sarah is.

Something Stan said to her stood out after the show was over and people were socializing, "If you sign with us you'll get a fairer count than if you sign with the Americans." I liked that, felt like I was an extra in Get Shorty watching Chili Palmer make his move. Loved the admission that businesspeople cheat, what else does it mean if you are offering a fairer count? And the insinuation was cute, his side would be more fair because of his word. Makes me think of all the crying about downloading and streaming as though there were good old days, as though musicians haven't always had other people taking percentages or positioned to control the revenue stream and divide up who gets what, people are supposed to trust the company's accounting . . . because it's their word.

There was a show called *RealTime* in the 90s on CBC and I was approached to suggest some ideas. One idea they liked was a Kingston Surf Party. We got together, Sarah on guitar and voice, Gord Downie on voice, Mike O'Neil from the Inbreds on bass and voice, Grant Etienne from 13 Engines on drums and me on organ and piano. It wasn't very good, I didn't know what to do or how else to facilitate than just turn on the recording machine. Just hoped throwing a bunch of good music people connected to Kingston in a room was enough, but everyone was so polite, the music was meandering and tentative. I have a copy, it isn't long and I don't think it even aired. Years before Gord's health problems it occurred to me that sampling from this recording might be a way to make something out of it. Thought I could take samples and create beats out of that and then farm it out to Gord, Sarah and Mike and see if they might write lyrics over it. That might make a better ending to something that only had a beginning and a middle. Show us your hits.

woodcutting

Jokingly said to the guy with the ponytail at Home Depot cutting the wood I was buying, "Is this the job you wished for as a kid?" He smiled, said no, he had a band 30 years ago and hoped to make it but got into a motorcycle accident, "Woke up five days later with a broken back, don't remember a thing, guy went through the intersection and nailed me, completely his fault. He paid less than $200 for the crime and I paid in headaches and physiotherapy the rest of forever." Said I was sorry to hear it, "But we were actually very close to getting a record deal, this close" — he put his thumb and index finger together. "You ever heard of South by Southwest?"
"Yes, I'm a musician too."
"No way. Well, we had an offer on the table from Chrysalis out of Los Angeles, you ever hear of Chrysalis?"
"Yes, I remember them."
"We had Steven something going through the contract, he was a big lawyer, but then I was hit, *poof* — life happens, eh?"
"Yes, life happens. Was the lawyer Stephen Stohn?"
"That's him. What do you play?"

"Accordion."

"That's funny."

"I guess."

"You have to admit it is a funny instrument."

"I guess."

"Not like you ever could be in a big band or have a record deal playing accordion."

"You might be surprised."

"Did you ever think of doing something more commercial?"

"Like?"

"Like guitar and voice."

"Too much competition. I have the accordion market all sewn up."

"That's smart, good for you. I still write, wrote something last night."

"About what?"

"About the birds."

"Tell me more."

"I love all their different sounds. I was writing about a guy who could talk to them and who convinced the birds to take him flying."

"Doesn't sound too commercial."

"It's not, I'm past thinking that way."

no mystery

Julia can play two open chords, E and A, but when she watches old Jimmy at the Jamzac comfortably playing bar chords she is in awe. Jimmy who can play bar chords doesn't feel anything special, doesn't remember what it was like to not know how to do this thing he has done for 40 years. He watches footage of Jeff Beck and is freaked out that he solos so incredibly well without using a pick. Jeff Beck doesn't think soloing without a pick anything special, he looks at Sheila the 11-year-old skateboarder and is blown away that she can do a kickflip and not crash and break her pelvis. He doesn't know how she does it. Sheila doesn't think her kickflip anything amazing, not like the velocity of Busta Rhymes's rapping, which she can't stop marvelling at. She thinks she could never do that. In fact they all think they could never do the thing the other does which knocks them out. Busta isn't as impressed with his own songs as much as he is fascinated by Evan Parker's effortless circular breathing. Evan

Parker yawns when people flatter his technique but the fact that North Americans can drive on the right side of the road is for him an endless source of amazement. He can drive at home in Britain no problem.

In another universe, Sherlock Holmes reads this and starts laughing to himself and snorts "not even a real mystery."

what new obstacles

Now $80,000 worth of previous gear comes with $200 music software. Used to be you couldn't afford to enter a studio, now the studio can be your bedroom or a rooftop, whatever you dream up. For the moment it seems more about talent than equipment, even though it always was. Wonder what new obstacles will fill the void.

when in rome

There was a story in Zen or Sufi anthologies about a student who couldn't understand what their teacher was talking about so they just imitated them and then something that was previously missing was found. When I worked with Henri Chislo I was so impressed with his piano style, which was very different than mine. I flail all over, but he was still. I tried to imitate his body language and very different experiences ensued. Wouldn't have had those insights otherwise. After, I concluded for all our conversations about music it might have been quicker to just imitate his posture. Maybe that's similar to painters sitting in front of older paintings copying them. Not that imitation is the goal but it sure can move you somewhere else.

gord downie's trance

A few years ago I learned that when orchestral players audition they do so behind a curtain. The hiring committee doesn't know what they look like, only the sound they generate. Equity thinking maybe, if the end result was the audience listening with their eyes closed. Might make more sense for the assessment to include seeing how they get down when they rock out. Aren't all of us with sight also entertained by watching the performer's technique and quirks? Certain performers are amusing for what they look like while playing. Chuck Berry's duck walk, Gord Downie's trance, Glenn Gould's crazy low chair, Nina Hagen's power isn't just her voice if you never saw her.

cheap fuck

Years ago I read in *Billboard* that Bob Dylan hired a 30-something guy named Jeff to be his manager. I wondered who this guy was and how he got the job. The article went on to say he previously worked with Elliot Roberts (Lookout Management — Neil Young). Around that time Blue Rodeo was hooked up with Gold Mountain Management, a corporate management company that farmed out mid-level managers and upper-level managers. Their roster included Sonic Youth, Nirvana, Cher, Beastie Boys, maybe 50 other big names. One of the partners was a guy named Ron Stone and I had a chance to meet him after our sound check in Vancouver. I read that Ron also worked with Elliot Roberts, so when we met I brought up the recent Dylan story and asked if he had any idea why Dylan hired him? He leaned in, "You wanna know why? I'll tell you, it's because Bob Dylan is a cheap fuck!" This was exciting. "Did you know Bob Dylan only pays him a salary!" He said salary like an especially vulgar swear. Threatened by an artist treating management as though they were employees instead of the other way around. I don't think he was aware of the fact that his story just made me admire Dylan more.

autographs

There are some unreal compilations on YouTube of people at fairs riding the Slingshot, which seems to propel people upwards at high velocities then allow substantial free fall. The amazing part, besides not being able to watch just one, is how many people literally faint during their chosen thrill. The brain has the intelligence to shut down the conscious part of itself as a response to heightened anxiety. How is that for proving who is in charge. It's like when you play something great, maybe even spectacular, you know it isn't "you" that deserves the credit. You can try to play a complicated passage but in the long run, the part of you that correctly executes it, if it does, will not be your conscious mind.

It's the synapses that should sign autographs.

grnt rjctn

Talked with a lawyer about simplicity and complexity. An artist has to have many irons in the fire, many grants, many prospective clients, jobs, collaborations because you don't know what could pan out and occasionally something does. To only do one thing is understandable, might work, but lays you out in the open, can more easily be thrown to the curb. Easier to destroy a simple structure, harder to break up a complex one.

When I'm waiting for good news, like results of a grant, I imagine bad news. If I daydream I filter it towards the kind of rejection letter that will show up. And when the rejection letter comes it's no big deal, it was already known. It's not like I'm so immature I need to spend time removing all of their vowels as if I get momentary revenge on the frustrating process of trying to convince gatekeepers that they should hold their breath and trust me. Got the rejection letter this morning.

H Bb -Lsl frwrdd yr ptch nd r tm hs hd chnc t rvw. Thnks for tkng th tm. t's rlly fn nd crtv d! Rght nw our pdcst dvlpmnt cmmtt s fcsd n fgrng t whch f th vry fw nw rd nd pdcst ptchs w r gng t dvlp, wthn th cnstrnts f r rsrcs. W r cmmttd t frsh, frwrd-thnkng, nnvtv cncpts nd stories. Whl yr prpsl s hmrs nd nq, r tm fls t dsn't qt mt th crtr v jst tlnd. W ls flt tht mny spcts f yr ptch r lrdy rprsntd n r xstng prgrmmng . . . s t hppns rglrly r-prpss cntnt n thr dly shw nd n thr ngng smmer srs, s t hppnd. t mght b wrth y rchng *t t s t Hppns's* xctv prdcr, Rbn Smth, t ptch yr cncpt s n ccsnl sgmnt, r wb xclsv srs. Y cn rch rn smt rn.st@cbc.c. m srry ths ws nt th nws y wr hpng fr.

Thnks gn fr rchng t.

courage

Director: Can you do that thing like Tarantino?

Composer: Like this?

Director: Perfect.

(next time)

Director: Can you add something Fellini-esque?

Composer: Like this?

Director: Perfect.

(next time)

Director: Can you make a small change like Jon Brion?

Composer: Like this?

Director: Yes I like that . . . perfect.

(next time)

Director: It still needs something.

Composer: What are you thinking?

Director: Maybe half Tarantino half Fellini.

Composer: Okay.

Director: And half Kurosawa too.

Composer: That's three halves.

Director: Am I a pain in the ass to work with?

Composer: No, you just need to hear things before you can figure out what you like.

Director: Perfect.

Composer: I'll try and do a blend of those three things.

Director: Waitasec. I just thought of something. Do you think it could be possible to try your own ideas?

Composer: It could be possible.

Director: Go for it.

(next meeting)

Director: I like the synth and the singing. And who is that singing?

Composer: She is an opera friend — because the film is about an opera singer I thought hearing some operatic texture might make sense in places.

Director: It works, great idea, I love it, perfect.

(next meeting)

Director: My friend in Los Angeles heard it and hates it, he had a
film at Sundance 3 years ago — he thinks you need to try another
Tarantino kind of thing.
Composer: Perfect.

unique universe

My friend once said to me you can say anything in a song. For some
reason it hit me suddenly that that is what makes it a superpower. It is
its own universe where you can design the conditions, the story, the
outcome. You can repair something that is otherwise broken.

god song

young songwriting student played her new song that presumes there
might not be god. said she is afraid to finish it, afraid of being judged
negatively when people hear it. told her there are also people who will
judge you for believing in god. that's true she said looking down at the
ground more confused. why don't you try to put the part of yourself that
is upset on hold while you finish it? you can always never ever play it to
anybody, even place it in a safety deposit box at the bank with a warning
never to be opened. she decided to finish it. i'm in the right line of work.

farters and burpers

Used to start my mornings at the end of high school listening to My
Aim Is True by Elvis Costello. Didn't remain a big fan as time went on
but I was thrilled to attend the first tour, plus he played my favourite
venue in Winnipeg — the Playhouse. With Blue Rodeo I played the
David Letterman show and Johnny Carson, but in my mind "making
it" has always been the Playhouse.

During intermission, I went outside to do something illegal which
ironically blew away from the strong back lane wind. Like the sneez-
ing scene in *Annie Hall*. After I returned feeling stupid, I ran into the
manager of local Winnipeg band, the Fuse. He said he was going to

ask Elvis to come jam with the band after the show, they had a gig that night at a local bar called the Norlander on Pembina Highway. I wasn't in a good mood — that wind was very expensive — and I responded cynically, sure, Elvis Costello is going to go play the Norlander after this, uh huh, have a great time.

That Elvis Costello did go and did sit in after the Playhouse with the Fuse was all anyone talked about for the rest of the year. That probably was the beginning of realizing famous people on stage also fart and burp or maybe that cynical people rarely get to enjoy magical moments.

cat power

At one point last night I was sitting on a doorstep with four people when a slender white cat steadfastly started climbing a tall tree. Everyone chimed in about how dangerous this was getting, then someone on the street got concerned and expressed its future would be only bad news. A three-year-old boy asked his mother if 911 needed to be called and was told that that's what happened the last time they saw a cat so high in a tree. But I knew this cat, it has survived a long time on its smarts. It scratched me one time and I didn't see it coming. And then it started to go backwards, everyone made encouraging sounds, on the edge of their seats, and it found its way down to the ground. Relief all around but until that moment everyone was thinking less desirable outcomes. Jumping up a tree, amusing everyone then scaring everyone. Creating a space where everyone doubted the possibility of a happy ending and then freaking them out by doing just that. Cat was just a good soloist.

lawyer fees

Got a call from a big company to score a movie. They spoke as though I was an interesting choice as composer. Then they asked if they could send me a couple scenes to score, then the people in charge would select who they liked most without knowing who they were listening to. I love that line of thought, wish everyone did that all the time. Give the job to who sounds best, not who is situated most powerfully. How radical.

Then before sending me the clips they sent me a legal paper to sign, stipulating every way I could be worth suing and that I am expected to work on this test for free.

I wrote back and said if they still want me to do this test for free no sweat, but if they want me to sign a form addressing reasons I could be sued, no thanks. It puts me in a position to use a lawyer and then I have to spend money, so maybe they should get someone else. Thanks anyway.

I'm curious to see if they decide I'm a flake or if they come back and say pretty please?

horror

There is a guitarist joke I'm fond of. How many guitarists does it take to screw in a light bulb? One hundred. One to do it and 99 to say "Oh, I could have done that." I like it because I don't think it is about guitarists, I think it is about everybody. The comedy I'm scoring currently is for a director in New York. Our back and forth led to us focusing on music from horror films. Not my area of expertise but I couldn't stop myself from saying, "Oh, I could do that, easy."

beware of great bob

I know a guy who plays piano. Used to see him studying years ago and he had impressive technique. This morning saw him for the first time in many years and when bringing up music he pointed out he no longer plays. Told me you lose it with time, as though it is a natural part of age to no longer play well. I guess he'll need an ambulance if he happens upon Great Bob Scott doing a drum solo.

ghosts

Writing a final paper for class about an idea that tickled my brain reading Avery Gordon on how ghosts haunt the present. It makes me think for instance of Bathurst and Bloor, now an empty lot but if you were around during Honest Ed's department store you might think about the ghosts here. For some people every time they look at whatever development next goes up at Bathurst and Bloor, they will also see the backstory. In music too, some people don't hear Cecil Taylor without thinking about the history of melodicism, and where does that ever end? Is there anything without a backstory? Nope. But if you follow that line of thought further, eventually there isn't an inciting incident, there is always an earlier history and another earlier history and another. In the bigger picture of life there is no beginning, middle or end, just perpetual motion. I don't think there is room in the class to have an opinion like that, to admit I don't really believe in ghosts.

interviews

In each interview I explained what I could teach instead of what they are offering. And the assignments — I would enjoy dreaming them up — that place students in positions where they might profit experientially. It might be pointless to admit my interest lies not in the course outlines they have in place but in altering old ones or designing new ones . . . but it would also be pointless to bullshit and pretend I was excited about things that don't move if you poke them. So far each called back with cryptic responses. One said maybe next winter, one said we're adding you to our system, one said so-and-so is going to reach out to you but I have not yet heard from them.

meditate

Critical voices in the head probably started off with good survival objectives. How to deal with encountering a bear or a storm. Critical thought probably saved the day. That's why meditation watches the breath, or a candle, or letting thoughts come and go. It relieves the dialogue that otherwise runs the show without stopping. And when there are no bears or storms the same mechanism chooses whatever else it can, like you and everything that's wrong about you. What do those voices have to do with performing or writing music? Nothing, but it can't stop itself. The trick is to dilute the concentration, seeing it for the software it is, like exposing Superman to kryptonite.

murder

There have been murders on my street three nights in a row. I don't know who is doing it but my guess is a squirrel. Two more dead sunflowers this morning. Evil bastard squirrel. Working on a new piece, familiar thoughts go through me about the balance of right and left, about rhythm and melody and especially the sequence of the material for an upcoming piano concert August 8th at Hugh's Room. Then it hit me, the transitions could be different, quicker and chaotic. Why not move between this and that and this and that with no explanation? Present my pieces like turning a radio dial, interrupting their motif or engaging a randomizer button? Might that not be a realistic nod to here and now? To YouTube life? To internet life? They might throw tomatoes at me or yawn but so what, it feels more correct to my aesthetic; abruptly zig-zag. Some won't get it, it isn't easy to follow my playing even when I make it straighter than that. Some will be annoyed and unlikely this will alter their ideas about what music should or shouldn't be. Maybe the squirrel is just trying to help a ladybug 25 blades of grass to the east and I'm stuck in a more selfish closet, unable to appreciate their greater goal.

teleportation

There is a woman I sometimes work with who regularly treats people with hostility. I very much want to tell her what I think of her meanness but what happens Monday doesn't exist the same way by Thursday. There is a concentration to anger that dilutes itself naturally over time. For me, that is the hardest thing in the world to remember, that this emotional state is not here to stay.

But how perfect upset feelings are for writing. When you set out to write music or paint or film, being upset is an advantage. Does anything seriously important happen when you feel neutral? And then there is the snapshot value. Art that is made under certain emotional conditions is like a photograph of time and place. When you make it, it is an exorcism and when you play it, even years later, it is like time travel, with the bonus that you aren't staying.

ronnie

My brother is coming to town, haven't seen him in over ten years. I owe him a lot, he showed my child hands how to play blues, Beatles and beethoven. I wonder how long we will go before making fists about right wing, right of return and Ron way of thinking.

flyshit

Two favourite musical boasts, that Billy Cobham could play a dime against the wall and the other that Stanley Clarke could sightread flyshit.

dream

There was a musician who had a dream that he was in a foreign country and his car was loaded with gear for a gig but it would not drive. He depressed the gas pedal but it wouldn't move and he was on the expressway. He thought to himself the transmission is dying, why didn't I have the mechanic look at that when I had the chance? He started to feel panic about being stranded in a strange country with a show starting soon and a car that didn't work and traffic shortly arriving with soon-to-be-hostile locals speaking in a language he couldn't understand. Every second built more layers of humiliation and panic. When he woke up, he thought if only he knew while dreaming that it was a dream and not based on anything real, then he could enjoy being asleep.

mri

A few years ago I had a problem with one of my hands and the sequence of doctors I saw inspecting this led to a 3:00 a.m. appointment at a hospital where I had an MRI for a few minutes. It was interesting to learn that these machines are in so much demand that people utilize the imaging round the clock but even more interesting was when we were almost ready to proceed they came to offer me earplugs. I asked why and they explained the sound was very loud and distressing to people. I put them on and lay down on the table, my arm extended so that my hand entered the cavity and then the machine started doing its loud blurting out of single bursts of sound without any coherent rhythm. Industrial ambient music. Afterward, I told the staff that I knew people who make music like this and perform it in front of other people who pay money to experience it. They laughed at me like I was a strange old guy who for some reason need to make up a strange story. Best to humour me and get on to the 3:30 appointment.

music and the mirror

When you think about the fact that nobody can say when time started nor when it ends, when you consider how long a line that is, an incomprehensibly long line, assuming it could even be a line. Then if you consider how long you are alive and how much space you occupy on that line of time, clearly you are so infinitely minuscule, arguably not even here, not even ever were here. Music is loved because it reminds us of ourselves, reminds us that it is something that appears to be alive, just like we do, but aren't.

just to leave you alone

Some Polaris Prize judges were overheard arguing about Gord Downie's last record. One said it was unfair to nominate him because he wasn't living, one said it was just another white guy, one said it was a great record and that was reason enough to support it, one said something incoherent about Jake Gold and Kevin Drew, one said Gord was famous enough and the prize should go to discovering artists . . . they went on and on trying to control the narrative.

Gord got the last word, he placed a song on the same record about trying to put a baby to sleep and concluded you can't control anything:

I held you
I rocked you to sleep
It'd take a long time
Eventually you'd go
And I'd try to get out
Of the rocking chair
With you in my arms
I'd get you to your crib
Slowly lower you down
And pull my hands away
As if from a bomb
Then I'd step away
One step at a time
The floors were full of sounds
All the creaks for time
Then I'd get to the door
Open it carefully
Trying to back out of the room so quietly
When I'd got to the door
Closed to within an inch
That's when you'd come awake
As if you'd been watchin' me
Watching me the whole time
As if you waited to see
If I truly intended
Just to let you be
Just to leave
Just to leave you alone
(from Bedtime)

dizzy miss lizzy: pow

On random, up popped Dizzy Miss Lizzy, which was a pretty import-ant piece of music when I was seven. I think this is the first time I ever listened to it as an adult familiar with the recording world. It killed me hearing George Harrison play the signature a million times with the same bend in the same place every time. During the last 25 years that would have been sampled once or twice and afterward spread evenly. At a certain point you get used to whatever they call french fries and then you go somewhere else, maybe from yesteryear, and they snip little pieces of thyme onto it and *pow*, the french fry has been reinvented and you realize where everything came from and where it is now and you are positioned to consider a whole other way of eating the next time you are hungry.

or barry manilow

Yesterday I counted five entitled morons blasting music at arena volume from slow-moving oversized cars. Four hip hop, one metal. Maybe it is the aggressive thing in the music but the surrealist in me wishes just once to pass a Hummer screaming Kenny G., Mel Tormé or Phoebe Snow, would make my day.

compelled

At an open stage on Monday, I heard a musician play some adventurous and nicely designed music he created on his iPad. He utilized portamento and glissando features which distinguished it musically and made it more memorable, to me anyway. Then one piece started off with more syncopation and an excited young woman seemed compelled to loudly clap her hands, slap her arms and stomp along with her feet. It is a tricky situation because an audience participating is in theory a bridge between the performer and the crowd, maybe it is unifying, but the downside is it locks the rhythm and repositions the performer to now be at the mercy of how good (or bad) the audience is at clapping.

pro pill

Directors give you clues but you have to constantly try to decode what they mean. Also they don't necessarily know what they mean. Isn't that awesome?

The hardest part about scoring a film is trying to keep my own taste in check which mostly never can I do. I watch it a zillion times, I get identified with it and have instincts about colouring it.

just like

Piano student told me she is so impatient about wanting to play new things that she plays the mistake over and over like a toddler trying to walk and falling on its face. Then I said like trying to juggle four balls without first mastering three. Then she said like trying to find the street without bothering to see the map. Then I said like mispronouncing a word and imagining time will correct itself. Then she said like counting eggs before they hatch. Then I said like planning your retirement before working a job. Then she said like taking the elevator when your calves need the exercise. Then I said like offering to pick up the cheque before seeing the total. Then she said like playing the opening harmonics of Roundabout without knowing how to play the rest of the song while being on live television. Then I said like being at a wedding and hearing the officiant ask if anyone opposes and raising your hand as a joke but then everyone turns expecting you to explain yourself. Then she said like making perfect kasha by bringing water to a boil but not actually waiting for the water to come to a boil. Then I said like being in a canoe trying to locate a spot to set up your tent when the sun has started to go down and not stopping right away even if it isn't the best place because soon you will be stuck in the night and have to spend many probably uncomfortable hours lying in a canoe assuming the weather doesn't get worse and it is mosquito season too. Then she said like showing how witty you are, writing about it instead of practising.

That pissed me off and I quit.

And then she called me a baby and then I called her an asshole and then she called me infantile and then I called her arrogant and then she called me a has-been and then I called her a no-talent and then she called me a takes-one-to-know-one and then I called her a Bryan Adams fan and then she called me a guy whose taste is up his ass and then I called her a wannabe and then she called me a fake and then I called her a music supervisor and then she called me a loser and then I called her a prima donna and then she called me a James Gray copycat and that's when it went too far. The truth is much stranger than her invention because I felt for James and his weirdness — lot of impulsive actions not necessarily with a lot of thought. I enjoy the memory his laugh when I answered his question about attending the Juno Awards inducting Greg and Jim into the Hall of Fame. The last time I saw him was doing his usual gig busking in Dundas West subway station, playing accordion. It stays with me when I pass that part of the station between escalators. Glad we had something not dysfunctional.

Practising a mistake is the opposite of practising it working.

pretending to talk about laura nyro

There is an interview with Todd Rundgren and he talks about Laura Nyro. He explains how her first record was so important and so amazing for so many people but when he met her he learned she wasn't happy about it or the process. Years later he works with her and she has her own studio where she records without any pressure or upset, but he finds it a so-so record, even says since she did so many takes "how will she be able to decide?" He concludes that pressure and pain are more useful for great records or great art. I didn't follow his logic. He assumes that Laura Nyro should regret the later record because he found it so-so and he thinks she should feel differently about her early record because others admired it, not her. He also thinks the artist who records many versions of their song won't be able to determine their favourite version because . . . ? I think he was talking about himself by pretending to talk about Laura Nyro.

watermelon man

York sent a letter to grad students today, sounds like nobody can balk about paying for the summer courses that are non-existent due to the strike or else you are no longer a grad student. Must reread it with a magnifying glass and dictionary. Wish they would ask me to score these emails. I could make them more enjoyable and easier to understand. I would start each one with the opening sample from Watermelon Man by Herbie Hancock just so all would remain interested in reading the whole email. The clever plucking might even make some sign up for another term. On to another short film, made by comedians who have no money but said pretty pretty please, sure thing. After I sent them the score they had many notes about what they like and what they don't like. I guess that is understandable but I was imagining a universe where if someone says yes I'll help you for free it means you don't get to complain about anything afterward.

Quiet

I'm looking for more work so sent out some resumés. While rereading one of them (that went out a week ago), realized typos were present like "media rats toring grant." At first I thought I might write them and correct it but maybe I should just act natural, like playing a clunker on stage. Calling attention to it results in everyone noticing something that might otherwise have snuck through.

forgetting or losing

There was a melody in my dream last night and when I woke up I thought I should play it right away or risk forgetting it. Then an hour flew by making her breakfast, getting her dressed and off to camp. Later I remembered the dream but no longer remembered the melody. There will be more dreams or melodies, no big deal. One time when word processors were thought modern I was getting ready to catch a cab to the airport, flying early to London, England. I had collected all my songs, especially unfinished ideas, on my word processor and accidentally erased all my files. The machine always asked at the end of each session Delete File Y/N? Something like that and this time it probably said Delete All Files Y/N? I was rushing and sleepy, I remember it in slow motion, my finger coming down on Y. Then 40 unfinished or unrecorded songs were gone in an instant. The next second I was catatonic, then the cab rang. Spent the flight trying to rewrite pieces from memory best I could, only managed one. Face-to-face encounters with unexpected loss eventually lead you back to thinking about attachment which in turn leads you back to the fact that you can't keep this life that you live. (Insert Earth Juice by Return to Forever.)

chubby checker

There was a drunk guy who was getting out of control at a gig one time. Seen it before. People pretend it isn't going on and hope the person and their trouble will go away or else they go for cover, it is someone else's problem. I can be sheepish too, I don't want to deal with a drunk person or potential fight. Sometimes someone who works there has to play the heavy. This time it happened in the back room at the Cameron and skinny young Kristiana who was friends with me and other musicians playing that night just reached out to the big drunk guy and nicely asked "are you okay?" — she was totally sincere. He melted, he spoke to her, she turned the outsider into a neighbour by just being kind. Taking a thorn out of the lion's paw. She helped him move on. It made me realize that was a possibility, a different way to be than anything I ever saw before. Maybe decent moments of learning require being surprised.

Short list of some favourite songs with twists:

Lola (kinks)
Roland the Headless Thompson Gunner (warren zevon)
Work with Me Annie (hank ballard)
Copenhagen (lucinda williams)
Sweet and Dandy (toots and the maytals)
Ambulance Blues (neil young)
You Never Can Tell (chuck berry)

rabbit trick

Playing a repetition in the left hand, soloing over it with my right hand. At a certain point what else can be said? Tried reversing which hand did what. Not as tidy but for a while a pleasing transition. Eventually similar problem returns, what else can be said? Deconstructing the rhythm became solution followed by deconstructing the melody. Then the same old question resurfaces, whether or not to return to the head because if I do then it is just that thing again that has been said so many times before . . . made a rabbit disappear but voila! made it reappear, take a bow. But isn't that every magic show? What if the melody etc. is deconstructed and we just stay in the deconstruction zone? That's way harder because there will be unsatisfied customers, maybe the whole place. What's worse, the disappointment of the player or the audience? Answer: asking the question in the first place.

see how they run

Pretty weird to realize that only a couple years ago there was a saxophone solo in Lady Madonna. That's what gets me about artists who knock me out, I'm surprised. Surprised by their relationship with their art and how many dimensions I can find in their work. Who doesn't like to be surprised and who doesn't get bored by the lack of it? Think about this when I hear/see popular artists with nebulous connections to the music. Do most bullshitters know they are bullshitters, that there are no surprises in what they call their work? Sometimes I'm ready to go on a rant about musical disappointments but then I recall if you speak ill of somebody popular, automatically a certain percentage defends them, even needs to attack you. It is like you are giving them a reason to tweak abusive back-atcha opinions. Isn't that dynamic more interesting than talking about the artist who started it? The energy behind the people who defended Jian Ghomeshi during the first days of his bullshit being outed. Herb had a theory that people naturally need to be abusive — if you pay attention, most conversations are about what's wrong with this or that, that people spend a lot of time attacking as a way of socializing. I don't know. His recording studio on Wright Ave. was a favourite because of the Wurlitzer, my secret love. Good thing I had one when a teenager playing in a basement band and having to figure out Bloody Well Right by Supertramp. Fifty percent of the problem was having a Wurlitzer. The guys were impressed that I figured out the solo (sort of). I didn't really get into Supertramp as much as the Kinks. Lot more surprises in Arthur than Crime of the Century. Uh oh, crossed the line again.

late night trinity

When I was 22 I had keys to Trinity-St. Paul's church. I had a job and our office was in the basement. There were seven other companies with offices in that church. Often after hours I opened it up with different music friends and we would have long improvisation sessions with the nine-foot piano in the sanctuary. Access to the church was for our offices, not playing the piano, sort of like asking a child in the hot sun to guard a bunch of purple popsicles. Those were unique evenings, echoey empty church, blue creation-themed stained glass, 400 empty seats between the floor and the balconies. Then some rotten loser broke into one of the offices and stole petty cash. They started an investigation; I threw away my key. Didn't want to risk becoming a suspect if they caught me now doing what I knew was unsanctioned. I knew the score, might not be believed and might be convenient to put the blame on me. Was once accused of breaking a window when I was a kid. I didn't do it but my friend's mother thought it was me and she called my mother and then my mother asked me in that tone of voice that meant everyone had already concluded guilt. The truth maybe is only for you anyway, like if you wrote a good song that is its own reward. Could never get behind people citing karma as magical mitigator. Pretty sure many a Trump or Jerry Lewis move through world feeling terrific about themselves then one last extended belch and die, no regrets.

vr manchurian candidate

The song originally called In Other Words was sung by Kaye Ballard, and it's a stunner. Just an A B A B A B, but a fantastic instrumental third verse with pizz strings against woodwinds and near the outro strings swell in unison moving quickly like drum fills. It became famous by its other lyric, Fly Me to the Moon.

In Sinatra's cover it swings hard and the drumbeat is very 60s and prevalent like Happy Together by the Turtles. As arrangements go it is very Pink Panther. Remakes are interesting or embarrassing. The former turns it on its head whereas the latter is boring.

Was thinking about all of this while pondering which was the best version of *The Manchurian Candidate*, Angela Lansbury or Denzel Washington, then realized Trump's version blows them both out of the water.

coexisting worlds

There is a moment in the documentary of recording Tears Are Not Enough when David Foster tells Neil Young his voice is out of tune and Neil Young replies "that's my sound, man." Then two other jokey musicians from the session chime in with jokes about how bad Neil Young sings but how wealthy he is. It sums up everything about everything.

poor technique

Many times people tell you about your art and who it reminds them of. They mean it to be flattering or useful — but if there was a compliment college I think that technique should send them to a meeting with the guidance counsellor.

what once was wild

Went to the Y and while entering the building I passed a man who looked so much like David, my old friend who died, that for an instant I thought he was alive and the whole sad story never happened. Really enjoyed that instant before the synapses to the cerebral cortex completed their job re stating facts of what happened. Years earlier, wrote a song about him called What Once Was Wild. One of the last times I saw David was touring in 2004 for the same record that included that song about him and when by surprise he showed up I told him I wrote a song about him. He asked if I would play it and I felt a bit awkward because it was about the dark clouds that followed him (and our growing apart). Later he seemed tickled, even a little thrilled. Maybe it was the posterity or maybe something else. We had American Stars 'n Bars always in the background when we hung out at his house in 1976 with Emmylou Harris singing Saddle Up the Palomino. Certain records will always be soundtracks to certain times of your life. Writing music about things that have happened is stronger than reviewing pictures of it, more emotional because when you sing and play you re-enter the space and position you previously lived, suddenly you sorta live it again. Close as one gets to time travel.

crown of accomplishment

There was a much sought-after flugelhorn player whose students appreciated them for their insight and technical expertise. One student complained his best states of playing remained elusive to which the teacher replied, "There is no there to arrive to. You imagine there is a crown of accomplishment, eventually you see the distance between you and the crown is constant. That imagined distance will always be just that — imagined."

switching sides

There is a brain thing I do at the piano which is when I realize my eyes are largely on the left hand or the right hand, I try to switch it. Whatever was previously comfortable or not requiring much thinking gets tossed out the window when I switch my gaze. It's like suddenly being thrown into a country where people drive on the opposite side of the road. The most interesting part is that if I return to the first view, the body already knows its role, the piece plays without struggle. I could play the first way and probably at the same time do mathematical calculations but if I change my gaze I lose my balance. I'm not sure if the thing that throws me is seeing new information or the distracting thoughts that result from taking in new information.

goo goo ga joob

Student: I know you don't like my music.

Teacher: Stop reading my blog posts.

Student: Is that a joke?

Teacher: Maybe.

Student: Why don't you like it?

Teacher: I never said I don't like your music.

Student: Do you or don't you?

Teacher: The class isn't about me liking or not liking your music.

Student: C'mon, what do you think?

Teacher: I like your capacity to listen selectively.

Student: Could you speak English?

Teacher: When did this paranoia start?

Student: When you gave Britney and Aaron an A and me a C.

Teacher: Right.

Student: Well.

Teacher: You handed that assignment in late and you missed a few classes. That affects your mark.

(Door opens, Britney enters)

Britney: Hi, excuse the interruption, just wanted to say thanks for the A, glad you like my music.

Teacher: Your mark isn't because I liked your music. Marks reflect the job of being students. Like maybe you would be the best prime minister but you don't get the job just because you think you are perfect for it.

Student: I don't want to be the prime minister.

Teacher: But do you get my point? You have to attend meetings with people and listen to them and discuss ideas and join committees, blah blah blah. Maybe later you get voted in but it's a job, there's things to do to prove it.

Britney: Am I interrupting something?

Teacher: I'm just saying making music and being a music student are different things. Britney got the mark she got because of showing up, doing the work and doing it well. It isn't about me liking her music per se.

Britney: You don't like my music?

Teacher: I didn't say that.

Student: You think I would be a good prime minister?

Teacher: Could you handle it if people didn't say you were a great prime minister?

Britney: What are you guys on?

Teacher: We're talking about marking and being marked.

Student: And that a teacher should like the music by their students.

Teacher: It's just art, it's just taste. Maybe you don't like my car but I can show you how to drive or how to change a headlight. It doesn't matter what you think of the colour of it.

Britney: (tiptoes out) I'm going to find Aaron, getting a little too weird, bye.

Student: You think music is like a car?

Teacher: In a way.

Student: You think a person shouldn't care what people think of them?

Teacher: Yes.

Student: You mean you never cared what people thought of you?

Teacher: Yes I did and yes I still might, but it's a distraction, that's why I'm telling you not to go in that direction. Trying to save you from wasting time.

Student: But you care what I think right now.

Teacher: Good point.

Student: Isn't that hypocritical?

Teacher: "To everything turn turn turn" — you ever hear the Byrds?

Student: "The eraser's here to twist your mind" — you ever hear Hypocrisy?

Teacher: Well, you seem so clever that's hard to believe. You're completely self-deluded, that's hard to achieve — you ever hear of Geoff Berner?

Student: F-U-C-K Y-A, F-U-C-K Y-A, eff you see kay why eh — you ever hear MacLean and MacLean?

Teacher: How does someone born in the 90s know MacLean and MacLean?

Student: How does someone who can't read music hold a job teaching it?

Teacher: How does someone who is just a composite of other students appear to be one?

Student: I am he as you are he as you are me and we are all together.

Teacher: I never made sense of that before.

Student: You're welcome. Change my mark.

after the paradiddles

Bill Kosinski decided to follow his dreams. In September he quit his job at the gas station and flew from a small Manitoba town to Mali in Africa to work with master drummer Drisa Drogipoju. Once he got there and started doing the teacher's exercises he became frustrated that his technique was less sophisticated than the other students'. Before October he decided to quit and return to Flin Flon hoping he might get back his job at the Shell on Highway 8. While packing his bags Drisa stopped by to thank him for his efforts and commend him for leaving. Obviously, said the master drummer, he would never be able to keep up with the other students, he was too slow. This enraged Bill and he decided to show him how wrong he was. He changed his plans again and remained and rededicated his efforts. By the spring he was the most accomplished percussionist among all the students. Then Bill asked Drisa if he meant it last year, when he told him he wasn't good enough. The teacher played a couple paradiddles and replied, "Everyone has a timekeeper in charge of them, but the one inside you was like an upset spoiled little cockroach who likes to be in attack mode, always pointing its fingers at the mirror and saying you are not good enough. Fortunately it was thin-skinned. The best way to help you get to where you wanted to be was to insult it, let it direct its venom elsewhere and create the necessary space for you to move with a better beat."

when they say see for yourself they're actually making a riddle

Even though the eyeballs are animated, they are just eyeballs. When you look in the mirror you see your parts, eyes or hair or chin . . . but just parts, all anatomical. Just as valid to look at your belly button or your pinky and say, "hey you, lookin' good." You can't explain to a piano why it can't play itself.

memorial

Met Domenic Troiano one time in the 80s at John Caton's office on Draper Ave. I tried to relay what a big deal his solo record Burnin' At the Stake was — on high rotation in my teenage bedroom. I could play guitar along to a third of the title song, the rest was too complex for me. Anytime I saw him on tv when I was growing up, playing in *The Midnight Special* with the James Gang or the Guess Who, I recognized the mark of a heavyweight releasing fireworks from his fingers, just the right amount. He wasn't interested in my gushing, he was trying to do business with John, discussing some commercial singer he was producing. I would have liked to have known him more, wondered what he was like as a person, great artists intrigue me. Poof, in 2005 I read he died of cancer, in his 50s.

I didn't know anybody at the memorial service at a church somewhere in a part of Toronto that is no-man's-land for me. His family did something very memorable, they manufactured large buttons of him in his signature beret playing guitar. It was for people to help themselves to after the service. Mine remained on the lapel of that suit jacket the next few years. I found it last week accidentally while looking through boxes of old things to discard but couldn't throw it away. Now in my guitar case pocket for extra strings, picks and slide. When I open it I'll be reminded to be good without being excessive.

mystery tattoo

The boyfriend of a guitarist bought her credit at a tattoo parlour for her birthday. When she returned from the shop she had the image of a bumblebee on the inside of her right forearm. The surprised boyfriend said he thought she would have contemplated whether to get a strat or a hollow body or a telly — why the bee? She said she wanted to add to life's mystery.

polyester vocals

Six-year-old is singing along at the top of her lungs to a commercial cover of Stevie Wonder's Don't You Worry 'bout a Thing. I'm feeling kind of proud. This is the last scene of the children's movie *Sing*. Then realize I hear a lot of autotune wrapped around the commercial singer's vocal. Not complaining, yet something about this situation gives me pause. Nowadays autotune is considered ordinary but performance-enhancing drugs are deemed unfair or untrue. I share my thoughts that this is a double standard with another musician and she gets testy about how wrong I am. Music is not a competition, she says. Maybe so, but still thinking that making someone who is pitchy artificially correct bears a resemblance to taking someone who runs great and making them artificially greater.

IIII

Some friends moved to La Push, Washington, to study with a shaman whose surname was Fourlines (signature was four vertical scratches) and they invited me to visit. After a show in Vancouver at the East Cultural Centre, I took a bus to La Push, stayed overnight, and one memory remains very vividly. While talking about the landscape and the locals, he told me about some trees near where we were standing and how they had been so parched they called over the clouds (he pointed across the sky) to come relieve them. I remember wondering after, who am I to assume the world is Cartesian? Wasn't Stevie Wonder trying to say something like that with The Secret Life of Plants? How sideways or underground might be the truth vs. how vertical we are told things are. Got on the subway yesterday and noticed the *Toronto Star* now has a slim miniature version for riders, the newsprint world so diminished from where it used to be. I heard that Fourlines guy in my head whisper maybe the trees asked for the manifestation of the internet so news would move online and keep more trees living. Robert Priest wrote a song that surprised me with something very similar to that idea called Who the Fuck Knows. Worth playing back on Soundcloud while reading this.

heisenberg uncertainty

The new tree, London plane, over this hot summer has been parched even though often put on drip hose. Many brown leaves fell to their end, compost, just like us. I try concerning myself with the unseen parts below, keeping on the drip hose. Similar to the new piece I'm creating, can't yet pull off coordinating ideas but until then placing energy into baby steps which are foundational to the overall concept of this piece, or it's just my imagination.

Wonder if some composers, especially the old uncomputerized ones, notated or conceived some works whether or not they could play their ideas in their entirety? I play a piano concert at Hugh's Room next Tuesday unless it is cancelled. Went last night but the doors were closed. Was supposed to be Marilyn Lerner and Lance Anderson. Marilyn and I played a delightful show together at the Music Gallery about 15 years ago.

I attended the piano series at Hugh's Room three weeks ago and the crowd was not the type that would be too interested in the kind of presentation I'm planning. But who am I to imagine I know? What does the crowd who is into what I like to play look like? In science departments or wherever they teach the Heisenberg uncertainty principle they should stop and discuss the profound implications of it. They should give the students a month to reflect on it or maybe a lifetime. On the surface it means our tools for measuring alter the behaviour of what we are measuring. What does that really mean . . . need to remember my imaginary ideas about the audience are just that, whether true or not.

long ago, far away

Someone who can solo on guitar is sitting in a room with three people who can't. The others are explaining how soloing requires this or that guitar, this or that amplifier. They argue about the merit of picks vs. fingers. But the person who can solo doesn't need to listen to them. Just doesn't mean anything to the person who knows how to do it. Sits quietly, nothing to add.

Lots of voices in my head certain of so many things I don't know anything about, occasionally easy to ignore.

cartalk

One time our transmission died in the rain after a show in Davis, California. Had to get a tow truck in the middle of the night to tow us to the nearest mechanic's shop relative to where we were staying, Carmaig's in San Rafael.

One time in Kiel, Germany, we hit the bar that you are supposed to clear and scraped the roof and worried we would have to pay a lot more to the rental company. I don't think later they inspected the roof.

One time the motor died after taking the mountains in Alberta on the way to play Banff. Bought a rebuilt engine and continued to honour the remaining two weeks of dates with Andras and The Previous.

One time my tire blew on the 401 on our way to Montreal. The car was a convertible. Greg was yelling at the driver not to use the brakes because they might seize up. All I could hear was him screaming "No brakes! No brakes!" I took it to mean the brakes didn't work and we were about to die.

One time the side door to the van broke and had to be held by David Lee while moving and we pulled into the nearest town, Belleville, and found a wrecker who was about to close (it was Friday) but found a similar side door. Installed right then and there, $50 and back on our way.

One time we drove through a blizzard to open for Ultravox at Barrymore's in Ottawa and we were way too close to the cars in front of us the whole time but we lived.

One time we lost a ball joint and a shock or two driving over potholes to Port Alberni and when we returned to Toronto an astounded mechanic explained why we should have died between there and here.

new hood

Some people stay on the same street in the same neighbourhood, nothing wrong with that, but some go to a new neighbourhood where they don't know where anything is. Walk around, go back again and again. Soon they know their way around part of it, even start to figure shortcuts, start to have favourite houses and trees. That's the kind of new music writing I like most.

bernie

I read an interview with Paul Thomas Anderson when he was still casting roles in the film *The Master* and asked Philip Seymour Hoffman what he thought of different actors trying out for the protagonist. Philip Seymour Hoffman said you should use Joaquin Phoenix because he scares me.

I could listen to Bernard Herrmann forever, same reason. Recently read his Wikipedia — made his own orchestra at 20, so so scary.

When Hitchcock gave him *Psycho* he said do not score the shower scene, don't play music in the shower scene . . . so glad Bernard Herrmann disregarded those instructions.

a few good men

When I was a kid I had a lot of favourite records and listened all the time. A few had lyrics with meanings that were different when I listened later in life. Didn't know what Joni Mitchell meant in Court and Spark. The male character was "looking for someone to court and spark." I am an oatmeal guy; when Mick Jagger sang "brown sugar how come you taste so good," I understood immediately. On the White Album, McCartney sang "why don't we do it in the road," I knew this probably meant soccer or ball hockey even baseball, right in the middle of the f'n road. Why not, I already did this after school with Barry, Elliot, Stuart, Boob and Jeff.

last words

As the old conductor lay there in an oxygen tent, tubes sustaining his last afternoon, Roderick arrived and leaned over the bed. The old man was pleased to see him. "I'm sorry I'm leaving," said the old man. "When I'm in heaven I'm going to miss the way you play."
Roderick touched his arm gently. "If that's how you feel then why did you often cut my solos?"
The old man struggled to breathe. "I love a lot of what you do, but you also play flowery and too ornate, can you handle the truth, Roddy?"
"Sure."
"You have any last words for me?"
"There is no heaven old guy, ciao."

listening again

A singing student told their teacher they can't sing the way they want and it depresses them. Teacher asked, "When was the last time you were happy?"
The student thought about it and replied, "I'm often disappointed with myself."
The teacher said, "I have some good news and some bad news and then possibly more good news."
"What's the good news?" asked the student eagerly.
"Singing isn't the problem, your singing ability is very good."
"Then what's the bad news?"
The teacher started to play with a ginkgo leaf. "The minds of people prefer to be depressed about something; even this message will likely be heard only as another disappointment."
"That's it?"
"Yes."
"But you said you had some good news and some bad news and more good news."
"Yes, possibly more good news."
"So what is it . . . the other good news?"
"I can't tell you, but it's there if you listen again."

10,000 times

Walking down the street, we hardly consider putting one foot after the next. The brain coordinates everything while that main part of consciousness thinks about what flavour of ice cream to buy. When musicians know something inside out, then they can do other things simultaneously. They can more or less hold a conversation while their hands play the piece. Same for actors, dancers, anyone who learned how to drive stick. The part of the brain that can't initially do it is no longer in that slow-processing position.

Been reading about the reticular formation, that part of the brain that decides what to filter towards consciousness or what to ignore. Makes me think about learning something new and how it is necessary to do it 10,000 times before autopilot exists. Wonder if it can be reduced to 9,000? I ask my students to recite the months of the year backwards while they practise or do a math calculation. Maybe it is a useful short-circuiting to try being as though we are in the future place before we are.

Like teaching French. Ask them to take a break, get an orange juice inside a French Café, hear a lot of fluent French by other voices unlike what they hear in the classroom. Many things will happen for their brain by standing in the middle of a French restaurant instead of a classroom slowly pronouncing *du jus d'orange*.

space is the place, cha-ching

I have to take three courses this fall to obtain my master's. My adviser made a course suggestion regarding my longer-term goals, writing about music and power (how songs can fuck shit up). The course she suggested is from the geography department and called Space, Place and Capitalism. Who knew geography professors were into Sun Ra's poetry and achievements.

passing pieces of paper

There is an exercise in the R. Murray Schafer book that knocks me out. He asked students to pass a piece of paper between them without making a sound. What a great shortcut to teach listening. Totally doing that at the start of next semester.

exposed

A PhD student was studying the 1,000-year-old works of composer Hildegard von Bingen when she came upon her old poetic axioms positioning music as a metaphor for all sound and suddenly it hit her that this is also true to every art form. For a sculpturist, every shape including all ordinary forms could be seen as sculpture and for a dancer every movement could be seen as dance whether it is human or animal or wind blowing branches and for the painter every colour is part of a composition and the canvas is perpetually everywhere we turn our gaze, and she started to explain this to her friends and family and then her mother slapped her across the face and said "Finish your degree and stop talking like a nut-bar!" The young woman put her hand to her cheek and shot back, "Are you from a work of fiction, 'The Abusive Mother Concerned about her Daughter's Future,' or are those your real thoughts?"
Having been exposed for the disposable character she was, the mother fled to the index.

first and second faves pt.1

Made another bread — so many YouTube tutorials, so little time. These are the inexpensive flours, wonder what the difference is with high-end stuff, maybe next time. They say Peter Gabriel always records through 58, that's cute but I am attached to the high-end microphones. Once upon a time CBC gave me a budget to "make a studio" to produce music for a sitcom — a purchasing budget of more than $10k. Maybe my all-time favourite moment of surrealism. Better than the cop I raced outside Hagersville (he won). I couldn't buy the things I really wanted like Mac stuff because back then it was all very territorial, only sold by certain retailers. The place that had the gear wouldn't serve me. Felt to me like they assumed I was riff-raff in my army pants and undershirt, they just wouldn't talk to me so

I left the store. Instead, bought an Atari Stacy laptop and ran Notator. Then the two main guys from Notator did a tour of North America. A meet-and-greet at the Diamond Club, 40 other people like me in the side room. There I was telling the actual creator of Notator from Germany that I missed a feature from a previous version and he said "That's interesting, I never thought someone would miss that, I'll put it back in." Second favourite moment of surrealism.

pt. 2

I was pissed off and more than a little on fire to write a letter about the salesperson who acted like I didn't exist, but I settled on a different response. In Toronto, during those midi and early music software years, usually I bought from Long & McQuade. It was mostly them or Steve's, and Steve's stopped a union from forming, which lost me as a customer even if it was more conveniently located when gigging on Queen Street. Instead of trying to write a letter to get the asshole fired from the store in the Yonge Street back lane, I wrote to Jack Long and explained what happened and how I decided now to buy an Atari Stacy (the only music computer that they sold) and commended the salespeople who had helped me many times on the phone for 20 minutes explaining a mark of the Unicorn synchronizer or why the JD990 string sound had disappeared. Jack wrote me a thank you and the next time I walked into Long & McQuade, Newton stopped me and thanked me for the letter and told me they photocopied it and my letter hangs in the office upstairs and all sorts of staff thanked me as they saw me and they gave me larger-than-usual discounts the next five years. Was such a better thing to do with my anger.

right and thong

There is a great film from 1979 called *The Shout* (Alan Bates, Susannah York, John Hurt), spooky subplot about sound/listening. Alan Bates's character lived years with Indigenous people in Australia mastering one aspect of shaman's power, a shout so loud it kills everything within a kilometre. The film is sort of filled with this mystery — is it true, is he deranged or does this shout and its fatal premise exist for real? I like the problem — we all know it is impossible, but is it? Are we willing to question whether or not our certainty about reality could be wrong?

I'm encouraged to think this is true. Trump, Taylor Swift, Doug Ford, Kanye — they all agree with me. There is another film with Alan Bates that made the same point without getting into the supernatural. *The King of Hearts*. I can't reveal the final scene without ruining the film for you but it turns itself inside out, a thing of beauty, as is the music by Georges Delerue, *incroyable*. Moves playfully and melodically between minor seconds, which keeps me amused and wondering how did he do that when ordinarily that is a tense unpleasant transition. The kind of choice that isn't how music is usually taught. If right and wrong are applied to harmony this is on the side of wrong but there it is being right.

back at pinawa fourth way music school

Somewhere near the Pinawa, Manitoba, Fourth Way music school, improvising students are divided into pairs. Instructor says, "we're going to practise listening." Then As are instructed to tell Bs about their family and Bs are instructed to listen.

Later teacher asks the As, when Bs heard them did they offer any other information? All the As answer in the affirmative. The Bs offered something, usually about their families too, for instance how they were similar or different.

Then the instructor says to the Bs let's try listening again. As tell Bs about your instrument, but this time Bs try to listen to your partner and if you find you have a need to talk about yourself, don't — we're practising listening.

the guy that knew a guy

The older British guy in the photo store at Walmer and Bloor said when he was in college he used to watch Brian Jones at gigs. He isn't bragging or looking for attention, came out when I wondered if he attended anything by any of the English legends at that time. Couldn't help asking after realizing he had been in his 20s in the 1960s in London.

Fun to get closer to anyone who was at historical intersections. When I realized Lenny Breau lived in Winnipeg in the 60s, I asked every hippie I met if they saw him. Very exciting to hear personal twisted stories about where he lived on Redwood, his musicianship and his heroin problem. Same thing when I realized Neil Young went to Kelvin High School, but the only person I ever encountered who knew him was the neighbourhood bank manager. I was 15, inquiring about a loan, just wanted to figure out how anyone could come up with $500 to buy a Prophet 5 in order to make the cool sounds Jerry Harrison did on More Songs about Buildings and Food or the first Modern Lovers record. Bank manager said,

"You want to know about a loan for buying an instrument?"

"Yes."

"I've known people who made it and people who didn't. Take it from me, you shouldn't bother."

"Who did you know who made it?"

"Neil Young," he said and added, "I used to play in a band with him."

"You were in The Squires?" asked wide-eyed Bob. Long pause — pleased and surprised a kid heard of The Squires. For a second he was no longer the bank manager.

"I was the drummer."

Ten years and three Junos later I went back to that bank looking for him so I could brag about not taking his advice. The tellers gave me such mean suspicious looks when I asked if they remembered him or knew where he worked now. They had no idea they were talking to a guy who knew a guy who used to play with Neil Young.

what you already know

Student: Sorry I didn't practise again. I don't know why because I really planned to but didn't. What's wrong with me?

Music teacher: You can't help it.

Student: You lie to yourself too?

Music teacher: It's the human condition.

Student: Like a political party spewing rhetoric about their moral values becoming silent if their president acts above the law when implicated by his lawyer or campaign manager or many mistresses?

Music teacher: Couldn't have put it better.

Student: You think the same thing is inside each of us?

Music teacher: Right, a hypocritical party in power inside you, even a hypocritical president. "I'm going to practise this week, it's gonna be the best practising ever. I am a genius practiser."

Student: Could there be a revolutionary movement inside me trying to overthrow the president?

Music teacher: Sure, but who is the you that wants a revolution vs. the you that is the corrupt president vs. the you talking with me right now?

Student: Like which one is the most for real?

Music teacher: Is any?

Student: How does this help me practise?

Music teacher: You already know how to practise.

the credit

Saw a play one time at Passe Muraille and it had a few different music cues including some amazing jazz music sounding exactly like sectional pieces from large ensembles like Count Basie. I looked on the program later to see who did the music and one local composer was credited for everything. Concluded that they were either a genius who can simulate the recordings and arrangements from the rich history of jazz more precisely than anyone I ever heard in 30 years, or they got 20 friends to play and record for free . . . or they used samples (long complex samples) and called that their composition.

business as usual

After his father the famous A&R executive died, the company gave the position to young Denny. Denny, who always believed he knew a hit when he heard one, made it his first order of business to sign his high school friend Blinky Swivelhead. The record went nowhere, he spent another $70k on a video which also went nowhere. Executive management had a meeting and discussed why they assumed the child of the person who did a job well should also be good at it just because their parent previously held the position. Just kidding, people don't reflect on that line of thought.

Meanwhile at Ivanka Trump headquarters they were planning her 2020 run at the Republican Party, someone suggested a song about being unique from that new Blinky Swivelhead. They negotiated a $300 fee for Blinky to sign away his rights to the song in perpetuity for use at future rallies and in all branding videos.

curry clan copeland

Made best curry but wrote down no measurements. If it was a movie it starred yams, onions, garlic, ginger, scotch bonnets, tomatoes, coconut milk, kale and the soundtrack was hot so hot. Saw the great new film by Spike Lee. If it was a recipe it featured organic everything blended with industrially processed stale shit and potatoes with rot and fungus brought to a boil and allowed to spill over and start a fire. The soundtrack had beautiful orchestral moments like *He Got Game* when he used some music of Aaron Copland on the basketball court.

jim keltner inside

Since wee-est memories, whatever musical connection I have, felt anybody can be same, like here is a key to a house and I don't own the house, but there's the door. Other people try it, some can open it, some can't make it work but that isn't their fault, they just have to keep trying to jiggle it in every way, they might get it tomorrow. The bigger deal is the house and we both know what's inside is Jim Keltner.

He lives in there with the others. His Wikipedia, so hard to read without spilling whatever's in my hand. Last night watched the dark documentary at the Bloor Cinema about triplets. For the people who separated these babies and carefully lied to their families and organized adoptions into specific socioeconomic settings, it was about studying nature vs. nurture. All for science or probably all for grant money. Have heard so much talk about whether you are born musical or not as if the important part is to prove whether or not things are genetically predetermined. I bet the desire behind knowing that, assuming it could be known, is the fear of finding out you don't have free will.

In the triplets film the adoption agency is of its time and place, fetishizing scientific research and inconveniences like informing people of their unknown siblings or surreptitiously spying on them is thought a reasonable price. They don't tune in to putting their bias under microscope which would be a more interesting movie — the bias behind the bias (good band name). That would be a better concept for exploring free will too. When they make a doc about Jim Keltner, I hope they skip the part about whether his genes positioned him to play with famous people.

marxist jazz

Reading about dialectical thinking in advance for the next York course, an introduction to Karl Marx's writing. I like the fact that Marx thought about everything being everything, no disagreement there. Last night played two sets with a jazz group. The songs mostly had heads and then improv sections. Careful to not step on any toes. Afterward two guys in the audience told me I was a punk-rock Thelonious Monk. They wanted to know what I listen to. They meant what do I listen to that informs how I play the piano, but there is a flaw with the assumption because taking the bus, cleaning the house and even paying attention to their question — is in fact what I'm listening to that feeds whatever the pianist in me is trying to do. For some people that won't make any sense but I bet some get it. I hope the professor in the Marx class is excited about discussing how everything is related to everything.

busted

I was recognized sitting alone at the front in a comedy show. Definitely a possibility when the comic started to probe random audience members and I knew him, but not so well. Acted together in a scene in a comedy he starred in five years ago. We became friends but I hardly ever saw him after that. Now his style was improvising with random audience members, unlike my sense of him five years ago; it was a little judgmental but understandable comedy method. He was on the youth network YTV, maybe now he is distancing himself from that or maybe that's ancient history. He turned his gaze on me sitting alone between two empty chairs with my thermos of ginger tea, he did his thing, asked about my posture, my clothes, my aloneness, the thermos and then fatal flaw —

What's your name?

Bob.

Bob. So what do you do, "Bob"? (said as if hard to pronounce).

Music.

Then his eyebrows had a moment, realized it was me, whispered into the microphone. Wiseman?

Yes.

Fell to his knees and said to the audience with a little bit of shock I know this guy!

I enjoyed the show, especially this part because he was challenging himself to work unscripted and now the stakes were . . . more unscripted. I think he felt our relationship might change negatively if he continued to work the same swagger. He started talking instead about his recent divorce. Next comic started her set acknowledging me to the crowd. I guess they spoke backstage.

You're from that band, what were they called?

Glue Rodeo.

Right, what did you play with them?

Saxophone.

Right right. Do you know the drummer?

There were three.

Right, but do you know the one with a drug problem?

There were three.

Right right but not you? No drug problem?

It's behind me.

What was their big song?

Baker Street.

Wasn't there another one?

Just Baker Street.

Did you have a saxophone solo in that song?

Yep.

Were you on drugs when you played it?
Probably.

hooked

My hook shot at 14 was often surprising, probably because I was short, it was unexpected but what other possibility did I have of getting around the height of other basketball boys? The hook shot was only my right hand. The difference between how I did that then and how I practise something on piano is that on piano I spend a lot of time working both sides. Seemed the natural place to go for development in tennis and ping-pong too. I don't know anyone who did but speaking pianistically it kept calling me or rather I kept noticing the shortcomings musically to only work one side.

What's similar however, is when you practise you are sort of a spectator of your own efforts. The new piece I'm working on right now cannot be played with certainty. I slow it down, try to find a speed where I can pull it off, but every so often I lose my patience and go for it at the speed I really wish I could already execute and if I'm lucky, for a second or two it might work. When it does I'm amazed because the I of I wasn't doing anything but watching. Sometimes as the hook shot left my hand I knew instantly it was a dud or instantly it was a contender. The ones that actually perfectly swoosh, you're hoping for it but the you of you can't take any credit except for showing up and having a great seat. The original virtual reality.

bank robber in times new roman

In the morning mail two rejection letters from the Ontario Arts Council. No funding to record the ten string quartets, nor to record a batch of new songs about Jian Ghomeshi's lawsuit, Donald Trump's pardons, why mangos rule, how children calculate interest rates, why Sarah Huckabee shouldn't be seated, what makes magnets play and luv — look out world, I'm on a roll. These rejections don't stop me (though I'm expecting a Juno nomination for most grant rejections in a lifetime), just would have made it easier to deal with capitalism.

On to plan B — bank robbery — if being at York University is a bank and if obtaining a degree is a robbery and if being on the run is like a job from a future employer. All that just to have enough to cover costs and proceed recording.

"Worth it," he answers, putting on his mask and cape and typing a 12-point double-spaced Times New Roman essay to slip the teller.

nobody's home pt. 1

Dmitri, a bass player, noticed the band he played in was always critical. Either they were insulting other groups or else envying how much better other groups were than them. Then he noticed inside his own head the same thing was going on. Always insulting himself for not being good enough, smart enough, handsome enough, musically accomplished enough or else wishing he was as good as others. By surprise one day he reached a radical conclusion — it was just in his head, none of it actually existed.

The bass was real, the amplifier too, but wishes or complaints were only clouds moving in the sky, apparently real for a few minutes, then no more. Dmitri wrote a song about it called Nobody's Home but the band didn't like it, rejected performing it. Two of them told him he wasn't a good writer, should stick to the bass. Next year they broke up. Life went on, they got straight jobs, started families, music came to a halt. 20 years later his son Smyrdnakov made a band and covered Nobody's Home. His friends liked the lyrics to the chorus: "There are bees in my head making honeycomb, buzzing with thoughts but nobody's home."

They made a video and dressed up like hornets. It went viral. After 23 million views, Amy Carnegie, who formerly answered telephones at Bruce Allen's office, approached Smyrdnakov and Dmitri and offered to do even more for them through merchandising Nobody's Home into t-shirts, hoodies, coffee mugs and a line of honey shaped in little houses that included randomly empty containers (literally nobody's home). This proved a successful marketing gag with the kids, lot of money flowed in. Dmitri's old bandmates called him up, said he should split the ownership of the song with them, especially insistent were the two guys who said he couldn't write.

He thought to himself after all these years nothing changes, people live and die complaining the entire time. He came to a new radical conclusion which was that the state of complaining which seemed outside and simultaneously inside himself wasn't something to struggle against because it wasn't possible to stop it. He became excited about simply noticing his own complaints and those of everyone else. Started to think all conversations were just excerpts of someone complaining about their job, their lover, the weather, the band, etc. He became more experimental with his music and his mind, trying to see if it was possible to move through life without complaints. No such luck except he had another realization, which was that the disappointment to not complain was another complaint.

His music became more experimental, now he played blindfolded and with a chopstick between the strings. Smyrdnakov videotaped him, threw it online and Universal offered to sign him. His YouTube channel, now known as Blindchop, developed a large following.

bar mitzvah questions

Last year I was asked if I would meet a 12-year-old in a Jewish family in the Annex who was looking to learn how to play something on the piano for his bar mitzvah. We arranged to meet. Was a nice meeting, liked the boy's mother and father, we had things in common about perspectives and living in Toronto. We moved to the piano room, a beautiful grand piano and their son took a break from video games, came downstairs and joined us. Shy guy with bright green hair, parents left us alone to talk.

I told him about my piano work and indicated whatever he might want to know, I might have useful ideas about where to start. After a while he said,

"I want to write a song for everyone at my bar mitzvah."

"Sure, I could help you with that. I write songs and produce records where songs get put under a microscope, you could say. Is there anything you want to know about right now?"

"Can I ask you anything?"

"Yes, sure," I answered.

"Why are we here?"

"Why are we here . . . like you and me now?"

"Like why are we in the universe?"

"Right. Well, nobody knows but some people believe there is a plan to everything, even life after we die, some think there is a God and that God has a reason for our existence; others think just because there appears to be arrangement in the world it doesn't mean there is anything more to existence, and basically for those people the question of why are we here presumes incorrectly that there is an answer. You follow me?"

"Yeah." Long pause between us.

"So, I guess if you want to work on a song, if you want some help or some piano ideas your father has my number. Okay?"

"Yeah, all right."

Never heard from them again but each time I subsequently walk by that house I glance at the window and like replaying that brief conversation and how surprising his question was, which on the surface didn't have anything to do with key signatures or rhythms but also did.

speed writing

The piece I'm writing surprises me because I want to develop it quickly, yet hours of practising are required in order to get it to a place where I can reliably execute it. Delays my quick-writing fantasies, can't write the next parts until I know the first parts, only then can I relax and imagine where I might go next. The last melodic piano piece like this happened over months. Didn't Bach write a bajillion pieces with 30 screaming children hanging off his shoulders? Wonder if people like him performed everything they wrote or if they also wrote (notated pieces) whether or not they could perform it.

classical music lesson

One time a classical music teacher asked for a lesson. They could technically execute whatever we discussed but they sounded like they were playing an exercise and disconnected from the part of playing that interests me. I shared my observation, but it felt as though I offended them, like a line was crossed, and they left soon after. A year later they asked for another lesson and when they sat down at the piano they wanted to get something off their chest, that the last time they were hurt by what I said. Then they asked for reassurance that I wouldn't say anything critical. I said what's the point of hiring me to talk about piano and my perspective if you also want to control me? They left. Angry that my personality was the same as it previously was, like someone hadn't learned their lesson.

trying to jump off the cliff while realizing it

I read retailers sold more when they were playing happy music. I hate statistics like that. I might only be a lemming but I hate being reminded. Then again, to hate being reminded sort of interrupts lemmingness.

ripped off from his solo and alienation

An adventurous guitarist was asked to play a solo on a record but not everyone in the room understood the solo and so he was asked to do another and another. Different members of the band had different favourite versions; so did the producer. In the end the leader of the band decided they should honour the version the guitarist felt proudest of. A splendid moment for the future of the band or at least the relationship between the guitarist and the leader. A week later the guitarist was called by the band's manager and told that the producer had a "technical problem" and the version the guitarist selected was "lost." As coincidence would have it, the version the producer liked most was found and used on the record. Same old story in the history of worker relations. I'm reading Karl Marx's theory of alienation; not very hard to prove even though he was born 200 years ago. What a difference when someone else takes credit for work not done by them vs. someone endeavouring to keep equity and respect in the room.

remembered all the words

I've seen all the Michael Hollingsworth plays, I enjoy them immensely. One time I insulted an actor without realizing it at a little party for everyone upstairs after the performance was done. In these plays, about Canadian history told from a left, feminist, Indigenous perspective, that illuminate where the church was, where the money was, where the army was, told in a zillion quick scenes one after the next after the next, all the actors play six or seven characters and the props are larger-than-life papier-mâché objects, the lighting is surprising, the music is usually by Brent Snyder whom I knew a little bit in the 80s, it sounds mostly like one synthesizer and adds another layer of unique — a lot is going on.

The actor was an old acquaintance and I wanted to say something nice. I shared how amazed I was with how much text they have to memorize and he said something in return very sarcastic, as if my compliment was worthless. The next days I thought about that and realized I wasn't saying anything about his acting.

Last night I played a set at the Tranzac, someone approached after to tell me I play real fast and they were really impressed by how fast I play, it's so blurry. I realize when someone says something like that they think they are demonstrating some understanding but it makes me shift away. They're impressed I remembered all the words instead of anything about what was done with the words.

eff it

One day the notes in the song realized they were alive and living notes. Soon they started to study who had similar pitches and where they were located on the scale. In fact they realized there were scales but what confused them was who was writing the music and was there in fact such a thing as a person. They understood notes because they were notes and they would submit to representing themselves accordingly when they were played as pieces but who was the pianist in relation to this? One weird note posited you can't know the source of being played and be the sound simultaneously. Not a popular idea. The other explanation was from F, whose perspective was that everything is always about your key only; "F it" was their motto.

the new drummer's character trait

In a universe not so far away there was a drummer in a band who liked to state the obvious. If the band started driving on the expressway, heading to a gig three hours away, he would point out that the old roads might be longer but more rewarding. Smaller towns would come to view whereas the expressway confined their drive to fast food corporate stops that monopolized who had the right to sell food and gas to the captive drivers. "You are so right," said everybody.

One time they were about to fly to tour Europe and the guitarist was required to sign a form acknowledging the airline had no liability if her guitar was damaged. The drummer who liked to say the obvious advised the guitarist to sign a blurry no thank you and the rest of the band said, "You're so right." The airline ticket counter person took the signed waiver without glancing at the signature. Fortunately everything arrived unbroken and they didn't have to test the strategy of the drummer who said the obvious but they slapped him on the back anyway for his intelligent insight.

The singer wrote the songs on piano, then brought them to the band, who in turn jammed them out, interpreting together what to do in the performance of each song, sometimes making up new parts. Then they had a hit song. Up until that hit, the band shared their money equally. Following the hit the singer announced a publishing deal and 96% of the income would be kept for himself while the remaining four members would each get 1%. Hence if one dollar came in from publishing the singer would be paid 96 cents and the remaining musicians would each get their own penny. The singer was proud of his generosity. The drummer who liked to state the obvious asked why the singer thought this was fair. They travelled together performing the songs — this is why the hit was added to the radio, because of the work distributed between them all. Who could say with authority that radio stations added the song because of the song or maybe because of the guitar solo? Maybe they just liked the name of the band or heavens no — could there have been payola involved because the sale of units was lucrative for the label?

The drummer who was hired to replace the drummer who liked to state the obvious got the new gig because partly they were disinclined to state the obvious.

oh please

Standing in Dollarama wondering when they will start selling cars, condominiums and coffee makers since they've moved in on everything else. Do You Think I'm Sexy comes on the overhead speakers. There is a saxophone solo. The chorus and reverb effect stands out like an announcement for simulated spaces. Weird, compressed and false. But success breeds instant imitation. Must have anchored the legitimacy of effects like this even if it does sound inorganic.

Like unapologetic use of autotune. Bet most recording people had the same reaction. This wasn't initially added to call attention to itself; probably singer thought it was cool then insisted it remain an audible effect. Song becomes a hit — poof — now a popular effect. Maybe politics same. Trump just imitating Jacob Zuma and Rodrigo Duterte since they were using the belligerent asshole psychopath plug-in with great success before him. Bet Aretha Franklin thought he could never be president.

Wall Street Journal: What do you think of the use of autotune by some younger singers?
Aretha: What is autotune? I don't even know what autotune is.
Wall Street Journal: It's a kind of way of electronically adjusting your voice —

Aretha: Oh please.

Wall Street Journal: So it doesn't sound pitchy, it doesn't sound wrong, it's hitting the note right on.

Aretha: That's ridiculous. That would be ridiculous, right? After 50 years? Please.

prefer the individual

I was reading some material that talked about contemporary composers extending the ideas of John Cage. I wonder what that means and how boring it might be. I love John Cage, for me he turned everything inside out and at the same time I find listening to music that removed the "individual" torture. The very reason why I admire him is why I can't stand him. Reflecting nature and challenging man's need to organize melodies and rhythms is as cool as listening to waves from the ocean, which is pretty cool but not what turns me on compared to whatever Gnarls Barkley is making up next with that unique voice. What a voice.

some say love

There was a woman whose favourite artist was Bette Midler and she fell in love with a man she hoped would share her musical taste but never really came true like in her imagination. He just didn't find Miss M. all that divine. She tried to persuade him, pointed out her fave moments of Bette Midler hoping he would be just as moved; he wasn't. At one point she became obsessed about it, even thought they should break up, but her high school friend Mimi assured her there will always be another Bette Midler–type situation looming, she added the universe works like that. She decided happiness isn't finding someone who reflects the same taste as yours, maybe it is just not giving a shit about judging the taste of others, then on second thought she decided fuck it — happiness is surrounding yourself with other people who like the same stuff as you. Mimi came over with beer and they blasted The Rose on repeat. When he came home from work he joined them, drinking and singing The Rose, and said he remembered the movie this song is from, liked it lots. Who is it anyway? She answered I have no idea and realized she stumbled upon another and better rule of the universe.

kombuchian

hard to believe durian on sale for $2.88 a pound but there it was three days ago. in the check-out line concerned people had to ask did I know what I had there in my shopping cart? not only knew but calculated saving $40 yet didn't consider the cost of making my house smell like durian. a sci-fi situation figuring out how to cut into it, probably arpeggiating synthesizers in the background score if a director should supply me with this footage. has to be experienced to understand. equally stunning discovering granadillas (three for $5). have to go to mexico one day now. the inside grey gel is gruesome but black seeds taste like crunchy refined bits of sugar, caught me by surprise like the online audio of trump talking with bob woodward. proud again to fly a bob flag. the new piece is unfinished, asked one person what they thought. always a dumb move to get an opinion when it isn't done, like adding a knapsack of rocks in the middle of my marathon. now every next part is distracted by recalling his response and this music sounds nothing like the spice girls but try telling that to the now infected voices of my mind. new kombucha, earl grey instead of green and english breakfast. end result two days away. Three litres. one is strawberry, one is blackberry, but the one i'm most interested in i'm keeping secret.

the nice guys

When the fan-who-loved-to-gush saw the drummer-who-liked-to-state-the-obvious she told him she was planning to take her vacation at the same time as the band was touring Europe so she could attend all their foreign dates. "Why do that since you've already seen our show a zillion times?" replied the drummer-who-liked-to-state-the-obvious curtly. "Because you're so fantastic!" answered the fan-who-loved-to-gush. She was used to the drummer not being the friendliest guy in the world but it didn't matter, she really wanted to see the person who was now emerging from the dressing room. The singer-who-was-more-of-a-leisure-suit-model-than-a-musician noticed the fan-who-loved-to-gush and tried nonchalantly to walk the other way but it was too late; she jumped in front of him and confessed she was planning to follow them across Europe. He opened his eyes widely and said, "that's wonderful!" He winked at her as she left and then the singer-who-was-more-of-a-leisure-suit-model-than-a-musician turned to the drummer-who-liked-to-state-the-obvious and said, "Old Barney strikes again." It was the name he used to insinuate she was unattractive and bore a resemblance to the cartoon caveman from the Flintstones. This was how he always referred to her, but the drummer-who-liked-to-state-the-obvious felt differently about how to treat the fan-who-loved-to-gush. He simply wasn't nice to her or, put another way, he discouraged her. He knew it and so did she. Thought this kinder than affirming her delusions that there existed an important friendship between them. It was annoying when the singer-who-was-more-of-a-leisure-suit-model-than-a-musician spoke rudely behind her back but kindly to her face. In fact the singer-who-was-more-of-a-leisure-suit-model-than-a-musician once told the drummer-who-liked-to-state-the-obvious, like a father to a son, "One needs to be nice to the fans, that's what it's all about." Inside each mind they had completely different templates for understanding the meaning of nice.

what would otis

Recently played a show, started by playing blues like my brother taught me. Wonder if Otis Spann would approve when I play. Love letting the right hand try telling the story. Hate it if left hand isn't having same respect. So that night played in two keys simultaneously. Allowed the creative exploration from my right hand as well as a brain kerfuffle reconciling the left hand in E and the right hand in B♭. This means the left and right were both juggling, it meant equal billing. Couple different audience members later praised what they heard. So then I asked if they understood what I was doing. No, they didn't. Funny in my head I thought it obvious, simultaneously ugly but beautiful, inside and outside. At least I didn't ask them until I had finished playing. Throws me a little off my game to know in advance people are listening and thinking it doesn't make sense.

what happened in hollywood

Long time ago we were in the movie *Postcards from the Edge*, quite the amazing moments, fancy hotel, easy work schedule. There goes Gene Hackman, there's Shirley MacLaine, and rehearsing every day with Meryl Streep. Especially fun for me since the song started with piano and voice. She was exactly how one would imagine — no airs, friendly to all, playful. I asked her if my brother could send her a script because he was a screenwriter, she gave me a PO box. Also asked the director, Mike Nichols, and he obliged, hope it helped my brother. Nothing as useful as eliminating the middleman.

Carrie Fisher, I didn't know who she was but someone said that's the author of the book that the movie is based on. I wondered if Mike Nichols was annoyed that the writer was walking around like a helicopter parent. I figured out years later they were all pals. I also figured out years later that lots of people were pinching themselves because she was Princess Leia. Star Wars wasn't part of my life. I didn't need any pinching.

She played my piano one day, it was a little amazing, River from Joni Mitchell's Blue album, note for note. I tiptoed behind her trying to watch over her shoulder — I never understood exactly what Joni Mitchell did and Carrie Fisher was nailing it.

But best lesson was Mike Nichols. Surprisingly they let us come to watch the rushes. A small screening room, Meryl Streep and Shirley MacLaine and some crew members. This was before computers and everything digital, it was radical to see something developed overnight. When the scene was over, the lights came up and everyone waited in silence for Mike Nichols's response. It was all obvious to me — there were no mistakes on the piano so it's all good, right? And any second he will say, "Okay, we got that," but instead he said, "Fuck that gold curtain! Fucked it all up! Shit, should be silver!" And then everybody on cue parroted same.

"Yeah, it's horrible, Mike."
"All wrong, so wrong, damn curtain."
"Soooooo wrong. Fuck that curtain, shoulda been silver, for Chrissakes."
Felt like a *Twilight Zone* episode or maybe something straight out of Bugs Bunny. Big dog and a little dog and the little dog is changing his own opinions just to remain on the good side of the big dog. I couldn't believe it — cowards, all cowards. They kept us a few more days and shot the scene all over with a different curtain. But now with years of recording I've had weirdly similar experiences and it makes me rethink what happened in Hollywood. People I work with don't necessarily tune in to all the sounds or arrangements that are my job to catch and question or repair.

"You hear that?"
"What?"
"That."
"Oh, you mean that. Right, should I record it again?"
"Yes, let's try that again."

So maybe the colour that Mike Nichols saw as totally wrong was actually totally wrong. And how would I know anyway? Sure was pleased about my small part with Meryl singing, plus none of them noticed it was a bogus midi keyboard.

where you are standing

Compassion struck me in my 40s because when I met people who were 15 or 20 years younger than me, some felt awkward or unrelaxed that I was so much older than them even though I knew there wasn't much difference between us. And I remembered what someone in their 40s seemed like when I was in my 20s — ancient. The whole thing was about compassion because if this dynamic between myself and people 15 to 20 years younger than me was true — what did it mean about people who were 15 to 20 years older than me? Probably that they knew something about me and them, just like what I knew about me and the youngers-than-me. Probably that I will be them too in a moment or two and might be surprised that I'm still the same. You would think one realizes these things before living it but it isn't necessarily so. A lot like that best piano lesson ever I had with Freddie Stone, who didn't play piano. A lot like my colleague who believes you cannot teach anybody anything but show them how things work, like where the on/off switch is concealed or where you change the fuses and then they can test that out but ultimately we all do our own learning. (Or not.)

lucky chance

Director and composer were struggling to make sense, things were not going well. She gave him a few scenes with temp music that the editor had added. He imitated the temp music (fast electronic or fast solo drums) but she told him it wasn't right each time. She felt self-conscious because she didn't know how to describe what she liked. He said that's all right and kept trying other ideas. Tried to score it as if it were a film he had made, what would he enjoy if no one had given him temp music, but again when she listened back she didn't like it. He asked to look through the music files on her phone where she kept what she enjoyed. Noticed slow acoustic guitar music mostly. Then he wrote some slow acoustic guitar music and later next week after she heard it she said she loved it, exactly what she was wishing for. How did you do that? He said I just took a stab in the dark.

the woman with the ramones t-shirt

Earlier in the morning the professor for the class on Marx's ideas asked us to say our name, what year we are in, what we want to get out of taking this course. When it was my turn I explained that I was looking at music and power and he became animated, went off on a tangent regarding how a socialist school could teach art.

He's taught this class for 20 years and yet he was just on vacation in Switzerland and had a book about Marx's life with him which he couldn't wait to return to each night before going to bed. More exciting than the Alps. He's teaching people something he knows and loves, up and down and sideways, he's living the dream. I envy him. Would love to teach a course on the White Album or Court and Spark or Songs in the Key of Life. Many musicians would understand this. To gab about a favourite period of a certain artist you feel suitably studied about and walk people through its greatness, design ways to share these values and intricacies to benefit new listeners.

Later I asked the woman sitting next to me on the subway about whether or not she recommended her phone. Because I hate my phone, which has been crashing when I'm in a pinch and need it. She explained the cost of the phone, and which mall she bought it from, and how much she pays each month, which somehow led to telling me that she is a chef in two restaurants and that she is originally from Jamaica. Couldn't help asking her next a bunch of cook questions about scotch bonnets, ackee and what is her favourite rice (parboiled). But one thing intrigued me more, does the Ramones t-shirt under her blue jean jacket mean she is a Ramones fan?

Since I had just left a long discussion on dialectical materialism, which I concluded is a much simpler idea to understand than its title, I felt like challenging my own habits like talking to strangers. Decided to abstain from asking any more questions, especially the one that really intrigued me. Instead wanted to question my questioning, which seemed more in keeping with what my new Marxist professor would find the more important question. I lost and it blurted out — pointing at her shirt, I asked are you a big fan? She looked momentarily at her top and said she didn't know what it was. I said they are a band that's very famous from the punk rock world of the 70s and 80s. She shrugged like she wasn't guilty of anything.

In my other new class we are discussing participatory research and the problem with people who don't participate. I wanted to speak up but I didn't know how to say what I thought or how to defend it because if people don't answer in a way that furthers one's supposition it still is the actual way that they did participate. Did the woman in the Ramones t-shirt not participate by shrugging? I think the question should be framed differently. Wondering if this line of thought will make me a Marxist or just positions me better to discuss what's common to Revolution #9 and Ob-La-Di, Ob-La-Da.

quoting rose winston

Looking for an agent. Had some recent exchanges that were pointless, questions like "Where do you see yourself in three years?" or "What were your sales like for 2015–2017?" or "Let me know when you're playing next?" to which I said why don't we have coffee this week and just meet and discuss the business of what I've done and what I want to do? No reply. I did the wrong thing by suggesting we be like ordinary people, like farting in email. Would I buy them dinner? That's my test. I usually book myself, as do most of my friends, but the truth is when the artist calls, the promoter lowballs them and if an agent calls they can't. I have my theories but ultimately, to quote Rose Winston, "That's the way 'tis."

why don't we do it in the road?

Can't buy me love. That means something.
I want you, she's so heeeeeaaaavvvvyyyyyyy. Totally get that.
All through the day I me mine, I me mine, I me mine. Totally get that too.

Recent live Paul McCartney in New York finishes by executing some of side B of Abbey Road building to the climax "and in the end the love you take is equal to the love you make." As far as axioms go, this only ranks around the level of a fortune cookie with K-tel as creative overseer. Wasn't convinced about its power, Sir Paul. Reminds more of Newton's third law of motion with musical accompaniment.

Why don't we do it in the road? — now there's a decent zen zinger if you ask me, which nobody is.

2 b more real

Being back at university I notice professors often assigning their own work for students to read among works by other scholars. I respect them more for keeping their own work out of it. The best open stages are the ones where the host does not play. If the host is also a performer then there are power relationships that can be disturbing; the person in charge can always punish you or do other immature things, give you a bad timeslot. Where the host is not a performer it feels more legit to use the word "open" in open stage.

outside sauna

Outside the sauna at the Y last night, heard two men try to outdo each other over who sold more records, The Eagles or The Pink Floyd. English wasn't their first language. It was tricky to follow their sentences, I believe both concluded by virtue of who sold how much that that determined who made the greatest music. Like the greatest at anything is determined by quantity. So best tomato sauce or best bicycle must be the ones that sold most units. I wondered how stupid they would think I was if I explained a counter-view. I settled instead for enjoying each reference to The Pink Floyd.

darius and fred

Fred, a songwriter booked by the Fab Acts Talent agency, played to audience sizes between 50 and 80. He was philosophical about the work when he did well or when he was thrown curveballs and in interviews sometimes said everyone is an actor and he was playing the part of singer-songwriter; even the audience played the part of an audience. Fellow Fab touring artist Darius also played to same-sized crowds and found Fred's perspective meaningless, even out of touch with reality. In the dressing room before every Darius performance they lit a scented candle and wore special socks and a special shirt and turned around three times before touching their magic guitar case and then they were ready to take the stage. Whenever things went well they felt that all their superstitions were paying off and whenever things didn't they concluded they needed to add more elements to the pre-show ritual.

secret is a secret

"Your premise is flawed," replied the old trumpeter who destroyed everyone each time she played, when the intern from *Exclaim!* asked what was her secret, during the phone interview.

real human being

The William Parker concert at the Guelph Jazz Festival Saturday morning was like discovering a new spice I plan to use in cooking. He played two pieces, great intensity. He explained the piece off the top had to do with an idea he had about a landscape where moments after Martin Luther King was murdered, his spirit hovering in the parking lot of the Lorraine Motel in Memphis and then Crazy Horse's spirit travelled to meet with him and shared insights about freedom and how it is an internal thing. I couldn't hear Parker's unmic'd voice as clearly as I would have liked but I think that was the gist of it. Fifteen minutes into it some loser's cell phone blared dumb ringtone for five seconds. I looked down from the balcony to see if his expression changed to something more disappointed but he didn't want to dignify the interruption and retained his focus with the music.

Later the second piece was as great an improvisation as you expect from someone introduced earlier as a world-class musician, even though it was the sales & marketing person from the college radio station making the claim. She might be the greatest sales & marketing manager in the history of jazz concerts, but seemed to me this situation should call for the poet laureate of Guelph, or at least Karen Houle (who probably is the de facto PL of G).

I liked the second piece more. He started with a concave bow made of something rigid. The bowing thread very taught. He playfully played with harmonics a long time, inspiring, and eventually morphed into a rhythm different than what usually passes for legit in freely improvised music. This pleased me much because I too like injecting melodicism or rhythmic grooves instead of remaining committed to playing free at all costs. Sometimes I think the players that avoid groovy rhythms or melodies are missing the point. Free means free, in the same record store you find William Parker you also find Avril Lavigne, has nothing to do with right and wrong, it's a reflection of what is organic, worth considering that everything is just coexisting.

Sometimes I think an interest to approach consciousness as the most urgent of priorities also makes for the development of the best realizations of music. A pleasant surprise when next he started to sing the following lyric inside his piece:
I want to be a real human being not an avant-garde,
I want to be a real human being not an avant-garde,
It is more avant-garde to be a real human being

some people

In my Marx class I had to write a paper on Chapter 1 of *Das Kapital* and during this week of reading it became apparent that Marx, like most famous dead people, gets his name thrown around a lot, not necessarily correctly. Ron Sexsmith wrote a fantastic song about this regarding Elvis Presley. It was on the record Grand Opera Lane (his best record if you ask any biased person that looks like me).
Some people just can't leave a dead man alone
They say "get back dead man get back to your throne"
If they just confessed he was only flesh and bone
Some people some people
Some people just can't leave a dead man alone
They'll dig up the dirty laundry right after he's gone
A man can't defend himself in the great unknown
Some people some people
Why don't they stay away, just let him rest in peace
He's living in Las Vegas on an isle in Greece
He's on the cover of another rag now

He's the father of somebody's child
Wasn't it enough for him to give his own life?
Without all this nonsense running wild?
Some people just can't leave a dead man alone
They say "get back, dead man, get back to your throne"
If to heaven I go, hope there ain't no telephone
Some people some people

in the strum

All the guitar strings except both Es had a secret meeting organized
by A who wanted to discuss how unfair it was that there were two
Es while the rest of them were represented only as single strings. A
said Es had more opportunities to be played, unfair. D and B agreed.
G argued that there was a view from which you could say each E was
their own sound but aren't they all from the same source and don't
they all vibrate at different speeds? A scoffed at G but it confused B.
D resorted to name-calling and said G couldn't understand since they
don't tune to a fourth.

When they returned both Es asked where they had been and what was
up? A said everything is fine, the others vibrated in agreement, except
G who was slightly out of tune (not unusual). Higher E had a thing
for being intuitive and suddenly with a tiny bit of distortion started
to scream, You guys want to get rid of me and low E, don't you? G
starting buzzing, Yes they do but I don't. You loser, said B to G. We
just think it isn't fair that the two of you are the same and we're all just
one of a kind said A while D stared at the ground, a little embarrassed.
So that's how it is, said low E. You think we aren't all one of a kind
and that you are unfairly exploited? Yes, that's true, said A, and D and
B nodded in agreement.

Low E thought what a shame they don't confront the guitarist instead
of fighting about position.

meeting of the creatives

(first mtg)

Director: so glad to meet you and let me say this — i love your music.

Composer: thanks, nice to meet you too.

Director: i have all your records. i would love to have you do the music for this film.

Composer: wow.

Director: i want you to do whatever naturally comes to you.

Composer: seriously?

Director: it needs a certain type of musician.

Composer: i have some ideas.

Director: can't wait, you da man.

(next mtg)

Composer: what did you think of the music i sent in yesterday?

Director: we need to talk.

Composer: sure.

Director: here's the thing, i don't think this direction you are going in is right for this particular film in this particular instance.

Composer: at this particular time.

Director: exactly!

Composer: forget the classical stuff.

Director: forget the bassoon or oboe or whatever that was.

Composer: I can try other things. no sweat.

Director: you know I really like what you do.

Composer: you have all my records.

Director: you da man.

(later)

Composer: hi.

Director: we need to talk.

Composer: okay.

Director: how is it coming?

Composer: pretty good, I'll have something for you to hear by the end of tomorrow.

Director: awesome. do you think you could listen to this? (hands him radiohead cd).

Composer: you want something that sounds like this instead?

Director: (proudly) i want something that sounds like you sounding like this!

Composer: i'll try, but you know it isn't what i do or what i hear in this film.

Director: here's the thing, when we made a rough cut we used this and we love it.

Composer: so why didn't you use that?

Director: do you know how much that costs?

Composer: too much.

Director: you da man.

(later)

Director: have you seen this on youtube? can you sound like that too? isn't it awesome?

Composer: it's a drum machine and a choir from estonia, not really like radiohead or me but if you want —

Director: i want!

Composer: okay.

Director: you da man.

(later)

Composer: did you check out the new music?

Director: (smirking) we got it.

Composer: you liked it?

Director: my daughter saw the first thing you did and she and her boyfriend loved it and when i played them the radiohead estonian choir drum machine thing they said it wasn't as good as the first thing. was that a bassoon or oboe, i fucking love it.

Composer: you da man.

eddie harsch & the soundwaves

One night six or seven years ago there was a blackout in our neighbourhood. We went for a walk in the blackness and electricity-less sky. At the bottom of the hill we stopped before a house where there was some slow piano emanating. Never saw the pianist but could identify with their decision that the blackout was a good moment to play.

I was sort of expecting them to reveal themselves and maybe I would play too and we'd make friends down the street. We sat down on the curb listening. In my imagination the pianist was an old woman playing pieces based on long-ago memories. We walked home.

A few years later I fell into a conversation with an older woman outside the same house and I took a guess that she was the pianist. I told her about the time I heard the piano during the blackout — was it her? "That was my son, he is ill but he used to be in a big rock band."

I thought on my street there was only room for one ex–member of a big rock band. Which band, I asked? The Black Crowes, she answered.

in the fishbowl

Fred: i hate bach.

Judy: bach is a genius.

Randy: i'm trying to eat dinner. why are you fighting?

Judy: we're not fighting, he's bragging about being stupid.

Fred: bach is a bunch of scales unlike music.

Randy: that's fighting.

Judy: you don't get it.

Fred: yes i do.

Judy: you play piano?

Fred: like a fish.

Judy: whatever that means.

Fred: swimmingly i play piano.

Randy: cute.

Judy: if you like dad jokes.

Randy: food?

Judy: in most piano music the left hand is like a bass player.

Fred: like perch and halibut — bass. (winks)

Judy: how did you get so funny?

Fred: read a lot of dostoevsky.

Judy: uh huh.

Fred: left hand is a bass player, I know that's not anything new.

Judy: and have you seen how it often follows the path of least resistance?

Fred: how is that?

Judy: duh, open your eyes.

Randy: stop fighting.

Judy: you can't handle the heat, get out of the kitchen.

Randy: you're the one cruisin' for a bruisin'.

Fred: you can lead a horse to water but can you make it drive a car.

Randy: that's not the correct —

Fred: thanks, randy.

Judy: in the left hand it's almost always single bass notes or octaves while the right hand tells the story, even if the left is chording the right is being melodic.

Fred: true enough.

Judy: if you go backwards and look at earlier piano literature the left hand is treated like an equal but over time people dilute its power over and over, like they don't want to think too much.

Randy: like language and everything.

Judy: listen again to bach.

Fred: it's exercise music.

Judy: whatever the right does the left does as well and the lines of movement are complicated for the fingers — almost all the time.

Randy: just like language — earlier words have weird pronunciations and later things become spelled more and more phonetic and slang-like? same thing.

Fred: slang-like?

Randy: people writing boys b-o-y-z, or fuze guys or dostoevsky sometimes is spelled with Y instead of OE. there's a million examples.

Fred: it was always that way.

Randy: no it wasn't.

Judy: bach was a musical mind unconcerned about easy solutions.

Fred: and boring.

Judy: for those without brains it's very boring, yes.

Randy: i like him but i don't play piano like you guys.

Fred: like yuze guys.

Judy: the point is he moved in various directions for reasons of musical taste vs. simplicity. he was playing what he heard because there's no other explanation for the crazy moves his left hand does.

Fred: you hurt my feelings when you say I have no brain.

Judy: it's hard to be a goldfish in the same tank with the same two fishes for four years.

Fred: were we ever not goldfishes?

Judy: we weren't born to be pets trapped in a bowl.

Randy: says who?

Judy: this is it exactly. when bach played, the piano was new, it didn't have a history of accepting the lowest common denominator. so he wrote equally for the left and right hands.

Fred: you're saying before we were in captivity we were daring and inclined to do things based on thinking things were limitless?

Judy: more or less, yes.

Randy: but the tank is great. we get food at the same time each day.

Judy: i guess if that's all you want then that's the way it goes. i'm just saying that bach came to his place with no history of shortcuts and it's interesting in that situation that he made up work that engages so much brain activity. he wasn't interested in dumb jokes and lazy technique.

Fred: then he wrote the well-tempered caviar?

set list

Singer: Let's start with Mona, people get into it off the top.

Drummer: Mona's too fast to start with, we need to build.

Bassist: Tomorrow We Hide would be good first, then the Instrumental, then Mona, that's hard to resist.

Singer: I don't want the Instrumental until after Midnight Toker because I need to relax my voice after screaming, okay?

Bassist: Okay.

Drummer: Then we'll put Midnight Toker in the middle and the Instrumental after that. Tomorrow We Hide off the top and then Don't Blame Her second — everybody cool?

Bassist: That's all right.

Keyboardist: Why not start with Ploughed Under and then Don't Blame Her, then Tomorrow We Hide and then Midnight Toker and then the Instrumental, that way there won't be three keyboard solos in a row.

Singer: Three in a row?

Keyboardist: Yep.

Singer: That's stupid.

Drummer: But the pacing of Ploughed Under before Don't Blame Her is too wishy-washy, we'll lose the crowd.

Singer: Right.

Guitarist: Why don't we cut up the song titles and throw them in a hat and then whatever order we pick 'em out is the order we play them?

Everyone stares silently at guitarist.

Singer: If you're not going to help us make a decent sequence, don't say anything at all.

Everyone: Right.

the twist

There is an idea out there in the world that when recording you should forget about the fact that you are being recorded. That to get the real you you need to fool yourself . . . something like that.

When you weren't being recorded, you did something brilliant, so now with a microphone you try to do it again but it didn't happen, remained elusive. You think if only it had been recorded the first time . . . because the first time you did something special but now that you are trying to capture the something special it isn't happening — must be because the presence of the microphone throws you . . . or so goes the usual wisdom.

What if altering one's performance is a good thing? What if knowing you are being recorded and knowing you are inclined to perform differently because the lights are on, people are watching, yada yada, was an advantage, was something to use creatively? Instead of planning to pretend you aren't aware (when you actually are) you planned to take the altered state and enjoy it for the purposes of making a recording — enter into it knowing it can't be what you had without a microphone. Maybe that's the way to fool oneself?

seeing stanley

For a split second sometime around 1989 Stanley Clarke made a pop band with Stewart Copeland. It was called Animal Logic. They played the El Mocambo and when I got there it was packed, shoulder to shoulder, but by that point I had already experienced being in a band where at showtime I had to walk through seas of people to get to the stage. That many people just opens up if you act like you have a job to do, so I said excuse me, excuse me, and by the time I got to the front there was enough room to sit down and experience being ten feet away from one of my ultimate music heroes.

What the fuck, Stanley? The music was horrible, so horrible. I didn't care about Stewart Copeland, not my guy, but Journey to Love, School Days and all the Return to Forever records were my vitamins in high school. There was a singer whom they were backing up and she was not memorable. There was a generic Los Angeles rock guitarist with big hair and fluorescent tape pieces on his guitar as was the style then, yawn.

Halfway through, the singer took a break, left the stage, and the band played one instrumental. *That's why we were there.*

Like we all climbed Mount Everest watching Stanley Clarke do his thing. The liquidity of his fingers, the fusing of his heart/brain/hands with his listening, felt like I was petting a lion. At one point the generic guitarist and Stanley started doing a call/response thing, a competition of who could play faster. Every zig-zag circular or vertical gesture the guitarist did, Stanley did back three times more complex and only used his pinky, very unlike the organic exchange between him and Jeff Beck from Journey to Love.

Then the singer returned and the band commenced to play more of their "pop" record. I couldn't handle the idea of waiting another 30 minutes to maybe experience one more instrumental and left.

the categories

and the Juno for venue that most often convinces bands that $100 is fair when they made 20 times that after expenses goes to . . .
and the Juno for greatest solo done while high on drugs that could kill a rhinoceros goes to . . .
and the Juno for manager who intimidates most people in the business and gets highest percentage of the artist's gross goes to . . .
and the Juno for journalist least familiar with their interview subject goes to . . .
and the Juno for best film score that sounds like another Philip Glass imitation goes to . . .

and the Juno for band member who drove safest back home after a gig goes to . . .

and the Juno for best ancient publicist with a British accent who breaks the ice telling sexist jokes goes to . . .

and the Juno for artist who did best job of avoiding all political opinions until it was obvious which way the wind was blowing and then got really vocal about it goes to . . .

and the Juno for most imaginative drum solo done wearing a bowler cap and unclothed while simultaneously singing operatically goes to — waitasec, there's only one candidate. Congratulations! 25 years in a row. Great Bob Scott.

invisible door

It's like the music business is a machine with an invisible door and people try to locate the knob. They go to school hoping someone can tell them where that handle is, but it's invisible. Yet you might get in and if so you have a golden opportunity to try to accomplish whatever your music fantasies were because it's an invitation-only party and if you're inside you can play.

Thinking about this while listening to a retrospective on the radio on Bob Dylan's birthday filled with a zillion people covering Dylan, which is no surprise because he's a brilliant writer, but I started thinking about the fact that because he got inside he had so many opportunities. We all know someone who's a special unique writer who isn't inside and they are not noticed . . . will probably die in obscurity.

An older music manager once told me that in early years people had heard a bit about Dylan but he was not the big deal he became until Peter, Paul and Mary did Blowin' in the Wind. Same goes for Joni Mitchell and Leonard Cohen whose careers became huge after Judy Collins covered Both Sides Now and Suzanne. Maybe the lesson there is if you have any access to more commercial people —

If you're a songwriter and somehow you find yourself inside the machine you should realize . . .

Don't assume there is no expiry date on the power and privilege that comes with being invited to an exclusive party.

Never give up your publishing, it is your future, your retirement, your ticket to not working at Long & McQuade (don't hate me, people at L&M).

Try to get your music covered. The more it's played, the more other people, other than fans you already have, get to discover you.

the cn tower ledge

For a certain type of musician, whatever they can do isn't good enough.

People new to piano have difficulty playing hands together. One forgets how real a complication that is in the early days. Their faces look at me like I'm asking them to step onto the ledge of the CN Tower.

The interesting thing is when they do get there, when they can play hands together, they have already moved on. I might say, hey, look you can do it! They don't care now; they're on fire about what I did in my right hand or my left hand or a record they heard and want to know how it was done.

The brain works like that. It's as though it always wants to compare where you are with where you wish you were.

Some people realize the great lesson learned from this. They know whatever they set their sights on they can learn, they know to be patient and stay the course, maybe there's another lesson in there too.

moment with cleave 3o years ago

Cleave: Why do you play the solo from our big hit song different every night?

Bob: Because I like the challenge, I like not knowing what I'm going to do. I like trying to make it different.

Cleave: When I go to a concert I prefer seeing someone play the solo exactly like the record.

Bob: I never thought of that.

memories of vienna

I worked on a film and they required me to sign a clause that stip-
ulated I could not say anything negative about them — ever. This
became weirder by the time I grasped they were absolute assholes. I
needed the money, I needed the job but I also need my dignity and it
took the fall.

Two lawyers later, I decided I won't do that again and addressed
it in subsequent jobs. If you have a clause like that, get someone else,
I'm the wrong guy, and the weirdest part is it's not a real problem. The
issue has absolutely nothing to do with whether someone is the right
composer for the movie, it has everything to do with out-of-control
power and insecurity.

singing is believing

Been in recording sessions where the producer (or the engineer)
seems ambivalent towards the singer and inattentive to listening for
the emotional content (isn't that the singer's job description?). With
printed lyrics they're ready to correct the singer about a forgotten
word or ensure the verses are in the right order, otherwise they act like
they're watching tv — worse, a rerun.

Even singers sometimes act blasé or perhaps get sidetracked by
criticism about their pitch or phrasing — maybe they got a parking
ticket, whatever — they're not in the best mood. Woe betide the singer
whose attention wanders from what the song is about.

My favourite part about producing is the part where it's just the
singer, the person representing the ideas of the song. Sometimes asking
where they were/what happened when they wrote the song leads to
best takes.

When I listen to Sister Rosetta Tharpe singing This Train
or I Want You (She's So Heavy) or Ballad of a Thin Man or The
Revolution Will Not Be Televised or Mississippi Goddamn, I believe
every vowel.

voyager 1 & 2

There was an idea to treat outer space like the ocean it is and in 1977 they launched spaceships Voyager 1 & 2 replete with messages in a bottle ostensibly for aliens to discover and consider.
What did they include to impress the aliens if either Voyager was successful?
Glenn Gould,
Beethoven,
Mozart,
Stravinsky,
Azerbaijani folk music,
Guan Pinghu,
Blind Willie Johnson,
Chuck Berry,
Kesarbai Kerkar,
Valya Balkanska and recordings of people saying hello in 55 different languages.
Music is our species' way of showing off intelligence. No paintings, no sculpture, no architecture and no modern dance.

same

The back stages
of lower level
performance places
have broken chairs
missing light bulbs
graffiti
doorless toilet stalls.
The back stages
of upper level
performance places
have security guards

fluorescent lights
fruit trays & deli platters
solid polished floors.
The first crowd pays less than $10
The second crowd pays more than $25
The same material is performed.

students who ask how

There's a million people trying to fit through a small opening, that's how it is. If you still want to try and fit through that small opening, be my guest, I don't think you shouldn't try, but beware the odds.

Forget about making cds or records, for now it's over. People get it online. If you must, just do 50 at a time.

The nature of networking isn't to send cold-call messages on LinkedIn or Facebook but to actually work with people. You will be surprised where they end up in five years or ten years and knowing them earlier might later pay unexpected dividends.

Make videos for as many songs as possible. YouTube is the radio.

Every city has a college/community radio station you can liaise with to promote your show. Don't worry about playing the entire country unless other people are putting up the money. Focus on playing Southern Ontario (and Montreal) if you are staying in Canada. Keep your job and try to play in all those cities on weekends. Say yes to every request of your musicianship if you can find a way to afford the trouble of doing it. (Unless it's Ken Finkleman.)

as it never happened

I had an idea for a CBC program and pitched it.
My idea was to comb through their 70-year audio archives and create conversations between people who are dead with people who are alive — as if they are in the same room. This would be easy for three or four of us nutty audio people cutting and pasting.
Title of show: As It Never Happened.
When I explained it to ordinary people, they laughed, got excited.

When I tried to pitch it (on three occasions) to folks in charge of new projects, they looked at me as though I hadn't said anything.

This was before the show *Rewind* emerged on CBC, which spoke a bit to what interested me, exploring the archives, but I was more interested in unexpected juxtapositions. It might have even facilitated an interactive experience, online contests for people to make their own mashups. If nothing else, rediscover their own history as recorded by CBC.

I still believe someone more creative might one day call me and say okay, let's try it.

as time passes

I like doing things myself including negotiations, I feel like I can sort out what's fair from what's unfair but the truth is whenever I have had an agent I get paid four times more and whenever a lawyer reviews the contract, bad shit in the deal is illuminated and corrected.

I don't think it means I shouldn't still do things myself sometimes, it's just worth remembering that people who seem nice, often are full of shit.

junejohn

Imagine people coming back to life and playing a concert   tonight. John Coltrane and Miles Davis. Tony Williams does an opening fill and June Tyson sings. Imagine the attention you would give that whole experience? Imagine giving that sort of attention to walking down the street and listening to the traffic, conversation bits or insects and birds? That's the present from John Cage, the compelling contribution he made to what is music; remembering to be amazed by sound and experience the music of sound events like a concert of super importance unfolding before you in real time . . . because it is.

The mind can't handle sustaining that sort of attention very long without wondering about a coffee or the phone bill or the person who took the seat on the subway before you but that's what's impressive about the greatest musicians, they seem to go a long time surfing that wave of being present in their listening and not cave to distraction.

!!!!!!

Some people I teach are notation-reading-only musicians and some have a similar story in their background being at parties where people are jamming and despite playing all their life they can't play along and feel like an imposter musician.

I love working with those types. I push them overboard. It's like they just told me they've been swimming all their life and we're on a boat and so I get them in the water, we both know they know how to swim.

"Life jacket!!" they scream.

"Swim!!" I scream.

"No!!!!"

"Yes!!!"

And then I ask them to pay in advance for the next four.

Okay, not exactly.

But sort of.

but the biggest kick i ever got

Maybe it's about the power of advertising. Never had any reason to sing Crocodile Rock but there it goes . . . me and Suzie had so much fun . . . everybody knows the experience of hating a song that's in their head. Some lift arrogant noses and say that's proof the song is actually good. True things we like we repeat in our heads but then why do we repeat things we hate?

It's added to the radio, it's played in the supermarket, in the elevator — opportunity to take up some of your mental real estate. That's why — advertising works.

If you win the lottery you could hire whoever is the payola-du-jour thus having radio stations and journalists busy working for you. Tried and true method to being established. Soon it's in the heads of the masses, like it or not, they'll talk about how great this new music is — that they "discovered."

spontaneous composition

Not-so-amazing improvisers start doing tricks or they start making noise for noise's sake as if it's proof they are an improviser. They lead no matter what others are doing, it's like showing off not listening, which is fair since anything in life is fair.

Improvised music reflects back life itself and the unknown sequence of events that is day-to-day experience — is it going to rain? is it sunny?

Exciting improvisers know they don't know, except possibilities which in a way are like knowing everything.

The improvisers who show how carefully they are listening, like birds in the trees singing back and forth with each other, are the most enjoyable.

Used to wonder if it was really true when they said Keith Jarrett was spontaneously composing. We had a lot of arguments as teenagers about whether that could be true. One thing that never occurred to us was whether the audience was capable of hearing it.

transparency

When things become bigger the advice of many managers is don't redistribute the money equitably. Just make a salary for everyone else . . . except of course you the artist and me the manager. Some people think that's fair; after all the artist wrote the damn song and now famous people are covering it or audiences of more than 500 people are attending the shows.

Then why did they share the money when it was a broke operation? If you rewind the tape the money was split. Check the first years playing to audiences of eight people — you can bet they shared the money (or loss) evenly. That was the cool thing to do, so why if it grows bigger shouldn't the same rules apply?

And what if the reason the song was added to commercial radio wasn't even directly because of the song? Who can prove why the decision was made that led to a whack of revenue for whoever owns the publishing? Was it because the station manager thought the lead guitarist made cool expressions during their solo? Was it because the chorus reminded the music programmer of their hometown? Was it because they thought the band's name was cute?

Let the whole band see the publishing statements from BMI or ASCAP or SOCAN, etc. When all is said and done, spreading around the wealth will make better conditions for the life of the artists' relationships or, to put it another way, hoarding will speed up a shitty death. There's nothing as cool as transparency.

not my cup of tea

Criticism hurts but so does bullshitting. Maybe lying is a better way to move through it?

When I asked our new American manager what he thought of my first record, sung in an unpleasant voice about the gassing deaths of people in Bhopal, the French secret service assassination of an environmental activist in Auckland and the exploitation of Indigenous people in Chile — he answered, "Nice, real nice."

Sometimes people gave me their music and wanted to know what I thought of it. I try to listen to everything I get because I love music that knocks me out plus I love producing people who knock me out, but truth is most things I get don't knock me out. More often than not when someone wanted my response and if I didn't like it, I would say it "wasn't my cup of tea." A neutral way of saying no thanks, I wasn't getting into it. Didn't want to look people in the eye knowing they sincerely wanted my opinion and say, "Nice, real nice."

Sometimes I meet those people years later and they say you despised my work, you hated my work, you thought I was shit. I said "it isn't my cup of tea" so many times, it's my go-to response. I never say I despise your work, I hate your work, I think you are shit.

new question on mensa application

A/ city licenses buskers
B/ penitentiary uses prisoner labour

C/ bands allow one member to profit from publishing money
D/ ticketmaster employs scalpers

How many on the list are similar?

(answer) None, these are distinctly different situations.

like a talking heads song

Hearing things like radio doesn't matter and it's all online, there's no corruption, it's a level playing field . . .
So then why can't poor slobs just be on iTunes or Spotify without paying an aggregator like Tunecore, CD Baby, etc. How very un-internet. How very much like . . . same as it ever was.

i see ghosts

I knew more than one player who could not keep going, couldn't juggle the conditions of selling labour, some dumb job, whatever it might have been, washing dishes or being a security guard when their real work was drumming or guitaring or producing, etc. Remember how people would speak about their mental health after they had a breakdown or took their life but I don't think those ends are ever a predetermined genetic condition, just too depressing that their talent wasn't worth something that positioned them differently in capital-ist world. Peter, Phillip, Mira, Babette, Charles and Clayton from Philadelphia who drummed for Roberta Flack.

a few favourite music moments

When June Tyson took the stage at the Sun Ra concert in 1984. The concert was underway for about 15 minutes, slowly different members emerged and joined the improvisation which was pulsat-ing and furious and musical. Seemed about nine men playing various winds, a drum kit, an upright bass and an actual large dead tree log and then out of nowhere walked on this creature with makeup on her cheeks as if they were her lips or eyes. Like a tiger she swooped the microphone into her hand and the band stopped on a dime as she sang "we travel the starship from planet to planet" and then the band played the same phrase in a free gesture accent for accent, imitating the language like some avant-garde performances would do 30 years later at the music gallery.

My older brother, Ronnie, had a friend named Larry Goldstein and he had a serious demeanour. He knew karate and I imagined he could chop through a pile of bricks with his pinky. He would have been 14 and me 9. He came over one time in the early 70s and had a copy of Abbey Road under his arm. I asked what it was and in the serious way he always spoke he said it was the Beatles' last record. This was too amazing. The very last copy of what the Beatles had done was for some reason acquired by Larry Goldstein and was simultaneously here in my brother's bedroom in Winnipeg. I felt so so so privileged and grateful that Ronnie knew Larry and hoped he might let me hear some of it one day.

Bruce Cockburn's guitar work was so original to me. That he would make a bass line with his thumb and simultaneously solo was a head-exploding phenomenon and at the same time a lot of those solo guitar pieces had folk or blues foundations. It fit my mind perfectly. But then near the end of the concert he sang a song whose lyrics made no sense to me (dialogue with the devil, why don't we celebrate). There was a vocal climax to the song, sung at the uppermost part of his range. Might be what for some people love of opera is about. It felt like a gamble, like he might not hit it, but did. A different, purer register. He did it two or three times in a row. I was melted by him hitting that note. Seemed to my teenage mind everyone was equally freaked out and bonded together by a voice.

I asked Darwyn Aitken who the photo was on his wall and he explained it was his teacher, David Saperton. He pointed at the guy in a tuxedo, said he was a maestro. It was understood he also meant this was a great achievement in his chain-smoking tiny Gerrard and Broadview house that a schmuck like him got to spend time with a golden artist like Saperton and then he added Saperton studied with Rafael Joseffy. He waited for me to acknowledge how amazing that was, but I just listened to the clock slowly ticking. Who's Joseffy? "Rafael Joseffy was a star student of Franz Liszt," he said, like solving a Rubik's cube. He was right, this was amazing. After that I treated the exercises he gave me, moving sixths and thirds and his "hop" technique, with reverence. I liked believing I was connected to Franz Liszt too.

Micah Lexier called me and said there was a woman playing the Arthur Street Gallery tonight — you shouldn't miss it. I trusted Micah's opinions; he had shared some pretty amazing weird records earlier, maybe Throbbing Gristle and John Giorno. He was right, that night with an audience of 12 people, Laurie Anderson playing Let X=X on a violin with a cassette tape head being stroked by one bow that had 12 inches of music on it or alternating to a Kodak carousel projecting images onto a black wall that she illuminated by windshield wiping her bow in the air — left me unable to speak for a couple hours and walking into walls. As close as I ever got to feeling like I saw the Beatles at the Cavern Club.

you're welcome

According to an unscientific student poll there are approximately six types of songs.

    a/   I want to fuck you
    b/   How can I get you to fuck me
    c/   Why did you fuck them?
    d/   I can't live without fucking you
    e/   Don't you know I want to fuck you?
    f/   I'm never going to fuck you again

I think their research is unsurprising. It's also why I enjoy something different than overused categories. Combine that with the fact that I hear a lot of things my young'n fixates on, and my favourite song of the last two years is from the film *Moana*. The character named Maui is a narcissist. When he meets Moana he presumes she's blown away to stand near him; he sings a song about how amazed she must feel to share the same oxygen as him. The chorus is "you're welcome," which is always funny and something about the design makes me think the arranger has a deep understanding of Earth, Wind and Fire.

sound advice

At school you are expected each week to read much and understand it as well as if it were really compelling. Most students I become friends with admit to often only reviewing the material the day before and some don't even do the readings. People look for shortcuts to demonstrate understanding instead of substantially knowing it. It defeats the point of why the teacher assigned this or that reading, no?

Makes me think of tours and different sound people every night. If you worked with one person each night you could experiment, build something unique. A lot of sound people laugh and double-check if I'm joking when I say we're done because my soundchecks are momentary, check everything works, that they have signal, we're done. They don't know any of my songs, doubtful it makes a difference to play them now. I've seen some people practically do their entire set in soundcheck as if the sound person will know all the cues later. Good luck with that.

harder

When my grandmother was in her 80s she walked slowly and was becoming a little more frail and I used to go shopping with her for groceries. I remember having two minds about it. At 13 I tried to hurry her up and impose my speed, not a pleasing memory, probably made her feel like a burden. The second was a year later and I started tuning in to trying to match her, slowing my steps and repeatedly catching difficulty with the new rhythm, playing in her time was way harder but more rewarding. Difficult-to-do things are like that.

Played a show one time with a big-shot visual artist/musician and it became apparent quickly that if I followed his lead, he would respond creatively and pleasantly, but if I took the lead he contributed less and was withdrawn and then the music was less interesting. So mostly I followed his lead, difficult but best solution, plus CBC was recording, which added another kind of simultaneous pressure.

rating surrealism

When I lived in the middle of nowhere in the 1990s, about 40 minutes from Hamilton, I came into Danny Lanois's orbit and asked if he would play on my record. He drove out and brought a small amplifier with an awesome sound. A local electronics guy converted old 16mm film projectors into guitar amplifiers using the projector's tubes. The sort of thing guitarists freak out about. Bernie Raunig was his name and so were the amps but later for short they were called Bernies. I bought one. Over time I learned I was in a club. About a dozen other musicians owned a Bernie, including Gord Downie and Maxine Pountney. Later, Bernie left Hamilton for another city.

One day in the mid-2000s while touring western Canada my Bernie started to fail. Some buzzing and intermittent sound. Tried replacing tubes using extras I wisely bought earlier but no difference. Can I find someone to fix an amp made from a 16mm film projector only an hour out of Osoyoos, British Columbia? Good luck. I made some inquiries to an old Hamilton friend, word got back that Bernie Raunig had actually moved to BC, near Castlegar, and I was two hours away. Found him in the phone book. Before you knew it I was in his garage, Bernie was repairing a Bernie, top-ten fave surrealist encounter.

concert at cbgbs

The fourth Blue Rodeo show was in New York at CBGBs. I never played in a band before. The first shows were at the Rivoli and the Isabella Hotel where the rooftop marquee advertised Tonight: Rock Like the Rolling Stones, Blue Rodeo. Always liked how that didn't make any sense, probably reflected an early conversation between the Isabella booker and Greg or else made up totally in a vacuum.

People were dancing at those first three shows but at CBGBs they stood there and watched. It felt dead and weird. Out of everyone in the band, drummer Cleave had the kindest personality and was the most experienced. Many times reframed what was going on. I said I guess they don't like us because they weren't dancing. He said when people aren't dancing he sees it as a different show, tries to play as best he can because they're just trying to listen like it's a concert. All I needed to hear.

bob wiseman likes having fun. He was on CNN lying about wanting to change his name to Prince; he played accordion on If I Had a Million Dollars by the Barenaked Ladies; he produced Kid in the Hall Bruce McCulloch's *Shame-Based Man*; he was the composer for *The Drawer Boy*, winner of the 2018 Best Feature Film at the Canadian Film Awards; and Odetta took his hands in hers and kissed them after hearing him play prepared piano at the Bitter End on Earth Day 2000. He was also a founding member of Blue Rodeo but he quit in the early 90s when he no longer found it as fun as when it started.